Supporting

Inclusive

Supporting Inclusive Practice

Edited by Gianna Knowles

 David Fulton Publishers

This edition reprinted 2009 by Routledge
2 Park Square, Milton Park, Abingdon, Oxon, OX14 4RN
Simultaneously published in the USA and Canada
By Routledge
270 Madison Avenue, New York, NY 10016

First published in Great Britain in 2006 by David Fulton Publishers

10 9 8 7 6 5

British Library Cataloguing in Publication Data
A catalogue record for this book is available from the British Library.

ISBN: 1 84312 420 3 (EAN: 9781843124207)

Typeset by RefineCatch, Bungay, Suffolk
Printed and bound in Great Britain

Contents

About the contributors

Katharine Amaladoss is head teacher of a primary school in west Sussex. She has been teaching for approximately twenty years in primary schools, ten years of which have been as a SENCO. Katharine particularly enjoys working with a range of agencies to support children's needs in an inclusive manner. She is fully committed to continuing professional development for all members of the school community. Her school has been praised as an excellent example of an Investor In People (it was awarded this status in 2002) and described as 'a family of people passionate about its people'. Her school is the locality base for the Social Communications Network, holding resources and a termly training venue for those working in children's services who particularly work with children with social communication difficulties/autism. Recently, she has been developing a range of therapeutic approaches to support pupils at her school, including therapeutic storywriting.

Carole Beaty is Programme Manager at Littlehampton SureStart, which opened in the spring of 2005. She has been working in the field of Early Years for nearly thirty years. She spent 14 years as an infant teacher and deputy head in charge of the infant department in a primary school, and for 15 years she worked within higher education in teacher education, working specifically with early years students. She gained her MA in 1991 from Southampton University. In 1999 she set up and ran the Childhood Studies degree at the University of Chichester. In 2002 she started to study for a certificate/diploma in play therapy, and this has involved placements within a local school and at Great Ormond Street Hospital, working with hospital play specialists. Carole has contributed children's titles to the Information series of the Longman's Book Project.

Jen Gardner is a senior lecturer in education at the University of Chichester. She has been working in the field of primary education for over thirty years. Jen spent the first 11 years of her teaching career in London schools, moving from ILEA to Haringey. There she was appointed as a home link teacher with responsibility for teaching across all phases in a large multicultural primary school and with the responsibility of integrating the school into the community in the post-Plowden era.

After moving to west Sussex she worked in a primary school where she had special responsibility for the children from a Bengali family who were in an isolated ethnic minority situation. She was able to use her prior experience to ensure that these children were fully included in the teaching, learning and life of the school community.

She gained her MA at the University in 1996 and completed her First Steps training in all areas of literacy assessment, teaching and learning in 1998, and is an enthusiastic member of the United Kingdom Literacy Association.

Sue Gilbert has considerable experience in many areas in the primary education sector. For over seventeen years she taught in Tower Hamlets in East London, as a class teacher and head teacher. Her teaching in Tower Hamlets involved working with children who had English as an additional language and their bilingual teaching assistants. At the University of Chichester her teaching as a senior lecturer has focused on professional values and practice, and ICT. She has been a member of the University's development team for the Foundation Degree for Teaching and Learning Support and is the deputy co-ordinator for this degree. She is involved in HLTA training and assessment and is the vice chair of governors of a local primary school with a strong commitment to inclusion. She has an MA from the Open University.

Gianna Knowles is a senior lecturer in the School of Teacher Education at the University of Chichester. She has been working in the field of primary education for over twenty years. Gianna spent 12 years in primary schools and advisory work before moving into higher education. She gained her MA in 1991 from London University's Institute of Education, and in recent years has been presenting research on School Improvement at BERA and the DfES teachers' research conferences. In 2004 she became head of provision for professional development courses for teaching assistants at the University of Chichester. This has included developing a foundation degree for teaching and learning support and developing provision for HLTAs. Gianna has also worked as a QAA subject reviewer and Ofsted inspector for nursery and primary school inspection teams.

Arvinder (Vini) Kaur Lander is head of the primary undergraduate initial teacher training programme at the University of Chichester. She has worked in education for the last 20 years as a science teacher and as a Section 11 teacher working with pupils with English as an additional language, and then as a senior lecturer in science education. She has an MA in Education from the University of Southampton. Her dissertation examined the place of multicultural education within initial teacher education. Issues of race equality have permeated her career, leading school staff and delivering staff INSET in this field. She is a qualified Ofsted inspector for nursery and primary schools, as well as for initial teacher education. In 2004 Vini took up the post of Deputy Director of Multiverse, a TDA-funded project exploring issues of diversity.

Barbara Thompson is currently head of the PGCE Primary Programme at the University of Chichester. Before moving into higher education she taught in primary schools in the Midlands and in Cleveland for 17 years. She has a long-term interest in gender issues, and before working at Chichester she was an Open University tutor on the MA module in Gender and Education. In 1989 she joined the primary team at Chichester and taught on courses in Race, Class and Gender. She now lectures in history and in professional values and practice, with a particular focus on inclusion issues, across the undergraduate and PGCE programmes. She also lectures on gender issues and research methods on the MA(Ed). She is currently undertaking her PhD in Women and Management.

Introduction

Gianna Knowles

What this book is about

> We have discovered how to engineer the blueprint of living beings but we are still search-
> ing for an environment in which children can learn with enjoyment and effect.
>
> (MacBeath and Mortimore 2001:1)

> An entitlement to learning must be an entitlement for all pupils...to ensure that all pupils
> have the chance to succeed, whatever their individual needs and the potential barriers to
> learning might be.
>
> (DfES/QCA 1999:3)

THIS BOOK IS ABOUT supporting those who work with children, particularly in preschool, nursery or primary school settings, in providing an educational environment and learning activities that will enable children to learn effectively and with enjoyment, whatever their individual needs. Defining what a school needs to do to provide an effective learning environment has been systematically studied through *school effectiveness* research since the 1960s (MacBeath and Mortimore 2001:3). However, the concept that an effective school is one that seeks to provide an *inclusive* curriculum and school environment, through seeking to address the particular learning needs of each individual, including considering their cultural background, gender and innate ability, is relatively new. The notion of an inclusive approach to education as a way of ensuring an effective education system was established by the 1999 revision of the National Curriculum:

> The National Curriculum secures for all pupils, irrespective of social background, culture,
> race, gender, differences in ability and disabilities, an entitlement to a number of areas of
> learning and to develop knowledge, understanding, skills and attitudes necessary for their
> self-fulfilment and development as active and responsible citizens.
>
> (DfES/QCA 1999:12)

The notion of inclusion has developed in response to the realisation that whatever educational measures are put in place, the success of any one child is dependent on that child experiencing an education that meets their individual needs. Each child is unique and needs an individual curriculum. While many who work with children have felt this to be the case for many years, the 'official' recognition that this is so brings with it certain challenges, perhaps unforeseen. Many who work with children have felt that the recent approach to education, particularly the curriculum documentation and requirements they have been working with, has failed to address the needs of some learners. That is, all children have had to be taught certain things, in a certain way, whether it is beneficial to the child or not. However, to now be told that teaching methods and, to some extent curriculum, content can be tailored to meet the needs of individuals raises the challenge of planning learning activities that benefit up to 35 individuals at any one time.

To help those working with children to meet this challenge, this book explores how the factors of ethnicity and culture, language, gender, special educational need, disability, and gifted and talentedness affect what children bring to the classroom, before they even begin to engage with learning activities. Having explored what makes children different it concludes with a chapter exploring something that unites all children, that is their learning styles. While home background, gender and individual needs may make children different from each other, the ways in which they learn are very similar. Planning learning activities that meet a range of learning styles will help all children learn and will go some way to help those planning the activities in their consideration of the need to provide for all children.

How have we got to this point?

Since the 1960s one of the major drivers of the British education system has been the concern to provide equal opportunities for all those who pass through the system (MacBeath and Mortimore 2001:3), in particular to meet the needs of those children who, for many reasons, schools were failing to enable to achieve. It has been a long-held view by many that to have 'a good education' is one of the most important factors in determining the quality of life a person will go on to enjoy after leaving school and, in the same way, the quality of their contribution to society as a whole. In this way, education is seen as being a way of changing a person's socio-economic circumstance, usually for the better. Not only may education be personally liberating and fulfilling in terms of the satisfaction and enjoyment gained from learning things, but it can also enable people to become more socially mobile by providing them with the opportunity to gain more rewarding employment, in both personal and financial terms.

Since 1997 there has been a concern about the standards that children, particularly 11-year-olds, are achieving in literacy and numeracy. The standards a school enables its children to attain have been used as a measure of the quality of the education the school is providing for its children. That is, to ensure children are on target to achieve long-term socio-economic benefits from their education we need to ensure they are meeting appropriate interim targets on the way. These targets are measured in the form of the end-of-key-stage tasks and tests children take at ages 7, 11 and 14.

To support schools in achieving these educational goals for children, the government has published a range of documentation, mainly relating to the academic curriculum, that schools have been expected to follow in order to help them improve the education they offer to children. For example:

- 1998 – National Literacy Strategy
- 1999 – National Numeracy Strategy
- 2000 – Revised National Curriculum
- 2003 – Curriculum Guidance for the Foundation Stage
- 2003 – *Excellence and Enjoyment*
- 2003 – *Every Child Matters*

The assumption has been that if schools take on board the practices advocated by the documentation and enable children to acquire the skills, knowledge and understanding contained within the documentation, standards of children's achievement will rise.

The notion of an entitlement to a certain level of learning

Since the 1988 Education Act, what is taught in schools in England has been largely governed by a series of government documents. As a result of the 1988 Act the English education system has for the first time in its history a National Curriculum; that is, a set of detailed subject-related skills, knowledge and understanding that every child in the country is entitled to have taught to them. It is exceptional for any child to be disapplied from the National Curriculum; that is, not expected to be taught the skills, knowledge and understanding that it covers. It is expected that all children, whatever their learning need, will be taught through the National Curriculum programmes of study, although it is recognised that the needs of some children will mean that their progress is at a different rate to that which might be expected from a child of similar age. The rationale for having a programme of learning that operates in such a way is that the National Curriculum provides a statutory entitlement, an entitlement by law (DfES/QCA 1999:3) to specific skills, knowledge and understanding, which is the same for every child.

The long tail of underachievement

Prior to the National Curriculum, schools had a much freer hand in deciding what curriculum they would provide for the children in their care. While for many children this resulted in a rich, exciting, appropriate nursery and primary school education, it was felt by many who worked in education and formulated educational policy that the system was too open to abuse and too many children were not being enabled to reach the standards of achievement expected of them by the end of their primary school years. Too many children were underachieving. By instituting a National Curriculum that is statutory, it can be better guaranteed that all children will have an equal chance of being taught at least a minimum of skills, knowledge and understanding.

To further ensure children are given this equality of opportunity in their learning, the National Curriculum brings with it expected levels of achievement for children. While schools monitor and assess children's achievement against the National Curriculum levels throughout the children's progress through school, at the end of each key stage children undertake formal national tests to assess their attainment. The end-of- key-stage tests provide an indication of how each child is attaining in relation to what might be expected from a child of that age and in relation to national attainment. More importantly, the tests provide a benchmark for the school to indicate how it is enabling its pupils to attain against the national norm. The school has a duty to teach each child, depending on their need, the skills, knowledge and understanding outlined in the National Curriculum and to expected standards of attainment by the end of key stages 1, 2 and 3.

Initially, for some schools, the introduction of the National Curriculum was felt to be a limiting feature on their provision. In view of this notion, it is worth noting that, the statutory element of the requirements outlined is a minimum expectation on which a school can build and develop its individual provision – 'a framework within which all partners in education can support young people on the road to further learning' (DfES/QCA 1999:3). The National Curriculum provides for a minimum of what must be taught and it says nothing of the methods by which the skills, knowledge and understanding may be taught. As long as schools can demonstrate that they are covering the content of the National Curriculum and are enabling children to reach the appropriate standards, schools can teach over and above the stipulated content of the curriculum and deliver it through the teaching methods they prefer: 'it is for schools to choose how they organise their school curriculum to include the programmes of study' (ibid.:17):

> The school curriculum should develop enjoyment of, and commitment to, learning as a means of encouraging and stimulating the best possible progress and the highest attainment for all pupils.
>
> (ibid.:11)

The first National Curriculum documents began to arrive in schools in the late 1980s and early 1990s. Testing children's achievement in relation to age-related expected levels of National Curriculum attainment began soon after. By 1997 the government felt it had enough evidence to claim that while many children were reaching the levels of attainment that might be expected from seven-, 11- and 14-year-olds, there were still too many children who were failing to meet their expected targets. Schools protested that not all children begin their education at the same starting point. Some begin their schooling having had a rich home experience of being read to and enjoying books, positive educational interaction with supportive adults around them who are fluent in spoken English and having had a positive nursery or playschool experience, all of which provide a strong basis for beginning the learning journey at school. Other children begin school with none of these experiences and find the adjustment to school culture very challenging. However, at the time, the government position was very much that it was for the schools to make up the difference in the children's experiences; that is, if a child failed to achieve at school, this was a failure on the school's part, not because the child might have an unsupportive or in any way inadequate home background.

To enable schools to better help children learn, particularly in the core subjects of English and mathematics, the government published the National Literacy Strategy (NLS) and the National Numeracy Strategy (NNS). These documents provide a framework or way of delivering aspects of the English and mathematics National Curriculum, but unlike the National Curriculum, they are a guide for schools – they are not statutory, although many schools have treated them as if they were. If the National Curriculum was significant in that for the first time the government laid down the content of what must be taught in schools, the NLS and NNS were significant because they provided government guidance on how things must be taught.

To this effect education policy has looked to schools to make the difference for children. However, while some difference has been made for some children, the policies of the government, particularly since 1997, have not delivered all that had been expected. Indeed the evidence for why this is the case has increasingly demonstrated that while schools can and do make a difference, school education cannot compensate entirely for society and the backgrounds from which children come (MacBeath and Mortimore 2001:2):

> children experience schools differently...achievement is not a simple linear progression but subject to ebbs and flows over time and in response to the influence of the peer group and pupils' own expectations on the basis of gender, race and social class.

This century has seen the acceptance by the government of the idea that children's backgrounds do make a difference to how children will attain at school; that if all children are really going to be provided with an equal entitlement to attaining the standard of education they are capable of, schools have to recognise children's individual starting points and differences and work from there. Children start school with individual expectations, experiences, cultural influences, levels of parental interest, skills, knowledge and understanding, and school is only part of the child's day-to-day experience and can only make some difference; having parents working alongside schools will make even more difference in enabling all children to reach the standards they are entitled to. In part, the acceptance of the notion that individual differences will affect attainment came about as the statistics showed that while the NLS and NNS had raised standards of attainment in literacy and numeracy it had not raised them to the expected target levels. In an endeavour to continue to raise standards the government went back to the research to explore what schools who were achieving high standards with their children were doing. The result of the consultation was the document *Excellence and Enjoyment*, the precursor to *Every Child Matters*. The research showed that children must enjoy a wide range of educational experiences, particularly ones that are motivating and interesting to them and, most significantly for this book, experiences that meet their particular needs. *Every Child Matters* also recognises that a child's background will impact on how well he/she does at school, and that in this way education is only part of the services that need to be readily available to children and their families in order for children to achieve not only a good standard of education but also well-being in all areas of life.

This purpose of this book is to explore difference and help those working with children to recognise differences between children and to remove the barriers to learning that those differences may create. To create the environment in which children can learn with enjoyment and effect, alluded to by MacBeath and Mortimore at the beginning of this chapter, this book discusses a range of needs children will come to school with and which schools need to make provision for. If a child's needs are recognised and barriers to their learning removed, it is more likely that the child will achieve appropriate standards of attainment in literacy and numeracy but also achieve general well-being. Each chapter provides practical help in enabling those who work with children, teaching them and supporting their learning, to recognise and use the unique qualities each child brings to the classroom to enable that individual's learning.

What is inclusion?

Chapter 1 explores what we mean when we talk of inclusion. It explores why it is important to have inclusive schools and an inclusive society. It discusses how schools need to be aware of children's cultural backgrounds, gender, special educational needs, disabilities, gifts and talents to ensure they are providing for them in an inclusive way. It provides the underpinning knowledge and understanding of the principles of inclusion. This knowledge and understanding will help in tackling some of the challenging issues raised by other chapters in the book. Chapter 1 briefly explores the history of the inclusion debate, outlining how inclusive practice is central to the National Curriculum and is becoming ever more central in the lives of all those who work with children through the *Every Child Matters* agenda.

Multi-agency working in the early years: a model of good practice

Chapter 2 picks up aspects of the *Every Child Matters* agenda, particularly as it relates to young children and the examples of good multi-agency practice that are being developed in early years settings. These examples of good practice are offered as an indication of the way the multi-agency working aspects of the *Every Child Matters* legislation can be made to work throughout the primary school range. In terms of inclusive practice it is important to consider the early years since, as the chapter explores, early years settings, including those set up through the SureStart scheme, are the start of the child's experience in education, and these years will lay the foundations not just for early learning but also for the way in which the child sees himself or herself. For this reason the early years specialist has an enormous responsibility to 'get it right' for each child within a differentiated learning experience.

Race, ethnicity and equality

Chapter 3 introduces the key terms associated with this area of inclusion. It challenges the assumptions on which we make our judgements about groups of people. The chapter asks the reader to examine their own preconceptions and beliefs and to explore their school's policies and practices in this area, to ensure we are all moving towards a truly inclusive approach. The chapter also provides an overview of the historical developments related to race, education and inclusion, since it is essential to understand the origins of the inclusion debate with regard to ethnicity in order to understand the contemporary societal climate, which inevitably impacts on school life regardless of the school's location.

Children who have English as an additional language

Chapter 4 aims to provide practical advice for those working with children for whom English is an additional language (EAL). In particular it aims to develop knowledge and understanding that will help the reader plan and prepare appropriate learning activities for EAL children. It identifies the importance of accurate assessments being made, assessments which will truly reflect individual children's stages of development in relation to subjects across the curriculum, and not simply in response to the child's developing knowledge and understanding of English. That is, having English as an additional language does not mean the child is not able to engage in learning activities at a level appropriate to their age range. The chapter also seeks to explore the key factors likely to affect the way pupils who have English as an additional language learn. It demonstrates ways in which professional values and practice can be developed in this area, including how to liaise effectively with parents and carers, recognising their roles in pupils' learning.

Reviewing gender issues in the primary classroom

Chapter 5 explores how the focus on gender and achievement has changed and developed over the last 20 years. The chapter charts how, perhaps surprisingly, the focus has moved from a concern with what was perceived in the 1970s as the educational disadvantages experienced by girls to a twenty-first-century national focus on the underachievement of boys. The chapter explains the history of the debate surrounding the issue of why gender affects achievement in school and how, as a result of intense media interest and Ofsted's attention on boys' underachievement, millions of pounds of government money has been spent on developing strategies to remedy 'the problem of boys'. A knowledge and understanding of the issues discussed are essential for those who work in schools who wish to make effective interventions in challenging gender inequalities, for both sexes, in the classroom.

Supporting children with autistic spectrum disorders in a mainstream classroom

Chapter 6 explores how the understanding and awareness of autistic spectrum disorders has grown in recent years, and as a result, more children with autistic spectrum disorder are being identified. The likelihood is that most schools will have children with these needs in their classrooms and therefore it is crucial for practitioners to understand how to best meet these children's social, personal and learning needs. This chapter sets out to provide you with an introduction to the current understanding of ASD and how these children may present in the school context. The chapter will also explore how the environment can be managed and learning facilitated. Finally, it will describe how the autistic child and their peers can be helped to understand the problem.

Physical and sensory disability

Chapter 7 discusses how, since the introduction of the Disability Discrimination Act (DDA), schools have been admitting children with disabilities not previously met in mainstream schools. Often many of these children with disabilities will have extra support, and the chapter highlights the importance adults needing to work as a team to ensure appropriate education and care for such children. The chapter also explains how the DDA relates to all aspects of school life, including extra-curricular activities and school visits. It seeks to provide a sound level of understanding of current legislation and requirements and a consideration of how physical and sensory disabilities impact on the child's experiences in school. Ways of offering structured support within the classroom are discussed, including the use of information and communication technology (ICT).

Gifted and talented

Chapter 8 explores what it means when we say a child is gifted or talented, particularly with reference to the definition used by the DfES. In particular, the chapter considers what constitutes barriers to learning for gifted and talented children. That such children can experience barriers to learning can be challenging to those working with them, since to a gifted or talented child more things seem possible than is the case for many other children. However, research has shown that where children do not have their giftedness or talentedness recognised and planned for, such neglect can lead to children failing to reach their potential, often becoming bored and disaffected, and in the saddest cases, becoming so disruptive that they are excluded, or so bored that they simply refuse to attend school.

Learning styles: overcoming barriers to learning

This book examines the variety of intellectual, cultural, social and linguistic backgrounds that individual children might bring to the learning environment. The different chapters explore a variety of factors that, if not considered and managed appropriately, may unwittingly lead to those managing the learning environment to place unnecessary barriers in the way of a child's learning. While this book explores the differences between children, Chapter 9 looks at children's learning from the standpoint of what unites them all; that is the learning styles they share. It discusses how to plan learning activities that seek to meet children's needs through considering the notion of multiple intelligences; visual, auditory and kinaesthetic learning styles; and Accelerated Learning Systems.

Bibliography

DfES/QCA (1999) *The National Curriculum: Handbook for Primary Teachers in England KS1 and KS2.* London: DFES/QCA.

MacBeath, J. and Mortimore, P. (2001) *Improving School Effectiveness.* Buckingham: Open University Press.

Slee, R., Weiner, G. and Tomlinson, S. (1998) *School Effectiveness for Whom?* London: Falmer Press.

1

What do we mean when we talk about inclusion?

Gianna Knowles

Inclusivity: how far all pupils benefit, according to need, from what the school provides.

(Ofsted 2003:77)

Educational inclusion is more than a concern about any one group of pupils...its scope is broad. It is about equal opportunities for all pupils, whatever their age, gender, ethnicity, attainment and background.

(Ofsted 2000:4)

Introduction

THIS CHAPTER AIMS to explore the principles that underpin the concept of inclusion and what inclusive practice might be. Its purpose is to provide the reader with knowledge and understanding which will help them approach the issues raised throughout the rest of the book. It explores why it is important to have inclusive schools and an inclusive society. It discusses why schools need to be aware of children's cultural backgrounds, gender, special educational needs, disabilities and gifts and talents so that all those who work with children may provide appropriate learning activities for all pupils, whatever their needs.

Every Child Matters: the next phase in the step towards inclusive schools

Developing an inclusive learning environment is a priority for all schools. Many schools have been working hard over recent years to ensure that all members of the school community feel wanted and respected and belong to a school that provides for their learning needs and enables them to achieve their potential. However, the Children Act 2004 heralds further developments for schools in their work towards ensuring their school is an inclusive one. This new challenge is presented in the form of the government's *Every Child Matters* agenda (DfES 2004b). *Every Child Matters*

(ECM) moves developments in inclusion policy forward. It recognises that the care, nurturing and education of children and young people is the responsibility of a variety of agencies. However, currently, separate agencies have responsibility for particular aspects of the child's and young person's welfare. For example, traditionally, schools are concerned with a child's education, and social services with the child's home background. While both agencies do have contact with one another there are tragic instances where some children seem to slip between agencies and where there has been a failure to prevent terrible abuse occurring. Indeed, it was the tragic death of Victoria Climbié in 2000 and the subsequent enquiry into the failure of the services involved in her care that has led to the development of the ECM agenda.

Case study 1.1

Victoria Climbié died on 25 February 2000. She had 128 separate injuries on her body, including cigarette burns, scars where she had been hit by a bike chain and hammer blows to her toes. The eight-year-old died from abuse and neglect while living with her aunt, Marie-Therese Kouao, and her aunt's boyfriend Carl Manning. Both were jailed for life for her murder in January 2001.

A public inquiry into her death in 2001 called for radical reforms of child protection services in England. The inquiry found that Victoria was seen by dozens of social workers, nurses, doctors and police officers before she died, but all failed to spot and stop the abuse. Lord Laming, who described Victoria's death as the worst case of neglect he had ever heard of, headed the inquiry. He stated: 'I remain amazed that nobody in any of the key agencies had the presence of mind to follow what are relatively straightforward procedures'.

In response to the findings of the inquiry, the then Health Secretary, Alan Milburn, said that the relevant agencies had more than a dozen opportunities within ten months to act to save Victoria but failed to do so. In a special statement to the House of Commons he stated: 'This was not a failing on the part of one service, it was a failing on the part of every service' (www.news.bbc.co.uk/hi/uk/2698295.stm).

Victoria's story is a particularly horrific example of child abuse and the failure of the agencies involved in her care to help her. However, for all the cases brought to the attention of the nation through media coverage there are many other cases where children are not being properly protected and looked after, cases that need to be addressed. ECM recognises that all those who work with children, in whatever capacity, have a duty, now enshrined in law, to be responsible for the overall welfare of those children and young people with whom they work. Through the ECM policy all agencies that work with children and young people will be brought together as Children's Services to work in a cross-agency, multi-disciplinary way to ensure that children are healthy, safe, achieving at school, making a positive contribution to the community and achieving economic well-being. The government thinking behind the ECM policy states: 'The Children Act 2004 secured Royal Assent on 15 November 2004. The Act is the legislative spine on which we want to build our reforms of children's services' (DfES 2004b:5).

The ECM policy applies to children, young people and their families, although for the purposes of this discussion, to save being too long-winded, the phrase will be abbreviated to 'child' and 'children'. Although the breadth of the agenda means all who work within a children's service, in whatever capacity, have a care responsibility for all children, young people and their families.

The underpinning principles of ECM are linked to five outcomes for children that the government has identified as being central to children's welfare. These are outlined below.

> Children and young people have told us that five outcomes are key to well-being in child-hood and later life – being healthy; staying safe; enjoying and achieving; making a positive contribution; and achieving economic well-being. Our ambition is to improve the outcomes for all children and to narrow the gap in outcomes between those who do well and those who do not.
>
> (ibid.:4)

Before further discussion about what changes ECM may mean for schools, the following activity will help you to assess how far along the path towards an inclusive educational setting your school already is.

Activity 1.1: Building an inclusive environment

Below is a set of indicators that any truly inclusive school will demonstrate. How many of the indicators apply to your school?

- Everyone is made to feel welcome.
- Children help each other.
- All adults support each other and work together.
- All adults and children treat each other with respect.
- Parents are welcome and there is evidence of a strong, mutually supportive partnership between the school and parents.
- The school has close links with the community, is involved in the work and activities of the local community, and the community has strong links with the school.

Schools that are able to demonstrate they are meeting the above criteria are well on their way to establishing an inclusive environment for children. The next phase in development is to continue to develop this inclusive practice, but within the school as part of the broader setting of a children's service, as required by the new legislation. For ECM to realise the ambition of improving the lives of all children and to ensure that all the five outcomes listed are met for each child, the following measures have been agreed by the government:

- the improvement and integration of universal services – in early years settings, schools and the Health Service;
- more specialised help to promote opportunity, prevent problems and act early and effectively if and when problems arise;
- the reconfiguration of services around the child and family in one place – for example, children's centres, extended schools and the bringing together of professionals in multi-disciplinary teams;
- dedicated and enterprising leadership at all levels of the system;
- the development of a shared sense of responsibility across agencies for safeguarding children and protecting them from harm; and
- listening to children, young people and their families when assessing and planning service provision, as well as in face-to-face delivery.

(ibid.:4).

What are children's services?

A children's service is a co-operative arrangement between 'among others, schools, social services, healthcare provision, culture, sports and play organisations, and the voluntary and community sector' (ibid.:12). All these agencies do not necessarily have to be on the same site. At present, local authorities are developing children's service provision in local areas and are exploring how best to secure co-operation between geographically local schools, healthcare provision and other partners. Therefore, in some cases, all the provision that comes under the umbrella of children's services will be on one site, while in other cases schools will be linked to specific local provision in their area, but on sites a small distance from the school.

Case study 1.2

The SureStart programme is a pioneer of the multi-disciplinary approach to meeting the educational, health and welfare needs of young children and their families. The principles that underpin SureStart, and its children's centres, provide a good model for the devopment of children's services for older children, young people and their families.

SureStart children's centres are places where children under 5 and their families can receive seamless, holistic, integrated services and information, and where they can access help from multi-disciplinary teams of professionals. These teams will include trained nursery staff and healthcare professionals, and often strong links to the community and community sport, culture and leisure programmes. SureStart children's centres enable all families with children to have access to an affordable, flexible, high-quality childcare place for their child. They provide choice for parents and the best start for children. In most cases, parents are directly involved in the descision-making and running of the children's services.

- SureStart is a government programme which aims to achieve better outcomes, helping services development in disadvantaged areas alongside help for parents to afford childcare; and

- rolling out the principles driving the SureStart approach to all services for children and parents.

SureStart provision brings together universal, free early education, and more and better childcare. A significant number of families with young children already benefit from good-quality integrated services. SureStart children's centres enhance these services and extend the benefits to more families, bringing an integrated approach to service delivery to areas where it is most needed.

The government is committed to delivering a SureStart children's centre for every community by 2010. SureStart children's centres are a vital part of the government's ten-year childcare strategy.

(www.surestart.gov.uk/surestartservices/settings/surestartchildrenscentres)

ECM recognises that schools already do much to support children's wider well-being (ibid.:14) and that schools have been working to make sure that individual children's needs are met. ECM acknowledges that schools have developed their inclusion practices to ensure that they:

- ensure that pupils attend school and behave responsibly and thoughtfully;

- engage parents and carers as partners in children's learning;

- offer a wide range of activities, from sporting and cultural activities to childcare; and

- have a formal duty to safeguard pupils and promote their welfare.

(ibid.:14)

Plans are also being implemented under ECM to extend the services offered by schools through the extended schools programme (ibid.). Extended schools will be those schools that offer childcare and other activities for children and families from eight o'clock in the morning until six o'clock in the evening. Schools are encouraged to work with the private, voluntary and community sectors to develop this provision, and many schools, as has already been suggested, already offer all or part of an extended schools service. Becoming an extended school is voluntary, whereas, by law, all schools will become part of a children's service. It is not expected that staff already involved in working in schools, either as teachers or support workers, will have to be involved in the extended schools activities; however, many support workers may see opportunities to develop their skills, knowledge and understanding or to use talents they have, and will want to be involved in the extended school provision.

One of the underpinning principles in the move towards children's services and extended schools is the need to involve parents in their children's education and development. Many schools already have very good policies and practices in place for working with parents and involving children. The next activity will enable you to gauge how effective your school is in working in partnership with parents. Look through the indicators of good practice and note those that apply to your school.

Activity 1.2

A school that has a good partnership with its parents is one:

- that does not patronise parents, that is it does not assume that, fundamentally, it knows what is best for the child and its family and has fixed views on how what is best can be properly achieved;
- to which parents are routinely expected to come as part of day-to-day school life, at the beginning and end of school, to leave or collect children, to 'help' around the school, or because school is part of the community life of the parents;
- that listens to parents' ideas, worries and concerns and acts upon them;
- that has open and well-developed communication systems to encourage parents to talk to school staff, for example:

    1 a named member of staff whom they can easily contact, by phone or by 'dropping in';

    2 parents can expected to be contacted quickly and appropriately in the event of any concern, or to communicate positive aspects of the child's behaviour and achievement at school;

- where parents are involved in the strategic decision-making of the school;
- where parents' particular skills and expertise are valued and accessed by the school; and
- where communication between school and home is accessible in the language a parent prefers to communicate in; while having printed matter translated easily into a variety of languages, a school may need to think more creatively about verbal communication in different languages; this is where using the skills of a bilingual parent may help.

So far this chapter has looked at the wider implications of the ECM agenda. The rest of the chapter will focus on how ECM will have a specific impact on schools and the general principles that underpin inclusion. In the ECM agenda, while all who work with children have a duty to enable a child to achieve in all five outcomes, it is recognised that schools have a particular role to play in enabling children to enjoy and achieve:

> Pupil performance and well-being go hand in hand. Pupils can't learn if they don't feel safe or if health problems are allowed to create barriers. And doing well in education is the most effective route for young people out of poverty and disaffection.
>
> (DfES 2004c:1)

The significant contribution schools can make to enabling the five outcomes for children to be achieved is in ensuring that they provide an inclusive, personalised education that will continue to raise educational standards. Building on the work on inclusion already begun by schools, schools also need to ensure that they:

- develop links with other agencies so that children with additional needs can be identified early and supported effectively;
- continue to develop anti-bullying and -discrimination practices and keep children safe;
- become a healthy school, promoting healthy lifestyles through Personal, Social and Health Education lessons, drug education, breakfast clubs and sporting activities;
- ensure attendance, encouraging pupils to behave responsibly, giving them a strong voice in the life of the school and encouraging them to volunteer to help others;
- help communities to value education and be aware that it is the way out of the poverty trap.

> (ibid.:1)

To help schools in determining how well they are doing in meeting the ECM agenda and providing appropriately for the children in their care, new inspection arrangements have been developed. How and what Ofsted will now inspect, to report what schools are doing well and how they can improve, will be discussed later in the chapter.

The picture as it is now

If the outcome of enjoyment and achievement is to be realised for children, then schools need to be sure that their educational provision provides for the needs of all children. The basis for what forms the content of the curriculum, and the skills, knowledge and understanding children are entitled to be taught, is contained within a number of curriculum documents. For children in early years and Foundation stage settings, this is *Curriculum Guidance for the Foundation Stage*. For children in key stages 1, 2 and 3, the document is the National Curriculum.

Inclusion and the National Curriculum

In 1999 the government published its revised National Curriculum. The document *The National Curriculum Handbook for Primary School Teachers* (DfES 1999) not only includes the programmes of study for each of the subjects covered by the National Curriculum but also sets out the principles that underpin the National Curriculum, its aims and its purpose. Indeed, these are very significant, but often overlooked, aspects of the document. Working under pressure to plan appropriate learning activities in line with the requirements of the National Curriculum's programmes of study for any given subject may seem to leave little time to consider the values, aims and purposes that underpin the curriculum. However, it is in this document that the government most clearly outlines what an inclusive school and education need to encompass. More than this, the document states that schools have a responsibility to provide a broad and balanced curriculum for all pupils, and that this is statutory; that is, all children have an entitlement to *effective learning opportunities* by law (ibid.:30). The National Curriculum sets out three principles that are essential for schools to consider if they are to develop an inclusive approach to education and the curriculum. They are:

1 setting suitable learning challenges;

2 responding to pupils' diverse learning needs;

3 overcoming potential barriers to learning and assessment for individuals and groups of pupils.

(ibid.)

Three principles for inclusion

1. Setting suitable learning challenges

Teachers should aim to give every pupil the opportunity to experience success in learning and to achieve as high a standard as possible.

(ibid.)

The National Curriculum aims to provide a 'balanced and broadly based curriculum' (ibid.:12), not only in terms of the subject knowledge and understanding children are expected to acquire throughout their compulsory school years, but it also seeks to 'promote the spiritual, moral, cultural, mental and physical development of pupils' (ibid.). As stated, the National Curriculum is a statutory entitlement for all children, that is to say all children are entitled to the skills, knowledge and understanding the National Curriculum embodies, by law. This is significant for two reasons: first, it means that all schools have a duty to all children, whatever their social or cultural background, differences in ability or disability, to teach them the skills, knowledge and understanding outlined in the National Curriculum. In this way all children can expect to have an education that develops for them similar skills, knowledge and understanding as for any other child in the country, thus providing a level playing field in terms of educational experience; and secondly, not only can a child expect a certain minimum entitlement to what constitutes their education, but also those working with children in mainstream schools have a legal as well as a moral duty to ensure all children are taught the knowledge, skills and understanding covered by the National Curriculum in ways that suit the children's abilities. This firmly places the emphasis on providing the expected learning challenges for all pupils in a way that they can access them with those planning and designing the learning challenges. Where children are receiving an education that matches these requirements, not only will they have taken on board a range of skills, knowledge and understanding, but also they will have been enabled to achieve self-fulfilment and develop as active responsible citizens, as set out in the National Curriculum (ibid.).

Activity 1.3

Below is a set of indicators that **inclusive learning activities** should demonstrate. Over your next few working days note how many of the indicators apply to the lessons you support:

- Learning activities are responsive to the diversity of the children's learning needs in all classrooms.
- All children are able to access the learning activities.
- Children are actively involved in their own learning.
- Children have the opportunity to learn collaboratively.
- Ongoing assessment is used to (a) monitor the achievement of all children and (b) set learning targets to ensure progress.
- Classroom discipline emphasises positive, wanted behaviours and is based on mutual respect.
- All children take part in activities outside the classroom.

2. Responding to pupils' diverse learning needs

The DfES has identified a number of different groups of children who may have particular needs when it comes to learning. These groups are: boys and girls, children with SEN, children with disabilities, children from all social and cultural backgrounds, children from different ethnic groups including Gypsy Travellers, refugees and asylum seekers, and those from diverse linguistic backgrounds (ibid.). This chapter outlines the main principles of inclusion; the remainder of the book will seek to look at these different groups in more detail and explore how schools can ensure that they are meeting the needs of this diverse range of children when planning for learning.

When planning learning activities it is important to be aware of these different groups of children, because our own background and experiences may, unwittingly, influence how we approach planning and delivering the learning experiences. Just as we need to keep updating our subject knowledge to ensure we have a good basis of knowledge and understanding of the subjects from which to plan and teach, so we also need to keep ensuring we have researched the knowledge and understanding that we might need in order to teach children in a group that we have less experience of dealing with. We need to do this since the place where a child comes from, geographically, culturally and socially, will mean that it will bring particular 'experiences, interests and strengths which will influence the way they learn' (ibid.). If the learning activities presented to the children are of a context outside their experience, it is unlikely that the children will be able to engage with them fully. For example, in the traditional stories of some cultures, fairies, dragons and witches may not figure, or may have very different attributes to the ones they have in traditional European tales. It may be necessary to explain the characteristics of these story beings, or what they are, before some children can access particular parts of the curriculum or certain learning activities.

3. Overcoming potential barriers to learning and assessment for individuals and groups of pupils

As discussed in the section above, the National Curriculum Handbook recognises that schools comprise children with a wide range of learning needs. It also recognises that a minority of children will have 'particular learning and assessment requirements which go beyond the provisions described already' (ibid.:33). These are specific learning needs that are likely to arise, perhaps because of a specific educational need or disability or because for the child has English as an additional language (ibid.). The National Curriculum Handbook details these particular groups of children as being:

- pupils with special educational needs;

- pupils with disabilities; and

- pupils who are learning English as an additional language (EAL).

The next two sections of this chapter outline the principles of inclusion with regard to these specific groups of children. The two sections below also explore the recent experiences of these groups, particularly how there have, in the past, been barriers to their learning, and why, therefore, inclusion is so important to ensure these barriers are removed and all children have the chance to achieve the standards expected of them.

Inclusion and pupils with special educational needs and disabilities

All those who work with children in early years settings and primary school classrooms know that no two children's learning needs are the same. Learning activities are routinely planned to differentiate for the varying learning abilities of the children in the teaching group. Similarly, those working in early years settings and the primary classroom know and understand that while it is straightforward to plan learning activities for a variety of learning abilities there are those children in the teaching group who have learning needs over and above what might usually be expected in other children in their peer group. That is, some children can be identified as having special educational needs (SEN); however, the routine planning for such children and the acceptance that children with SEN should be in mainstream classrooms is a relatively new idea in education.

Before the 1980s it was likely that those children who seemed to have profound learning difficulties, perhaps because of a physical disability, would attend and be educated in special schools. However, since then, there has been a growing awareness of the need to ensure that everyone has the opportunity to take equal advantage of the opportunities afforded by our society. These may be opportunities that are linked to education, health or social and economic well-being, and that the principle of equality of opportunity extends to children who are deemed to have SEN.

Here we are concerned with the principle of equality of opportunity as it relates to the education of children with SEN. Since the 1980s there has been a range of legislation put in place by successive governments to ensure that children with SEN can have wider access to mainstream schooling. The 1981 Education Act began this process; it required that schools make formal, documented arrangements for identifying and meeting SEN (Ofsted 2004:3). This legislation was further strengthened by the 1993 Education Act which enshrined in law the principle that children with SEN should – where this is what the parents want – be normally educated in mainstream schools (DfES 2001:1). However, while this principle seemed to ensure that children with SEN would have greater equality of opportunity in terms of deciding where they could go to school, before a child could be placed in a mainstream school the families of the children had to fulfil a number of conditions. It had to be demonstrated that the mainstream school of choice could provide appropriate educational opportunities for the child, given the child's learning difficulties. It also had to be demonstrated that the school could provide the education the child's difficulty called for, 'while also ensuring the efficient education of others with whom she or he would be educated and that resources would be used efficiently' (ibid.). While the legislation was designed to broaden SEN children's access to mainstream schooling, it was found that these conditions were open to abuse and children who would have benefited from inclusion were denied access to mainstream education (ibid.).

Since 1993, the concept of inclusion with regard to SEN has developed significantly. In 1994 the United Kingdom agreed to support the statement drawn up by UNESCO's world conference in Spain. The statement calls upon all governments to 'adopt as a matter of law or policy the principle of inclusive education enrolling all children in regular schools, unless there are compelling reasons for doing otherwise' (ibid.). This statement changes the emphasis from the need for families to demonstrate why the school should accept the child, to the expectation that the school will accept the child unless it can demonstrate compelling reasons for doing otherwise. Not only is it expected that where families want a mainstream education for their child everything possible should be done to provide it, but also the range of special educational needs under consideration also broadened. Since 1993 the concept of inclusion for pupils with SEN related to learning difficulties has broadened to include a range of other particular needs, for example children with physical disabilities and conditions such as autism and Asperger's syndrome, which may affect behaviour and the child's ability to socialise.

In 2001 the Special Educational Needs and Disability Act provided a new legal framework for the inclusion of children with SEN in mainstream schools. The Act significantly:

> strengthens the right of children with SEN to attend a mainstream school, unless their parents choose otherwise or if this incompatible with 'efficient education for other children' and there are no 'reasonable steps' which the school and LEA can take to prevent that incompatibility.
>
> (Ofsted 2004:3)

In the same year, the Disability Discrimination Act placed new duties on schools not to treat disabled pupils less favourably than others and to make 'reasonable adjustments' to ensure that they are not disadvantaged (ibid.).

From these most recent pieces of legislation we can see the government firmly signalling the principles of what is to be seen as an inclusive education:

> The new legislation expects mainstream schools to include all pupils fully, making appropriate changes to their organisation, curriculum, accommodation and teaching methods. It places duties on schools and LEAs to ensure this happens.
>
> (ibid.).

Activity 1.4: Training to become an inclusive environment

Many schools have been undertaking in-service training and other review activities to ensure their school is an inclusive environment. Below is a checklist of some of the activities schools have undertaken to move towards a more inclusive environment. Read through the list and note how many of the activities listed your school has been involved in and what your role in the activities has been:

- developing strategies to improve children's self-esteem;

- staff development – for teaching and support staff in how to ensure learning activities are accessible by all children;

- considering how support staff are managed and deployed to better ensure inclusion;

- improving the school environment for all children and adults with a disability;

- improving the induction process for children new to the school;

- reviewing the way in which children have a 'say' in school issues and evidence that the children's ideas and concerns are implemented or resolved; and

- improving the partnership with parents.

Inclusion and children for whom English is an additional language, including children from minority ethnic groups

As information about the achievement of children in the National Curriculum end-of-key-stage tasks and tests began to be collected and collated during the 1990s, it became evident that a number of trends were emerging in terms of those children who were achieving or could achieve what was expected of them given their age and normal performance and what they were actually achieving. The evidence showed that children from African-Caribbean and Bangladeshi cultural backgrounds particularly were achieving less well than children from other cultural groups. While measures were put in place to begin to combat the issues, in 2003 the DfES launched a consultation document on the achievement of children from minority ethnic groups that stated: 'the attainment of minority ethnic pupils remains a matter of serious concern' (DfES 2003a:10).

If we are to begin to understand and explore why children from ethnic minority cultures achieve less well in school than children from other cultural groups, and if we are to consider how we might ensure a more inclusive schooling for them, we must first address the issue of racism.

> Racism has always been the major enemy of democracy and of liberal societies. The fact that institutional racism persists in liberal societies, including Britain, even today, means that the whole basis of democracy and citizenship is constantly undermined.
>
> (Osler 2003:4)

Modern Britain is often referred to as a multicultural society (ibid.:9). Osler explores what this means, outlining how the policy of postwar immigration encouraged Afro-Caribbean individuals and families to come to Britain to fuel the depleted post-Second World War workforce and to enable Britain's rebuilding, and how this has led to the 'growth of visible minority communities' (ibid.:10). The growing diversity of cultures and communities in Britain has brought with it the problem of racism. The racist behaviour that occurs in schools can be complex and falls into a range of categories. The most observable form of racism is racist behaviour, for example name-calling, intimidating behaviour by one individual or group towards other individuals or groups of children, deliberate exclusion from social activities and, more recently, the use of mobile phone text messaging to pass racist texts and pictures.

However, racism is not always observable. The Macpherson Report, published in 1999, which reported on the inquiry into the racist murder of the teenager Stephen Lawrence, identified a further type of racist behaviour, that of institutional racism. A central part of the report was concerned with a discussion about what constitutes racism:

> Racism in general terms consists of conduct or words or practices which disadvantage people because of their colour, culture or ethnic origin. In its more subtle form it is as damaging as in its overt form.

> (Macpherson 1999:6.4)

In exploring the 'subtle' forms that racism can take, the notion of institutional racism developed:

> the collective failure of an organisation to provide an appropriate and professional service to people because of their colour, culture or ethnic origin. It can be seen or detected in processes, attitudes and behaviour which amount to discrimination through unwitting prejudice, ignorance, thoughtlessness and racist stereotyping which disadvantage minority ethnic people.

It persists because of the failure of the organisation openly and adequately to recognise and address its existence and causes by policy, example and leadership. Without recognition and action to eliminate such racism it can prevail as part of the ethos or culture of the organisation. It is a corrosive disease. (ibid.:6.34)

For many years schools have developed and abided by their anti-racist policy, policies which outline procedures for dealing with racist behaviour when it is found to be occurring. However, the drawing up and subsequent modification of these policies has often been in direct response to government legislation. That is, in some cases, schools wrote the policy because they 'had to do so' as a legal requirement. In 2000 the Race Relations (Amendment) Act was passed. This Act came after the Macpherson Report and requires schools to work within the statutory Code of

Practice produced by the Commission for Racial Equality (CRE). In the light of this legislation, and through the development of the concept of institutional racism, school policies now need to be proactive, not reactive, in tackling the issue of racism and equality of opportunity for all children, whatever their cultural background. That is, schools must seek to prevent racism occurring, not simply react when it does occur. In the light of the 2000 Race Relations (Amendment) Act, school policies must aim to:

- eliminate racial discrimination;
- promote equality of opportunity; and
- promote good race relations.

Schools are not being inclusive simply by dealing with racist incidents as they occur; they must actively put in place strategies and actions that ensure equality of opportunity and promote good race relations. To ensure that equal opportunities policies take effect, schools must:

- monitor pupils' achievement and behaviour, including attendance and exclusion by ethnic group, and set targets for improving these areas of schooling, in part through deploying grant-aided support more effectively;
- keep curricular and pastoral strategies under review to ensure they benefit all ethnic groups;
- give clear priority to ensuring pupils from ethnic groups make good progress; and
- counter harassment and stereotyping.

(DfES 2003c:9).

Mainly white schools

The concept of multiculturalism is often exclusive of white communities, which may mistakenly be assumed to be culturally homogeneous.

(Osler 2003:10)

This shift in emphasis, in terms of legislation, policies and actions with regard to ensuring the inclusion of minority ethnic cultures, is perhaps most challenging for those schools that have an entirely white, or mainly white, pupil intake. While all schools have policies which outline how they deal with racist behaviour, when it is found to occur, mainly white schools have often felt this policy to be redundant, as they have claimed that since they have no children from minority ethnic cultures, no racism occurs. However, this is the very institutional racism that the Macpherson Report highlights. There is a duty on the school to promote race relations and to counter stereotyping. Simply believing that because there are few, or no, children from a minority ethnic culture attending the school, inclusion of such groups is irrelevant, is 'unwitting racism' (Macpherson 1999:6.17), in as much as it shows 'lack of understanding, ignorance and mistaken beliefs' (ibid.) about the cultural diversity of the Britain we now live in. If children in mainly white schools are not provided with the opportunity to explore and engage with the diverse cultural heritage of Britain they will continue to view children from cultures different to their own as 'other' and 'alien'. As the government document *Aiming High: Understanding the Educational Needs of Minority Ethnic Pupils in Mainly White Schools* states:

- many teachers in mainly white schools minimise the significance and value of cultural diversity;

- many minority ethnic pupils, in consequence, are discouraged from appreciating and expressing important aspects of their identity and heritage;

- mainly white schools are frequently not sufficiently aware of racism in the school population and in the local neighbourhood;

- in general, mainly white schools do not adequately prepare their pupils for adult life in a society that is culturally and ethnically diverse.

(DfES 2003c:3)

That is to say, because there may seem to be no incidents of racist behaviour in mainly white schools, it does not mean that racism does not exist, or that racist beliefs are not held. Indeed the challenge for such schools is to find ways of exploring the beliefs of their pupils and finding ways of helping them to be prepared for 'adult life in a society that is culturally and ethnically diverse' (DfES 2004b:3).

So far this section of the chapter has dealt with inclusion as it relates to the diversity of cultures within Britain in terms of white, non-white or black cultural groups. However, minority ethnic cultures also include white minority ethnic groups.

Recent constitutional reform in the UK, including the establishment of a Scottish Parliament and Welsh Assembly, and the development of a new settlement between Britain and Northern Ireland, have led to increased interest and debate on what it means to be British and how citizenship is related to national and regional identities. So, for example, what does it mean to be British and Scottish? Meanings of nationality and identity are being re-examined and re-defined.

(Osler 2003:11)

As Osler states: 'the diversity and range of identities within the white population is something that tends to be overlooked when we are thinking about minority ethnic cultures' (ibid.).

We need to acknowledge that racism and discrimination in British society are not confined to 'visible' and established minorities, but that other individuals and communities, including refugees and asylum seekers, Jewish and Irish people, and Gypsies and Travellers, may currently experience racism, prejudice, disadvantage, harassment and violence.

(ibid.:13)

Indeed the government has identified children from Gypsy Traveller families as those being most at risk of being failed by the education system (DfES 2003c:7). Schools with Gypsy Traveller children are most often located in rural areas that mainly serve village communities (ibid.:6). It is often the very same schools that claim to be all-, or mainly, white schools with no minority ethnic diversity.

Inclusion – other groups

In exploring the background to and principles of inclusion, this chapter has looked in detail at three particular groups of children: those children with SEN; those with disabilities; and children from minority ethnic groups, including Traveller children, refugees and asylum seekers. Other groups of children to whom these principles apply are those who are deemed gifted or talented and those who have particular needs because of gender. The subsequent chapters of this book will look in specific detail at the needs of all the different groups outlined above and provide ideas on how to plan for and avoid barriers to their learning.

How does a school know when they have got it right?

In developing an inclusive approach to education a school needs to ensure its policies are underpinned by the following DfES key principles:

- with the right strategies and support nearly all children can be successfully included in mainstream education;
- an inclusive education offers excellence and choice and incorporates the views of parents and children;
- the interests of all children must be safeguarded;
- schools should actively seek to remove barriers to learning and participation;
- all children should have access to an appropriate education that affords them the opportunity to achieve their personal potential.

(DfES 2001:2)

Activity 1.5: How are inclusive values evident in your school?

Look for the following indicators:

- every child is known well by a teacher or support worker, or other appropriate adult;
- children feel that people in the school like them;
- children feel valued for themselves rather than for what they have – or can achieve;
- all adults who work in the school, in paid work or in a voluntary capacity, feel valued and supported;
- significant events, such as births, deaths and illnesses, are appropriately acknowledged;
- it is recognised that everyone belongs to a 'culture' or 'cultures';
- staff avoid demonising particular children;
- basic facilities such as toilets, showers and lockers, are kept in good order;
- children's wishes for modesty, such as in changing for activities, is respected.

(QCA 2001:59)

All schools will be developing their inclusive practice in line with these principles and many schools are very good at self-monitoring and self-evaluation of how effective their policies are. What has been outlined so far is the model of good practice, with regard to inclusion, that the government proposes for schools. Ofsted is the agency that, through inspection, monitors and reports on how well schools are doing in response to the proposals. The framework for inspecting schools changed in September 2005 to enable schools to be inspected in line with the ECM agenda (Ofsted 2005a). Ofsted's purpose in inspecting schools is to provide 'an independent, external evaluation of the quality and standards of the school' (ibid.:4). During an inspection the inspectors will look for a range of evidence to base their judgements upon. In terms of what they are looking for with reference to inclusion, they will be seeking evidence about how well the school:

- meets the educational needs of the range of pupils at the school;
- provides for the spiritual, moral, social and cultural development of the pupils at the school; and
- the contribution made by the school to the well-being of those pupils.

(ibid.)

As part of the inspection process, inspectors also seek the views of parents, pupils and other partners about the school's work (ibid.:10); and throughout the inspection, inspectors will talk to children to canvass their views and gather evidence about how well they are achieving. Some of the indicators, with regard to inclusion, that demonstrate schools are meeting the five outcomes are that the school:

- provides challenging targets for learners in relation to their capability and starting points;

- enables most groups of learners, including those with learning difficulties and disabilities, to make at least good progress;

- enables children to enjoy school a good deal – children feel safe and adopt healthy lifestyles; and

- ensures children develop a commitment to racial equality.

Some of the indicators of schools that are failing their children are where:

- a significant number of learners do not meet targets that are adequately challenging;

- a considerable number of pupils underachieve, or particular groups of children underachieve significantly;

- children, or significant groups of them, are disaffected and do not enjoy their education;

- children are exposed to bullying, racial discrimination or other factors that mean that learners feel unsafe and, when threatened, they do not have confidence that they can get sufficient support; and

- healthy lifestyles are not adequately appreciated or pursued.

(Ofsted 2005b)

Copies of the frameworks for inspection can be downloaded free from the Ofsted website or ordered from the Ofsted publications centre. All frameworks come with guidance for inspectors, an additional document that provides more detail on the evidence inspectors are looking for and making judgements about, against each aspect of the framework. In beginning to research good practice in any aspect of education, Ofsted are often a useful place to start as the frameworks for inspection are set out in such a structured way that they provide a sound model for exploring aspects of educational practice that schools and those working in them need to consider. Ofsted also collate their inspection findings and publish reports of how particular aspects of education are developing and progressing across the country. In this way they provide a good benchmark of what is happening in schools and examples of schools where things are going well.

This chapter has provided the starting point in terms of considering what inclusion is, who we are considering when we are thinking about inclusion and how a truly inclusive school can be developed. The following chapters will provide more detail about the inclusion of specific groups of children and provide guidance for you in supporting the teaching and learning of all children you work with.

Conclusion: inclusion good practice checklist

An inclusive school is one that has, as a minimum, the characteristics listed below.

- **A school ethos of respect,** which includes policies, good leadership and all adults and children following it.

- **Training** for all staff to develop their knowledge and understanding of the different groups of children who may be experiencing barriers to their learning.

- **A culturally relevant and affirming curriculum**. It is important for all children to see their culture, history, language and values reflected in their school experience. This applies to white children, too, and children in mainly white schools, if you think of the wider society they live in. All schools should have resources in classrooms and libraries which give a positive view of the diverse cultures and lifestyles found in Britain as this adds to the quality and accuracy of knowledge about diversity for all children (DfES 2001:5).

- **Effective teaching and learning**. Lessons need to be planned to ensure the needs of all children are met. Where support staff are being deployed their role and focus needs to be planned. They need to be part of this planning process and have time to prepare any relevant material for groups or individuals.

- **Parental involvement**. Parents and the wider community should be positively encouraged to play a full part in the life and development of the school.

- **Induction procedures for new children**. This helps if schools have a policy for helping a child new to a school, joining an established class part way through the school year, to settle in. This might include welcoming parents, providing sensitive support in offering to fill in forms if necessary, allowing the parent to spend some time in class with the child, and providing the child with a 'buddy' who will look after them at break times and explain school procedures and routines.

- **Learning partners**. Children are paired with others in the class who can offer peer support for particular classroom activities. As seen in the case study above, this can be beneficial for the child who is providing the support, as well as the child being supported. The support child may have needs of their own – low self-esteem for example – which will be helped by being able to offer support to another child.

- **Targeted use of peripatetic support services and materials they offer**. This enables those working with children needing this sort of support to offer access to the curriculum.

- **A sanctuary area**. This is where pupils worried about bullying or harassment, or who are overwhelmed by the school environment, can retreat.

Bibliography

DfES (1999) *The National Curriculum Handbook for Primary School Teachers*. London: HMSO.

DfES (2001) *Inclusive Schooling*. London: DfES.

DfES (2003a) *Every Child Matters: Change for Children in Schools*. London: DfES.

DfES (2003b) *Aiming High: Raising the Attainment of Ethnic Minority Pupils*. London:DfES.

DfES (2003c) *Aiming High: Understanding the Educational Needs of Minority Ethnic Pupils in Mainly White Schools*. London: DfES.

DfES (2003d) *Aiming High: Raising the Achievement of Gypsy Traveller Pupils*. London: DfES.

DfES (2004a) *Removing Barriers to Achievement: The Government's Strategy for SEN*. London: DfES.

DfES (2004b) *Every Child Matters: Change for Children*. London: DfES.

DfES (2004c) *Every Child Matters: Change for Children in Schools*. London: DfES.

DfES (2005) *Leading on Inclusion*. London: DfES.

Learmonth, J. (2000) *Inspection: What's in It for Schools*. London and New York: Routledge/Falmer.

Macpherson, W., (1999) *The Stephen Lawrence Inquiry Report*. London: HMSO.

Ofsted (2000) *Evaluating Educational Inclusion: Guidance for Inspectors and Schools* (ref. HMI 235). London: Ofsted.

Ofsted (2003) *Handbook for Inspecting Nursery and Primary Schools* (ref. HMI 1359). London: Ofsted.

Ofsted (2004) *Special Educational Needs and Disability: Towards Inclusive Schools* (ref. HMI 2276). London: Ofsted.

Ofsted (2005a) *Every Child Matters: Framework for the Inspection of Schools in England from September 2005* (ref. HMI 2435). London: Ofsted.

Ofsted (2005b) *Using the Evaluation Schedule: Guidance for Inspectors of Schools* (ref. HMI 2005). London: Ofsted.

Osler, A. (2003) *Citizenship and Democracy in Schools: Diversity, Identity, Equality*. Stoke-on-Trent: Trentham Books.

QCA (2001) *Planning, Teaching and Assessing the Curriculum for Pupils with Learning Difficulties*. London: QCA.

QCA (2000) *Index for Inclusion: Developing Learning and Participation in Schools*. London: QCA / Centre for Studies in Inclusive Education.

Vincent, C. (2003) *Social Justice, Education and Identity*. London: Routledge/Falmer.

Web links

http://www.surestart.gov.uk/surestartservices/settings/surestartchildrenscentres/

http://www.surestart.gov.uk/

http://news.bbc.co.uk/hi/uk/2698295.stm

Multi-agency working in the early years: a model of good practice

Carole Beaty

Inclusion in the early years

FOR THE SAKE of clarity, the early years will refer in this chapter to the period from birth to age 6, and in Framework terms it will cover the time in which a child is at home or in a preschool setting of some form, and is then starting their more 'formal' settings in school. Clearly, because this is the start of the child's experience in education, these years will lay the foundations not just for early learning but also for the way in which the child sees him/herself. So whatever the child's needs, the early years will set the scene for the rest of life, determining to a large extent whether the child has a 'can do' approach to learning and development or perceives him/herself as different and somehow apart from other children. The early years specialist has an enormous responsibility to 'get it right' for each child within a differentiated learning experience. However, the early years specialist has a great advantage in the flexible way in which they might create their learning environment. Within this environment the creative use of play can and must incorporate a wide range of needs, providing both support and challenge for all children, while enabling them to set their own challenges.

Inclusion means welcoming and accepting all children, whatever their background, gender, ethnicity, religious belief or ability. It means within an early years setting, or through outreach work, creating an atmosphere that, without being bland, is truly inclusive. This is far more complex than it sounds and will involve many ingredients to be truly successful.

Background and research context

Early years policy and practice in the UK is currently undergoing a revolutionary change in developing integrated working, pulling together the range of different agencies that work with both children and families. This is in response to the *Every Child Matters* document. This document was written after the Laming Report highlighted the difficulties that had arisen in cross-professional communication surrounding the Victoria Climbié case. Laming felt that significant changes must be made to ensure that we do not just provide a multi-professional approach, but that work is integrated properly; that is working from a shared understanding, a shared vision.

Integrated working also springs from a greater understanding of early brain development, specifically the work of neuroscientists like Susan Greenfield. This research into brain development has endorsed the work of Vygotsky and Bruner in that it has shown the social nature of early learning and the impact of early experiences on subsequent development, emphasising the importance of support-ing the development processes of young children within the context of family and community. Research on brain development also demonstrates how essential touch and early bonding and interaction are to the young child in laying down essential neural pathways, as well as creating an individual's sense of themselves. It has also shown clearly what the Jesuits always knew, that the young brain is infinitely adaptable and receptive to the range of stimuli it finds about itself:

> The brain of a two-year-old has energy consumption at the full adult level; by three years old it is twice as active as an adult's brain, at which level it remains until nine or ten years of age when (amazingly) it starts to decline ... The brain continues to 'rewire' as it is greeted with successive forms of stimulation and each novel experience that requires a response. Experience changes the brain. Everything that a baby sees, smells, hears, tastes and touches alters the way the brain develops in an increasingly situation-appropriate way.

The findings of this neuroscientific research appear to provide sufficient evidence powerfully to reinforce an argument for an enriched environment and sensitive adult support in early life. (Riley 2003:2).

Theoretical contexts

Integrated working and the development of children's centres in the UK are supported by a range of child development theories for their authority.

Sociocultural theory

The whole field of developmental theory has been strongly influenced by the work of Russian psychologist Lev Vygotsky (1896–1934). According to Vygotsky, social interaction – in particular co-operative dialogues between children and more knowledgeable members of society – is necessary for children to acquire the ways of thinking and behaving that make up a community's culture (Berk 2002). Vygotsky believed that as adults and more expert peers help children master culturally meaningful activities, the communication between them becomes part of children's thinking. Once children internalise the essential features of these dialogues, they use language within them to guide their own actions and acquire new skills (Berk 2002).

Case study 2.1

The young child playing in the garden talks himself through a pattern of behaviour observed from an adult or older child. The child may rehearse a visit to the garden centre where he helped a parent to pick out different coloured flowers to go in the garden. He takes them to an imagined till and then into a car to drive home, all the time talking the situation through to himself.

This notion of the social and cultural context for development has a large influence on the integrated approach towards services for children and families, seeing the task of child-rearing and development as a shared responsibility that all members of a community have something to contribute towards. The child brings with them to the early years setting a whole range of behaviours and mores that they have learnt from home and community. Their sense of their own identity is wrapped up in that community evolution. A children's centre can support this aspect of the child's identity by drawing upon the wide range of professionals who are knowledgeable about the child's context. For example, in an area where different languages are spoken, the bilingual community worker can bring the home language and culture more clearly into the setting.

Ecological systems theory

It takes a whole village to raise a child.

(Old African Proverb)

Urie Bronfenbrenner, an American psychologist, put forward an approach to child development that has recently gained in significance in relation to recent social policy in the UK:

It offers the most differentiated and complete account of contextual influences on children's development. *Ecological Systems Theory* views the child developing within a complex system of relationships affected by multiple levels of the surrounding environment. Since the child's heredity joins with environmental forces to mold development, Bronfenbrenner (1998) recently characterized his perspective as a *bioecological model*.

(Berk 2002: 27)

Bronfenbrenner looked at the range of environmental and cultural influences that form the developing child. He characterised this model as a series of expanding circles of influence (Figure 2.1).

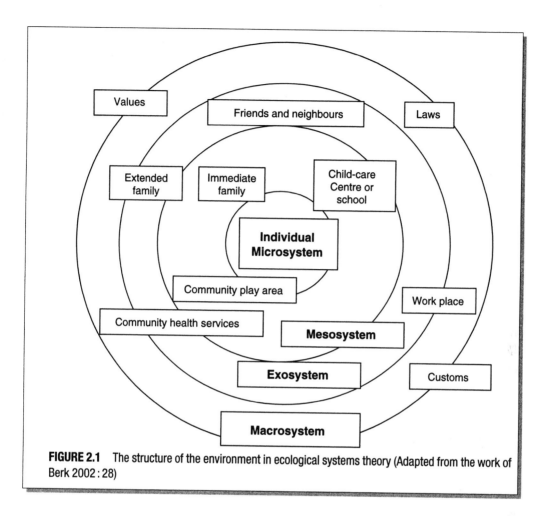

FIGURE 2.1 The structure of the environment in ecological systems theory (Adapted from the work of Berk 2002 : 28)

The microsystem

The innermost level of the environment is the microsystem, which refers to activities and interaction patterns in the child's immediate surroundings. Bronfenbrenner stated that to be able to understand child development at this level we must keep in mind that all relationships are bi-directional. That is to say, adults affect children's behaviour, but children's genetically and socially influenced characteristics – their physical attributes, personalities and capacities – also affect adult's behaviour. For example, a friendly, attentive child is likely to evoke a positive response from parents whereas a distractible youngster is more likely to receive restriction and a negative response. When these reciprocal interactions occur frequently over time, they have an enduring impact on development (Bronfenbrenner 1995). Third parties will also affect whether parent–child (or other two-person) relationships enhance or undermine development. If other individuals in the setting are supportive, then the quality of relationships is enhanced. For example, when parents encourage one another in their child-rearing roles, each engages in more effective parenting (Cowan *et al.* 1998, cited in Berk 2002). In contrast, marital conflict is associated with inconsistent discipline and hostile reactions toward children. In response, children typically become hostile, and their adjustment suffers (Hetherington *et al.* 1998, cited in Berk 2002:28).

The mesosystem

For children to develop at their best, child-rearing supports must also exist in the larger environment. The second level in Bronfenbrenner's theory is the mesosystem. This level encompasses connections between microsystems, such as home and preschool/school, neighbourhood, playgroups etc., that foster children's development. For example, academic progress depends not just on activities that take place within the classroom but also on parental involvement in school life and the extent to which academic learning is carried over into the home (Connors and Epstein 1996). Similarly, parent–child interaction is likely to be affected by the child's relationship with the caregivers within their particular childcare, and vice versa. Parent–child and caregiver–child relationships are likely to support development when there are links, in the form of visits and exchanges of information, between home and the childcare setting (Berk 2002:28).

The exosystem

The exosystem refers to the social settings that do not always contain children but which affect their experiences in immediate settings. These may be formal organisations, such as parents' workplaces or health and welfare services in the community. For example, work settings can help parents in their child-rearing roles, and, indirectly, they can enhance development by offering flexible work schedules and paid parental leave. Exosystem supports can also be informal, such as parents' social networks, friends and extended family. Research confirms the negative impact of a breakdown in exosystem activities. Families who are socially isolated because they have few personal or community-based ties, or who are affected by unemployment, show increased rates of conflict and child abuse (ibid.: 29).

The macrosystem

The outermost level of Bronfenbrenner's model, the macrosystem, consists of cultural values, laws, customs, ideology and resources. The priority that the macrosystem gives to children's needs affects their experiences at the inner levels. For example, in countries that require high-quality standards in early years childcare and education, supported by a well-paid, well-trained workforce, children are more likely to benefit in their immediate environment. Early interactions and attachment are more likely to be promoted by the whole community. The consequence of this is that social exclusion is less likely (ibid.).

Clearly, the above way of looking at the world of child development has enormous implications for families and for practitioners in getting it right for each child. Social policy has been much in the news lately: can the engineering of social fabric and early intervention and support really lead to better outcomes for children?

Activity 2.1

Consider the way in which a setting in which you have worked makes use of this model to help the child make the transition from home to early years setting. How do practitioners gather information about the range of contexts that affect the child's capacity to grow and develop? For example, do they carry out home visits before the child starts in the setting? What form do these visits take?

An ever-changing system

According to Bronfenbrenner, we must keep in mind that the environment is not a static force that affects people in a uniform way. Instead, it is ever-changing. Important life events, such as the birth of a sibling, entering school, moving to a new neighbourhood, or parent's divorce, modify existing relationships between children and their environments, producing new conditions that affect development.

(ibid.)

Case study 2.2

For example, many early years settings have key workers who develop and maintain an ongoing close relationship with the child. This will help the whole family to feel closer to the setting. A children's centre will have a range of health staff working on site or in close proximity to the setting, so when a new baby is expected in a family the midwife can fully involve the rest of the family in this process and can visit the early years setting to set up a mini baby clinic where dolls can be weighed and measured and each child can have early experiences of visiting babies with their parents.

If a child experiences a loss in the family due to bereavement or separation, the key worker could work with centre staff, such as play therapist and educational psychologist, to help to support the whole family.

The ecological model provides us with a very particular framework to consider integrated working. It urges us to look not just at the child but also at the range of environments that revolve around that child, constantly influencing their development. So the parents' self-esteem, relationships and contact with educational, health and social caring services will make a big difference to how the child sees themselves and whether they are in a position to benefit from the opportunities that life presents.

Crucially, the way that governments legislate on family issues and conceptualise the nature of childhood and parenthood will affect day-to-day development of the child. Spending and intent, as well as legislation, are an important indicator here. The important thing is to see the child as a whole, not as separate parts, and those concerned with their development – family, friends, health workers, social and caring workers, educationalists, politicians – should listen to each other and develop or work upon a shared philosophy that permeates all their work.

Activity 2.2

List all the elements of good practice you would hope to see in an effective children's centre that would support young children's learning and development. For example, list all the staff from education, health, family support services and the voluntary sector that should be working together under government legislation.

Typically, the Scandinavian countries, particularly Sweden, are held up as a model of good practice as the Scandinavian governments are generally committed to supporting family needs with legislation that encourages attachment by providing appropriate maternity/paternity pay. Nursery education, with an emphasis on play and experiential learning, is offered until the age of six, sometimes seven. In northern Italy, the Reggio Emilia approach to childcare and education is often given as an example of good practice in integrated working, that involves family and community supporting the individual needs of the child.

Case study 2.3

Littlehampton Children's Centre, in west Sussex, that grew out of a SureStart local programme, provides a range of possible childcare provision from nursery care, childminders, drop-in parent and toddler group and spaces indoors and outdoors that invite creative play with a variety of media. The needs of the whole family are considered, and the centre offers a range of training and employment opportunities, an all-day café/restaurant and a wide variety of exercise classes. Opportunities exist to try out new skills in art classes, cookery and alternative therapy training. A wide range of professional staff are also there to offer informal advice and support.

The Italian Reggio Emilia approach to the care and education of young children

The Reggio movement began in 1945 in a fairly affluent region of northern Italy. As the people of this area set about the task of rebuilding their homes, towns and villages, they were determined to create opportunities for the next generation through excellence in their childcare and education. As they started to build their nurseries and preschool settings, Loris Malagussi, pedagogist and educationalist, rode past on his bicycle. He stopped to ask what they were doing, and was so inspired by their work and ideas that he stayed to offer his own skills in shaping and directing this work. Today the Reggio approach serves as an inspiration to all those working with or for young children. In developing community projects it seeks to involve all those people with day-to-day impact on children's lives. So local politicians, town planners and architects are knowledgeable about early years philosophy and child development. They seek to learn from each other when creating policy, practice and environments that will affect children. Central to the Reggio ethos is the importance of creativity in supporting learning and development; so architects and town planners seek to create spaces that allow for this creative growth in both adults and children and allow them to explore and learn through their senses in a climate of mutual exploration and challenge. Central to the work of Reggio is the notion of inclusion of all children, whatever their needs and backgrounds. So this highly creative approach is offered to all children and their families. Centres work in an integrated way with a range of professionals offering their own particular interventions.

Creativity offers children a way to explore their feelings and engage with learning in a truly unique manner that must aid and support concentration.

Case study 2.4

A four-year-old in a nursery had always found it hard to settle and was often disruptive and could be aggressive. One day a group with drums arrived in the setting. The drums were of all different sizes. Ben was immediately attracted to the deep, resonant sound that the large drum made. When all the children and staff sat in a circle with their drums he was delighted to maintain the rhythm that was set. He listened carefully and took the lead on several occasions. He maintained concentration for a considerable period. When the group left, Ben made his own drum and set up his own group with the other children.

Creative activities help practitioners to discover individual learning styles and support children's emotional as well as their cognitive development.

Research in the UK

The Effective Provision of Pre-School Education (EPPE) was set up in 1997 to investigate the effects of preschool education and care on children's development for those aged three to seven. This was a study undertaken by the Institute of Education at London University and commissioned by the Department for Education and Skills. The EPPE team included a range of highly reputed early years researchers: Kathy Sylva, Edward Meluish, Pam Sammons, Iram Siraj-Blatchford and Brenda

Taggart. This was a five-year longitudinal study that collected information on 3,000 children who were recruited at age 3-plus, and studied longitudinally until the end of Key Stage 1 (DfES 2005a).

The aim of the study

EPPE explored five questions:

- What is the impact of preschool on children's intellectual and social/behavioural development?
- Are some preschools more effective than others in promoting children's development?
- What are the characteristics of an effective preschool setting?
- What is the impact of home and childcare history on children's development?
- Do the effects of preschool continue through Key Stage 1 (ages 6–7)?

DfES (2004)

When the findings of this research were released in 2005 it was found that integrated centres that drew upon a range of professional expertise and knowledge in supporting children's development consistently scored higher than more traditional models of preschool provision. The nature of adult–child and child–child interactions were seen as a central area that supports cognitive growth and social development. Levels of training and ongoing professional training were also seen as essential in the development and maintenance of effective levels of growth and development. The quality of home–school links and the way in which families were involved in their children's learning were seen as very powerful in influencing outcomes for children.

Activity 2.3

Read your school's policy for setting up home–school links. Note where, around your school, you see examples of good practice in this area.

The impact of the EPPE study on policy and practice

From the outset, EPPE was designed to inform policy and everyday practice. The impact has been seen at four levels:

- on national policy – through evidence to parliamentary select committees, ministerial briefings and contributions to the spending review, and departmental and treasury evidence to teams preparing government reports and policy documents;

- on local authority policy – through dissemination to local officers and elected members of local authorities seeking to reconfigure their early years services. Also locally, through workshops and training, usually organised by the Early Years Development and Care Partnerships;

- on practitioners and parents – through lectures, seminars and workshops focused on practical pedagogues; and

- on the academic research community – the team has published 12 technical papers that have informed new areas of research as well as supporting the development of curricular provision.

(ibid.)

Developing practice in the United Kingdom

In 1997 the UK acquired a Labour government for the first time since 1979. They came to power with a strong emphasis on education and childcare. They also aimed to support a range of family issues and sought to deliver quality services in childcare and education. Their definition of 'quality' was an environment that emphasised the value of play and early intervention in children's lives to minimise the effects of disadvantage, parental stress and community disaffection. Through the SureStart programmes, the government also sought to engage the community in developing their own programmes, asking parents and families what would support their needs. The Children Act of 2004 developed the work started by Lord Laming and introduced a range of legislation in the document *Every Child Matters: Change for Children*.

SureStart is a national programme, with local programmes based in areas of most severe deprivation. The original concept of these programmes was to target children of 4 and under and to try to ensure that no child was living in poverty. To do this the government sought to implement an approach, which is based upon Bronfenbrenner's ecological model in that it looked not solely at the child but also at the circumstances in which they grow and develop. So programmes help to create a joined-up service that would offer opportunities both for the child, in terms of play-based experiences, and parents, with access to employment, counselling and training opportunities. Often located in the same building, or nearby, are health professionals, individuals offering financial advice and a range of other services.

SureStart must work in collaboration with partner organisations, such as the Primary and Acute trusts, social services, CAMHS, local schools and colleges, Connexions and the voluntary sector, as well as local faith groups.

SureStart works to a range of government targets which help to monitor its effectiveness. These include those which relate to figures, to the number of people accessing services, as well as targets which are more specifically health-related or to education, such as the numbers of mothers who breastfeed, the number of parents who stop smoking and the numbers of teenage mothers. Education targets relate to the number of childcare places offered and children's progress in language development as recorded on the Language Measure. For the family support aspect of the programme, the government would be looking to see the number and quality of parenting groups and classes offered. Parental partnership targets would look at the number of parents who were on the Stakeholders' Board. SureStart is evaluated by NESS (National Evaluation of SureStart: www.ness.bbk.ac.uk).

Since Labour was re-elected in 2005, the emphasis has increasingly moved towards the development of children's centres, with one being promised in every area. These centres build upon the experiences of the SureStart programmes. In the SureStart children's centre Practice Guidance (DfES 2005b) a clear vision for these centres is set out:

> SureStart Children's Centres will be central to all Local Authorities' efforts to develop mainstream early years services as part of wider local provision for children. The main purpose of children's centres will to be to improve outcomes for young children as set out in *Every Child Matters*, with a particular emphasis on the most disadvantaged.
>
> (ibid.)

The context

If we are to achieve this vision we need to be aware of the changing context for children's centres. First, we are moving from the development of different local initiatives such as SureStart Local Programmes (SSLP) to children's centres that will be a mainstream national service. The responsibility for the development of children's centres is with the local authorities, working with partners, increasingly through children's trust arrangements (ibid.:5).

Case study 2.5

Littlehampton Children's Centre works in partnership with the local church and a voluntary organisation (WIRE: Wick Information Recreation and Education) that provides activities and training opportunities for young people. The Children's Centre, which opened in February 2005, is based in a large centre of population and is within pram-pushing distance for many young families. Its services are always evolving in response to local needs and regular evaluation. Currently it offers the facilities listed below.

- A 50-place nursery for children from three months to five years, open 8am till 6pm every day.
- A childminding network, with a co-ordinator, that supports the need for choice in childcare and education; the network provides training and assessment for the childminders themselves as well as advice on the business side of their work.

- A health support team which works in conjunction with local hospitals and health centres. The centre's staff include: community midwife, health visitor, community nursery nurse and speech and language therapist. Health staff run a range of services to meet the needs of families in the local community; for example, a post-natal depression group, exercise classes, baby massage and baby sign, as well as more conventional services such as baby checks and pre- and post-natal checks.

- Education support through a range of classes and informal parent-and-child groups; for example, the educational psychologist runs a music group to talk with parents about the importance of early interaction and bonding; the library outreach worker runs a book group; the speech and language therapist is starting the First Words project so that she can capture each child's precious first utterance; the portage worker bases her work on home visits and sets up play sessions within the centre; she works closely with the centre's staff and the nursery to address the global needs of each child. The centre's early years teacher works closely with the nursery manager (also an early years teacher) to promote learning across the centre in all its forms; and the early years teacher runs a range of physical activity and creative groups in partnership with parents and local occupational therapists.

- Family support is offered through home visiting and parenting groups as well as one-to-one sessions. There is a counsellor based within the centre and a range of home visitors support the needs of vulnerable families. Job Centre Plus offers advice on training and applying for jobs. There is a basic skills counsellor. Because Littlehampton has a large Portuguese population, the Portuguese community worker offers a range of support in terms of translation and English as a second language classes.

- A wide range of training opportunities are offered at the centre, many providing a qualification; for example PLA run courses from level one to level three. First aid, cookery and food hygiene courses are run on a rolling programme. Breastfeeding peer supporters are trained to work with new mothers, and also gain a qualification themselves.

All these areas are offered within the centre, where there is a coffee shop, a place to relax and many places for children to play and enjoy the wide selection of books from the library.

The key elements of *Every Child Matters*

The Children Act 2004 secured royal assent on 15 November 2005. The Act is the legislative spine on which the government seeks to build reforms for children's services. It establishes for England:

- a Children's Commissioner to champion the views of children and young people;
- a duty on local authorities to make arrangements to promote co-operation between agencies and other appropriate bodies (such as voluntary and community

organisations) in order to improve children's well-being (well-being is defined in terms of the five outcomes – being healthy; staying safe; enjoying and achieving; making a positive contribution; and achieving economic well-being), and a duty on key partners to take part in the co-operation arrangements;

- a duty on key agencies to safeguard and promote the welfare of children;

- a duty on local authorities to set up Local Safeguarding Children Boards and on key partners to take part;

- provision for indexes and databases containing basic information about children and young people to enable better sharing of information;

- a requirement for a single Children and Young People's Plan to be drawn up by each local authority;

- a requirement on local authorities to appoint a Director of Children's Services and designate a Lead Member;

- the creation of an integrated inspection framework to conduct joint area reviews to assess local areas' progress in improving outcomes for children and young people; and

- development of provision relating to foster care, private fostering and the education of children in care.

(DfES 2004)

Working towards better outcomes for children in an early years setting

The Government has worked with partners from the statutory and voluntary and community sectors to define what the five outcomes mean. They have identified 25 specific aims for children and young people and the support needed from parents, carers and families in order to achieve those aims.

(ibid.)

Every Child Matters: five outcomes for achieving well-being

- Be healthy: physically, mentally, emotionally, sexually, healthy lifestyles, choose not to take illegal drugs. Parents, carers and families promote healthy choices.

- Stay safe: from maltreatment, neglect, violence, sexual exploitation, accident, injury and death, bullying, discrimination, crime, anti-social behaviour in and out of school. Have security, stability and are cared for. Parents, carers and families provide safe homes and stability.

- Enjoy and achieve: ready for school, attend and enjoy school. Achieve stretching national standards at primary school. Achieve personal and social development and enjoy recreation. Achieve stretching national educational standards at secondary school. Parents, carers and families support learning.

- Make a positive contribution: engage in decision-making and support the community and environment. Engage in law-abiding and positive behaviour in and out of school. Develop positive relationships and choose not to bully and discriminate. Develop self-confidence and deal successfully with significant life changes and challenges. Develop enterprising behaviour. Parents, carers and families promote positive behaviour.

- Achieve economic well-being: engage in further education, employment or training on leaving school; ready for employment. Live in decent homes and sustainable communities. Access to transport and material goods. Live in households free from low income. Parents, carers and families are supported to be economically active.

(ibid.)

If ECM is going to have a positive impact on children's lives the key to its success is the realisation of the duty on children's services agents to co-operate and work constructively with families. All those services working with young children and families would need to acknowledge the importance of seeing the child and his/her family in a holistic manner and work within a framework of joint understanding. It is now a legal requirement for the local authority to provide policies that actively promote co-operation. This means seeing every child within the context of their family, culture and environment when planning early interventions.

Within the SureStart/children's centre agenda, partner agencies must be knowledgeable about different services and the most productive way in which each facet of the service could work together to achieve better outcomes for each and every child. This means true co-operation and a willingness to learn from each other and listening to local parents in their local community.

Below is a case study of how this might work for one particular child.

Case study 2.6

Yasmin lives with her mother in a large block of flats. She has cerebral palsy and although they live on the bottom floor of the building, getting in and out of the flat is difficult. Yasmin's mother, Chloe, is depressed and feels isolated. A portage worker visits the family weekly and has set up a play plan for Yasmin. After some persuasion the portage worker encourages Chloe to accept a place in the children's centre nursery. The co-located occupational therapist arranges a sitting and standing frame for Yasmin and provides training for all staff. The portage worker visits the nursery regularly and acts as the key worker.

Chloe has time to visit the counsellor based at the centre. She is also able to access health staff on an informal basis over a cup of tea in the centre's café. She regularly sees the aromatherapist who works on site. A multi-professional case meeting is set up at the centre with all those involved with the family contributing. This group includes a representative from Housing who is able to arrange more suitable accommodation for Chloe and Yasmin.

Each SureStart is different and is determined by community need. Services are led by parents and co-ordinated by professionals.

From the SureStart programmes in areas of deprivation, the Labour government came to the 2005 election with a promise to create a children's centre in every area. Children's centres should be physical manifestations of integrated working with, in many cases, co-located services; that is different agencies working from one site to offer a 'one-stop shop' for family services.

Children's centres would be expected to offer the following:

- integrated early learning and childcare for babies and children until they are five years old;
- a choice of childcare for children under five. This would include a nursery offering childcare and education for at least 48 weeks of the year and from 8am to 6pm every weekday. The centre should also provide access to childminders and should provide ongoing support and training. This childcare and education should be fully inclusive.

Family support and parental outreach:

- visits to all families in the catchment area within two months of the child's birth (through the Child Health Promotion Programme or agreed local arrangements);
- information for parents/carers about the range of family support services and activities available in the area;
- support and advice on parenting including support at significant transition points for the family (e.g. pre-birth, early days, settling into childcare);
- access to specialist, targeted services for those families which need them, e.g. support for parents/carers of a child with a disability;
- activities which increase parents'/carers' understanding of the child's development;
- specific strategies and activities which increase the involvement of fathers.

Child and family health services:

- antenatal advice and support for parents and carers;
- Child Health Promotion Programme;
- information on breastfeeding, hygiene, nutrition and safety;
- promoting positive mental health and emotional well-being, including identification, support and care for those suffering from maternal depression, antenatal and postnatal;
- speech and language and other specialist support;
- support for healthy lifestyles;
- help in stopping smoking.

Parental involvement:

- consultation and information sharing with parents/carers, including fathers, on what services are needed, and systems to get user feedback on services;
- ongoing arrangements in place to ensure parents/carers have a voice, e.g. Parents' Forum.

Links with Job Centre Plus

- centres will link with Job Centre Plus to encourage and support parents/carers who wish to consider training and employment.

Other services which may be included:

- SureStart children's centres may also offer parents/carers help with accessing training, work, advice and information and may well offer a range of other services.

Services should include:

- effective links with further and higher education institutions, and local training providers;
- training for parents/carers, including English as an additional language, basic skills or parenting classes;
- specialist services for children with disabilities;
- benefit advice, including maternity benefits;
- childcare and other services for older children, e.g. siblings of families receiving services;
- adult relationship support;
- contact centres;

- toy libraries;
- support for the delivery of Bookstart baby bags, toddler bags and 'My Treasure' boxes.

(DfES 2005b)

The children's centre concept was promoted in the report to the government *Interdepartmental Childcare Review*, published in 2002. This review found that an integrated approach which ensures the joining up of services and disciplines such as education, care, family support and health is a key factor in determining good outcomes for children. The integrated approach that children's centres offer provides holistic support for children's development and support to families with young children, as well as facilitating the return to work of those parents who are currently unemployed.

Children's centres are not about lots of new services, but rather re-orientating existing services and, where possible, co-locating services in order to meet the needs of parents and carers, as well as creating more childcare places that might enable parents to return to work.

Why are children's centres being developed?

- All the research that led to *Every Child Matters* considered that integrated services would best support the needs of young children.
- All the outcomes of the 1997 childcare review found that:
  1 deprivation raises the chances of social exclusion;
  2 services are often unco-ordinated; and
  3 most under-fours miss out on service provision.

So if we return to Bronfenbrenner's notion that the eco- and exo-systems in which children grow and develop are essential in influencing how children perceive themselves and their place in the world, then children's centres hope to make a difference to the whole of a child's experience and must therefore be fully inclusive in nature.

What will children's centres look like?

There is no typical children's centre; they will vary a great deal as they respond to the needs of the local community. However, it would be expected that the following staff would be co-located within the centre or would be part of a virtual team:

- health
- community midwife
- health visitor

- community nursery nurse
- occupational therapist
- paediatrician
- physiotherapist
- education
- early years teacher
- speech and language therapist
- portage worker
- educational psychologist
- childminding network co-ordinator
- library outreach worker
- crèche supervisor
- crèche workers
- neighbourhood nursery staff (not all children's centres have nurseries)
- nursery manager

With this range of staff and spread of expertise there is the possibility of working with the many dimensions of a child's life, pooling expertise and resources.

Early identification and intervention

All early years settings will be subject to the *Every Child Matters* agenda and all will be subject to the Core Offer as well. In the past it might have been felt that matters of maturity need to be considered when working with very young children and that identification and intervention could wait. There is now a feeling in education that children should have the help and support that they need at an early age, and that this should not be delayed. Professionals always feel that they do not wish to label a child too early in life. However, early identification and remediation can make all the difference. Often a child's progress in development, or lack of it, is a direct result of the context or situation in which they are growing. For example, a mother's postnatal depression can have a severe impact on a young child's growing speech, and possible delay may be an outcome. The alert midwife and health visitor will be on the lookout for signs of depression and will seek to support the family in every way. If the child attends the children's centre, there can be ongoing support from all the health and education staff, including the speech and language therapist. Postnatal depression groups are often led by someone who has experienced this same challenge; informal advice and support is often more appropriate than professional intervention.

Co-ordination of services

Every county will have an Early Years Development plan that will:

- co-ordinate practice within a given area, offering choice to parents in childcare and education;
- provide training and development to all settings;
- offer evaluation of all settings, whether in the maintained or non-maintained sector, through given Quality Assurance schemes; and
- provide specific support for inclusion of children with additional needs in all settings, depending on parental choice.

All local authorities are working to ensure quality experiences for all children whatever their needs and abilities. All settings, including childminders, need to ensure that they make all experiences accessible to all children.

Each setting would need to have:

- an accessible environment/including accessible toilets;
- a philosophy that embraces inclusion; this will mean careful training and education of all staff;
- an equal opportunities policy that truly embraces all children and enables staff to challenge discrimination;
- a special educational needs co-ordinator who will bring together resources, staff and family to ensure that all children's needs are met;
- a curriculum that is fully differentiated in line with the *Birth to Three Matters* framework and the Curriculum Guidance for the Foundation Stage;
- a committed staff that is well trained and wishes to carry on with their training;
- staff who have an understanding of the *Every Child Matters* framework and work towards it;
- a record-keeping system that records children's individual achievements, but also considers the next steps in their development and how these might be achieved.

The early years curriculum

Fundamental to inclusion is a commitment by all staff working within a nursery or children's centre to equal opportunities for every child. All staff need to have a good understanding of stages of development and the way in which children learn most appropriately. This is a real challenge at the moment, with the development of so many new childcare places. There is a responsibility on local authorities to ensure that staff in nurseries and children's centres are well paid and have a clear career pathway, in order to create and maintain a valued workforce. If we were to take the Scandinavian model of pedagogues, care and education staff who are educated to degree level might represent a strong and empowered workforce.

To ensure full inclusion it is essential that practice is rooted within an understanding of developmental theory. The current curriculum guidelines create a framework for practice rather than a rigid set of rules. The *Birth to Three* documents emphasis the essential nature of relationships and observations at a time when a child is coming to terms with themselves as an individual and when early attachment is so essential.

The Foundation Stage curriculum offers areas of experience for children from age three to six. Both documents emphasise the holistic nature of children's learning, and the importance of differentiating the learning experiences of every child through play-based opportunities. Drawing upon earlier discussion on brain development, it is essential to provide challenging and unusual opportunities in the early years setting. For example, a visit to the local farm, where animals can be stroked and fed, might lead to the setting up of a play farm in the outside area of the nursery. In the children's centre a visit by the nursery children to the baby clinic might lead to a play- based baby clinic in the imaginative role-play area. This could contain scales, dolls, appointment books and a feeding area.

The government has now set out its plans to amalgamate *Birth to Three* and the Foundation Stage curriculum within the Early Years Foundation Stage (EYFS).

'Well-planned play will continue to be central to children's development and learning, ensuring that learning is both challenging and fun', according to a *Direction of Travel* paper published by the DfES (2005c). The paper lays down the current thinking and proposed schedule of implementation of the new Early Years Foundation Stage. It says that the final EYFS document will include a series of principles and/or standards which will underpin practice. These will replace the existing principles from *Birth to Three Matters* and the Curriculum Guidance for the Foundation Stage, as well as the national standards for under-eights daycare and childminding. The six areas of learning will remain, with mathematical development being replaced by problem-solving, reasoning and numeracy (*Practical Pre-School for the Foundation Stage* magazine, January 2006).

The Primary National Strategy Key Elements of Effective Practice (KEEP) document (DfES 2005a) provides guidance for reflecting on practice, evaluating this and changing and adapting. In its introduction it states: 'Effective practitioners use their own learning to improve their work with young children and their families in ways which are sensitive, positive and non-judgemental'.

Therefore, through initial and ongoing training and development, practitioners need to develop, demonstrate and continuously improve their:

- relationships with both children and adults;

- understanding of the individual and diverse ways that children develop and learn;

- knowledge and understanding in order to actively support and extend children's learning in and across all areas and aspects of learning;
- practice in meeting all children's needs, learning styles and interests;
- work with parents, carers and the wider community; and
- work with other professionals within and beyond the setting.

(ibid.:3)

This document provides a valuable tool for all early years practitioners to assess their own delivery of the curriculum. It is essential to acknowledge that the curriculum is everything that we do around the early years setting: the relationships we have with children and with parents, and the ethos of acceptance care and enjoyment that is provided. This is an essential element of inclusion, creating a curriculum through knowledge of individual children that responds, day by day, to their growth and development, but which takes in the whole context of a child's life: home, street, family, friends, pets, health, inclination, self-esteem and identity.

Young children learning

When working with young children, most specifically those with additional needs, it is essential to always bear in mind the ways in which young children learn. From experience and through observation, practitioners are aware that young children learn:

- through first-hand experience;
- from setting their own challenges and being involved;
- by building upon what they already know and can do;
- by working alongside more experienced others;
- in contexts which are meaningful for them; and
- through rich, involving experiences.

Research on child development and on effective early years practice points the way to inclusion being fundamental to all practitioners' thinking and must inform training and reflection. Settings must provide culturally relevant, responsive experiences for each and every child, whatever their background and level of need.

Conclusion

We live in exciting times in early years research and practice. Neuroscientific research confirms much of what earlier researchers in the field of child development postulated, that those first years of life are critical in forming a sense of self and belonging, and in creating neural pathways that will provide a blueprint in the brain that will often determine later behaviour patterns. We have a government committed to early excellence and to an understanding of true integrated working. Children with additional needs must have well-informed, well-trained and motivated staff who are able to respond to the whole spectrum of the child's life experience. Whether we work in local government, health, the voluntary sector, education and care or in the social services, if we are a parent, grandparent, aunt or uncle we must not fail to respond to this change; we must grab it while we may and talk to each other about the needs of children and viable resolutions. This is not a time for complacency.

Bibliography

Berk, L.A.E. (2002) *Infants and Children* (4th edn). Boston, MA: Allyn and Bacon.

Bronfenbrenner, U. (1995) 'The bioecological model from a life course perspective: reflections of a participant observer', in Moen, P., Elder, G.H. and Lüscher, K. (eds) *Examining Lives in Context.* Washington, D.C.: American Psychology Association, pp. 599–618.

Connors, L.J. and Epstein, J.L. (1996) 'Parent and school partnerships', in Bornstein, M.H. (ed.) *Handbook of Parenting: Vol. 4 – Applied and Practical Parenting.* Mahwah, NJ: Lawrence Erlbaum Associates, pp. 437–58.

DfES (2004) *Every Child Matters: Change for Children.* London: DfES.

DfES (2005a) *Key Elements of Effective Practice: National Primary Strategy.* London: DfES.

DfES (2005b) *SureStart Children's Centres: Practice Guidance.* London: DfES.

DfES (2005c) Direction of Travel on the new Early Years Foundation Stage (www.surestart.gov.uk).

National Evaluation of SureStart (NESS) (www.ness.bbk.ac.uk).

Practical Pre-School for the Foundation Stage (January 2006 edition). Leamington Spa: Step Forward Publishing.

Riley, J. (ed.) (2003) *Learning in the Early Years: A Guide for Teachers of Children 3–7.* London: Paul Chapman Publishing.

Siraj-Blatchford, I., Sylva, K., Muttock, S., Gilden, R. and Bell, D. (2002) *Researching Effective Pedagogy in the Early Years.* London: DfES.

Race, ethnicity and equality

Vini Lander

Introduction

THIS CHAPTER AIMS to introduce the key terms associated with this area of inclusion. Although an understanding of these terms is not absolutely essential to engage with the idea of race equality, the terms provide a useful supporting framework within which to develop an understanding of race equality. It should be noted that the subject of race equality and racism is challenging because it makes us examine our preconceptions and prejudices. It challenges the assumptions on which we make our judgements about groups of people. If we are to move ourselves, school policies and practices towards a truly inclusive approach then the reader needs to remain open to the ideas within this chapter and reflect on the tasks set. The chapter will also provide an overview of the historical developments related to race and education. It is essential to appreciate the origins of this debate in order to understand the contemporary societal climate, which inevitably impacts on school life regardless of the school's location.

Basic key ideas and concepts

This chapter cannot elucidate all the terms associated with race equality. The following key terms are addressed to provide a basic understanding of the conceptual framework.

Race, or 'race', is not a scientifically recognised term, nor does it have a biological basis. There is one race, the human race, or one species, homo sapiens, to which we all belong. The use of the term race and the associated idea that men and women could be classified as belonging to a particular race, for example, Indian, African etc., is a societal construct which emerged in the Victorian era. At that time it was thought that there were biological differences according to one's race, for example the notion of intelligence and race. There is no scientific basis for this; it is a superficial construct, a convenient way to label people, very often based on skin colour and other physical features. These days the term is used as a means to make a social distinction between groups. Gaine and George (1999:5) describe a working definition of race as 'a group of people who may share some physical characteristics to which social importance is attached'. So race is a social construct, and by placing the term in inverted commas, we indicate that it is a contested term. Other writers choose not to use the inverted commas, indicating that the term is evolving and changing as we develop our understanding of the area of race and race equality. Some have argued for the term to be dropped since it is used to denigrate people (Miles 1982). Others (e.g Tizard and Phoenix 1993) have suggested that the term be retained since racists base their discriminatory behaviour on what the term represents. Therefore, to lose it would be to lose our focus on racism and racist behaviour. But since the most expanding part of the population consists of people from mixed-heritage backgrounds, the use of the term is rendered impotent. However, Omi and Winant (2004) point out that race should no longer be a term, which denotes power relationships, nor should it be seen as an objective notion. They suggest that with increasing globalisation race should be seen merely as a means to signal the infinite variation that exists within a species and should be considered a positive force for the future without losing the significance that race plays in the formation of our identity.

Nowadays we tend to use the term 'ethnicity', which is seen as a more preferable term. It is the expression of the way people define themselves. It refers to the person's culture. I can define myself as Sikh or Indian or Punjabi, and this self-identification is based on cultural reference points such as religion, language, nationality and cultural customs such as food and dress. All people possess ethnicity, for example English, Welsh and Scottish. However, although the notion of ethnicity is more palatable for some, others have argued that it dilutes the issue of racism (Sivanandam 1985). Hall (1992) suggests that ethnicity is also a contested notion, but it is part of our identity, as illustrated by the example above, and an important aspect of our sense of self. It is important to note that ethnicities should not be hierarchical, that is, that white British culture is seen as the norm and other cultures and customs are compared with it and seen as 'abnormal' or aberrant.

Activity 3.1: Cultural equality

Can you think of contemporary examples of how we fall into the trap of thinking that one ethnic group or tradition is better than another?

Who is ordering these ethnic groups – the powerful, or the less powerful groups?

Can you think of how you would ensure you would maintain an ethnic minority child's sense of self in subjects such as science or art?

What are discrimination and prejudice?

It is important to establish the difference between prejudice, discrimination and racism. We all hold prejudiced views about one group or another. Prejudicial views tend to be unfavourable, based on limited knowledge or stereotypes, which may indicate a dislike or even an intolerance of certain groups. Such views can be to the detriment of certain groups. Discrimination leads to the singling out of one group for favourable or unfavourable treatment due to perceived differences. It is normally seen as unfavourable or unfair treatment, which is based on prejudice. So we may discriminate in favour of women who support a particular football team since they demonstrate qualities that positively predispose us to them. Conversely, when there are people or groups who possess qualities, cultural norms or customs that appear to be strange to us because we represent the 'norm', then our prejudicial views may lead to discriminatory behaviour towards them. Prejudice and discrimination are powerful forces operating throughout everyday life, but they can become destructive when we consider issues of race and culture.

Racism is based on the belief that one 'race' is better or superior to another and this belief is underpinned by 'the power to put this belief into practice' (Gaine and George 1999 : 5). Racism can be a destructive force and many think that it takes on a violent or extremist persona, for example the violence perpetrated by teenage racist thugs against a Chinese takeaway owner in Manchester (10 November 2005, www.bbc.co.uk). Most writers propose that racism arises from the power relationships that exist between black and white people. This arises from the fact that most political, social and economic decision-making lies in the hands of white people and that these decisions disadvantage black people (www.multiverse.ac.uk). The Stephen Lawrence Inquiry (Macpherson 1999) defines racism as 'conduct or words which advantage or disadvantage people because of their colour, culture or ethnic origin' (www.archive.official-documents.co.uk)

In other words, racism = prejudice + power. So although there may be a number of African-Caribbean and Indian pupils in a school, they are not in a position of power to exercise their prejudicial views on the minority (Gillborn 1990). Essentially, the root of racism lies in the belief that one group is superior to others who may be distinguishable by their colour, language or culture (Gaine 1995). At its extreme, racists will not distinguish between those that have assimilated themselves with the host culture and those that have chosen to maintain their culture within the host culture. Indeed, Gaine (ibid.) draws stark attention to this when he states that in the 1930s the German Jews were the most assimilated group in Europe but suffered at the hands of the most abhorrent racist regime. But racism does not always manifest itself in an overtly violent way, as it did in the case of the murder of Anthony Walker, a teenager killed with an axe in a Liverpool park because he was black (*Times* online, 16 November 2005).

Racism can be more subtle and can exist within organisations such as schools and LEAs. This is termed institutional racism, and the Stephen Lawrence Inquiry (www.archive.official-documents.co.uk, para. 6.34) defined it as:

> the collective failure of an organisation to provide the appropriate and professional services to people because of their colour, culture or ethnic origin. It can be found in the processes, attitudes and behaviour which amount to discrimination through unwitting prejudice, ignorance, thoughtlessness and racist stereotyping, which disadvantages minority ethnic people.

This implies that there are forces operating which, left unidentified, can lead to disadvantage of black and minority ethnic groups. One example, cited by Gillborn and Youdell (2000 : 120), was the predominance of black pupils entered for the Foundation tier GCSE mathematics paper. Gillborn (1990) notes that black and minority ethnic people can be the unintentional victims of well-intentioned liberal actions. He urges the need to recognise the distinction between what he terms 'popular racism', as described above, and the equally damaging, but non-violent and implicit, institutional racism. For example, institutional racism can occur when a rule is made which is intended to apply to everyone but excludes other groups of pupils. The rule that girls must wear skirts for PE or that skirts are a compulsory part of the school uniform would exclude Muslim girls from undertaking PE and from going to a school which insisted on maintaining this uniform rule. You may be thinking, 'when in Rome . . .', but would you think in a similar way if a school insisted that a disabled child should climb the stairs because they could not afford to install a lift? We must retain the notion of inclusion as we read through this chapter and tackle the examples. Inclusive education is defined as follows:

> . . . the process by which a school attempts to respond to all pupils as individuals by reconsidering and restructuring its curricular organisation and provision and allocating resources to enhance the equality of opportunity. Through this process the school builds its capacity to accept pupils from the local community who wish to attend and in doing so reduces the need to exclude pupils.

> (Sebba and Sachdev 1997, cited in Fredrickson and Cline 2002 : 66)

Activity 3.2: Institutional racism at work

Can you think of other ways in which the education system, through its 'normal' working practices, can operate in an institutionally racist way against groups such as:

- black and minority ethnic pupils and their families;
- asylum-seeker and refugee pupils and their families;
- Traveller, Roma or Gypsy pupils and their families?

Discuss your examples with a colleague. How could you or your school change these systems or processes to eliminate the institutional racism you have identified?

Gaine and George (1999) cautions that we need to avoid generalisations and try not to see black and minority groups as victims. While you have identified instances from your practice which could be deemed institutionally racist, there is a list of facts and statistics which need to be examined critically and, most importantly, addressed by the education system. These are listed below.

1   Black boys are three times more likely to be excluded from schools than their white peers.

2   Black African-Caribbean and Black African pupils make relatively greater progress on entering school than do white pupils; this statistic is being challenged by recent research by Gillborn who claims that the new Foundation stage profile assessments which assess pupils' ability when they start school show that white pupils gain better results than their black or minority ethnic peers. This may indicate unconscious teacher racism or, more importantly, institutional racism on the part of the QCA, which devised the profile. Gillborn asserts that this new trend may have emerged because the profile relies more on teacher observation, and since research shows that teachers have lower expectations of black pupils, this is now manifesting itself in the results of the Foundation stage profile (www.tes.co.uk).

3   Black, Bangladeshi and Pakistani pupils perform less well than white pupils throughout compulsory schooling.

4   Many children from minority ethnic groups are from lower socio-economic groups; over 30 per cent of Pakistani and black pupils are eligible for free school meals and over 50 per cent of Bangladeshi, Gypsy/Roma and pupils of Travellers of Irish heritage are eligible for free school meals. While socio-economic factors explain a large part of the inequality of attainment, there are still differences in attainment between ethnic groups among those pupils eligible for free school meals.

5   Proportionately, more black, Pakistani and Bangladeshi pupils are recorded as having special educational needs compared with white, Chinese and Indian pupils.

6   There are proportionally more Black African-Caribbean and other black pupils in pupil referral units compared with the proportion of these groups in mainstream schooling (www.multiverse.ac.uk).

Despite these statistics, Tony Sewell, a black educationalist, argues that teacher racism is not the only factor which leads to the under-performance of minority ethnic pupils despite the evidence that the achievement gap between white and Pakistani and black pupils has widened. Sewell's argument rests on the fact that although teacher racism and low expectations are evident in schools, the underachievement of black pupils, particularly African-Caribbean, is also influenced by cultural factors; to be precise young black culture, which considers 'learning or intellectual activity as anti-black' (www.bbc.co.uk, 27 October 2000).

However, Gillborn and Mirza (2000) indicate that social class, gender and ethnicity are factors influencing the attainment of black and minority ethnic pupils. They conclude that in terms of social class and gender, African-Caribbean, Pakistani and Bangladeshi pupils are underachieving due to the inequality of educational opportunities. African-Caribbean and Pakistani youngsters do not share the success of other ethnic groups whose GCSE attainment has increased.

Doreen Lawrence, the mother of Stephen Lawrence, notes in the foreword to Richardson (2005): 'Tell it like it is: how our schools fail Black children', and describes it as 'scandalous' that the education system still continues to fail black children as it did 30 years ago when the aforementioned book was first written by Bernard Coard.

Activity 3.3: Why do you think black children fail within the education system?

Debating this question with a friend will serve to consolidate your understanding of the issues raised so far.

Racist bullying

As a professional group, those that work with children may well find that although they condemn the manifestation of popular racism, they may well have acted in a way to disadvantage a black or minority ethnic child. Some teachers and other professionals think that racist behaviour is the same as bullying. However, racist name-calling is not the same as bullying; the names do not just damage the individual but serve to denigrate a whole culture – the family, relatives, cultural past and traditions to which the individual belongs. In this way, racist bullying is more pervasively damaging than bullying. In addition, racist bullying, like bullying, can affect a child's attendance and, consequently, their attainment. A recent Ofsted report (2005, www.ofsted.gov.uk) indicates that supportive LEA guidance on tackling racist incidents and strong leadership from the head teacher on this issue instils confidence among staff, pupils and parents that racist incidents will be treated seriously and dealt with appropriately. Following the Stephen Lawrence Inquiry recommendation that all schools should record racist incidents and report them to the LEA, all schools are required to establish and operate a procedure for doing this. But it is insufficient to merely have ways to report and record such incidents; schools must also take steps to prevent racist bullying (Commission for Racial Equality

2002). Ofsted inspections will gather evidence to ascertain whether pupils feel safe from bullying and racist bullying.

But what is a racist incident? It is normally appropriate for schools to seek guidance from the LEA, which in turn will be informed by the definition in the Stephen Lawrence Inquiry. But many schools work on the assumption that if a pupil feels the incident is racist then it should be treated as such.

Activity 3.4: Is it a racist incident?

Are there any advantages or disadvantages to this approach?

Can there be racist incidents in a mainly 'white' school? Say more.

What happens when incidents are reported? The school should report the incidents to the governors and the LEA. Some LEAs will then instigate staff development and support to improve understanding and, in better schools, the trends in the reported incidents are monitored and a member of staff responsible for Race Equality will work with staff to improve the inclusion of race diversity and racism issues within the curriculum (Ofsted 2005, available at www.ofsted.gov.uk).

Case study 3.1

Harjinder is a bright, intelligent, high-achieving Year 5 Sikh boy in a mainly white school in a shire county close to London. He has been subjected to racist comments and bullying since he was in Reception. His various teachers have all had differing responses to him when he has reported that Darren has called him racist names such as 'Paki'. One teacher said, 'Oh, just ignore him, you are better than he is'. Another said, 'I'm sure that can't be right'. How would you feel and what would you do if you were:

1   Harjinder?

2   Harjinder's parents?

3   Harjinder's current Year 5 teacher or a teaching assistant in his class?

4   The head teacher of Shire Primary School?

A history and critique of race and education

In order to understand the debate and concepts associated with the area of race equality, students need to appreciate the evolution of the debate from its earliest days. This section seeks to outline the educational response to race equality over the last 40 years. The debate, government policies and teacher practice impacted on my life as a school child and that of others. Where pertinent, I have illustrated the effect of the differing approaches on my own educational experience.

The immigration of people from new commonwealth countries such as India, Pakistan and the Caribbean occurred in response to the labour shortage in Britain after the war. At first it was the male members of the family who migrated to Britain to work and once they had secured living accommodation and a sound financial base their wives and families joined them. Massey (1991) states that the change in the nature of the British population resulting from postwar immigration led to subsequent educational changes. At first it was thought that, given time, these new-comers would adapt to being in Britain and to British life. They would, given time, eventually 'fit in' or be absorbed into British society. In fact, there was no policy to address the education of immigrant pupils or pupils from overseas, as they were called in school. Troyna and Williams (1986) state that this non-response could be classified as a policy response in itself since the decision not to respond is an active process. But early race tensions, resulting in disturbances in Notting Hill in 1958, led society to re-examine this *laissez-faire* approach. Assimilation was seen as the way forward to developing a more cohesive society. Assimilation involved the newcomers adapting to, and adopting, a British way of life. In order to do that, they and their children needed to speak the language. So new arrivals found themselves in dedicated language centres where they learnt English, made friends with other pupils from immigrant families and, once they gained a certain level of proficiency in English, were sent to mainstream schools where they had no friends and had to adapt to new teachers, new systems and new pupils. Some found themselves in schools with few black and minority pupils and they encountered racist attitudes and abuse. I write with personal experience of the isolating and frightening ordeal of being one of only a handful of black and minority youngsters in a mainly white school. It was unpleasant, disorientating and demeaning to be called racist names when you were new to the school, in a new home and in a new country, all at the age of six. Massey (1991) notes that this policy of assimilation assumed cultural superiority and was premised on prejudice because local education authorities in the 1960s would bus immigrant children to other schools when their numbers within the school population exceeded 33 per cent. This was seen as a means to further cultural assimilation, but was quite clearly racist since no white children were bussed to schools and there was no evidence that such dispersal would facilitate assimilation or, as some white parents thought, affect the education of their children if there were too many immigrant pupils in the school.

In the mid-1960s the notion of assimilation evolved into the idea of integration, whereby immigrants would become proficient in English as the first step to becom-ing culturally integrated into British society. Immigrant children were not encour-aged to maintain their mother tongue, the prevailing view being that it would impede the acquisition of English. As a child at that time, I remember my parents 'buying into' this and telling me to speak English at home. This was at the expense of reduced proficiency in Punjabi. I now speak Punjabi at a basic level but I am not literate in my mother tongue. This policy of integration served to substitute aspects of cultural identity with a view to helping pupils to become British. But cultural and linguistic integration did not lead to full integration within society, since these new British citizens were still subject to racial abuse and discrimination in the playground and in the street. The lack of linguistic and cultural integration served as a convenient excuse to explain the underachievement of black and minority ethnic pupils. So as Massey (ibid.) explains, this ideological stance meant that there was no examination of the school and the processes they employed to educate black and minority ethnic pupils.

The ideology of assimilation is flawed; Gaine (1995:38) argues that there are a number of weaknesses to the approach. Some of these are listed below.

■ The notion of Britishness on which assimilationist thinking is based, is itself flawed and any attempt to define Britishness is inadequate and often based on a middle-class notion.

■ The lessons of history show us that groups do not assimilate. He outlines the American example where groups have retained their cultural identity, for example, the Irish-Americans.

■ The curriculum is itself not devoid of the influence of other cultural dimensions so those that call for 'British culture in British schools' need to re-examine the curriculum which covers the Egyptians and colonialism, and in geography covers issues related to the third world.

■ The assimilationist approach has been tried and has failed because minority ethnic groups have sought to maintain their mother tongue, recognised that the education system fails their children and have called for separate schools. These are not indicators of success for this approach.

■ Assimilation no longer applies to second-, third- or fourth-generation black and minority ethnic pupils. But Britain does not acknowledge black and minority ethnic people as British; instead they are still considered as foreigners. I believe now, in 2005, this perspective is changing as black and minority ethnic people such as myself begin to define themselves in terms of their culture and their Britishness. I would describe myself as a British-Indian, but a more accurate self-identity would be British-Sikh, a description which draws on my religious identity and not my cultural identity. The term 'Indian' is very wide, and while I can identify with some aspects of being Indian, I have only been to India once in my life and I feel that I have greater affinity to my religious, rather than my cultural, identity.

■ The notion of assimilation is itself based on an idea of cultural superiority or, as Gaine (ibid.:39) states, 'at least the greater appropriateness of it [British culture] in the British Isles'.

It is important that education acknowledges the experiences of black and minority ethnic people. An educational perspective that does not include this perspective is inadequate, inappropriate and racist. It does not meet the need of either constituency, neither white nor black and minority ethnic pupils (ibid.). A secondary trainee teacher recently asked me 'why pupils with English as an additional language cannot go somewhere to learn English before they attended his English class'.

Activity 3.5: Let them learn English before they learn my subject

What assumptions have been made about pupils who have English as an additional language? How does his comment reflect a possibly assimilationist stance?

Gillborn (1990) criticises assimilation and integration as approaches that were a partially racist response, clearly identifying black and minority ethnic people as a problem. He adds 'such an approach was bound to fail' (ibid.:147). Elements of this thinking, that 'these people are a problem', still exists within schools and pervades some teachers' thinking and practice.

Integration evolved into the notion of pluralism, a term introduced by the then Home Secretary, Roy Jenkins, in 1966. It is described as 'equal opportunity accompanied by cultural diversity in an atmosphere of mutual tolerance' (Massey 1991:13). Within education, some teachers came to realise that assimilation and integration, with their focus on English language proficiency, were inadequate responses to the education of pupils from overseas. They felt that an understanding of the cultures and traditions from which these pupils originated would help mutual tolerance and promote an acceptance of cultural diversity. They termed this approach 'multicultural education', a term borrowed from American education. The term served to move the approach and thinking away from a superior monocultural stance to one which acknowledged the need for all pupils, regardless of their ethnicity, to appreciate the multicultural nature of Britain, and one which appeared to acknowledge the equal status of different cultures. Initially, the approach was concerned with providing opportunities for culture and language maintenance. The approach appeared to recognise the enrichment of 'British culture' by other communities and was based on a pluralistic view of society. But in the 1970s this approach slipped into rather tokenistic practice, which is still prevalent in some schools. It became characterised as the three Ss: saris, steel bands and samosas. This approach was premised on the notion that black and minority ethnic pupils' attainment was due to their poor self-image, so a recognition of their culture within education would serve to improve their performance, but the existence of low self-esteem was not evident in research (Massey 1991; Stone 1981). Some schools introduced courses on Black studies, which were designed to positively develop black students' self-esteem. But such courses were compensatory, and the minority ethnic child was seen as the problem. But the problem was not the child, but the system (Gillborn 1990). The term 'multicultural education' slipped from use in school into government policy documents. Indeed, it was a term used in the Swann Report (DES 1985). Gaine (1995:41) suggests that multicultural education 'arose from strangeness, inadequate recognition and understanding of each others' cultures and from "prejudice"'. Gillborn (1990) describes multicultural education as an umbrella term, which may encompass three broadly different approaches. The first is described as having a 'compensatory ideology' that resulted in promoting the learning of English as a second language. The second was a more reflective approach involving the use of discussion to analyse and reduce racism. Thirdly, an approach described as socio-political ideology focused on the notion of identity as a prerequisite to establishing a pluralistic society. It is no wonder that even today people have differing opinions and views about the term 'multicultural', whether it applies to education or society as a whole. There has never been a central government definition of the term. At the time, I witnessed some teachers who would teach about, for example, Divali and present it to pupils as strange and exotic. The customs and traditions of others were compared to 'normal, white, middle-class' culture, which served to highlight differences. As a nine-year-old I remember thinking 'it's not good to be different'.

The underachievement of black pupils, particularly those of African-Caribbean origin, initiated a government inquiry in 1979 known as the Rampton Committee, charged to investigate 'The education of children from ethnic minority groups' (the original title of the inquiry). The committee's report, in 1981, was met with disappointment from the opponents of the multicultural approach who felt that racism was the fundamental cause of black underachievement. But Rampton had little to say on this aspect, merely indicating that schools needed to deal with and oppose the ignorance, which is the basis of racism. There were some problems within the committee, and after the resignation of Lord Rampton, the second-in-command, Lord Swann, was appointed to complete the work of the committee. The Swann Committee's report, 'Education for all' (DES 1985) represented a clear shift in perspective from the original title of the inquiry. The report represented an interesting juncture for teachers and educators involved in the field of multicultural education. The Swann report recommended that:

1   the problem was not the education of ethnic minority pupils but the education of all children;

2   education had to involve the education of all pupils to live in a multicultural, multiracial and multilingual Britain;

3   the challenge of educating all pupils for a multicultural society was the responsibility of all schools and not just those in areas of high diversity;

4   education has to offer more than a reinforcement of pupils' values and beliefs;

5 it is important to tackle racism, particularly to challenge the stereotypes that persist and influence individual and institutional practices;

6 multicultural dimensions need to permeate all aspects of the curriculum.

The Swann Report stressed that only through the above approaches could a school begin to offer true equality of opportunity. The emphasis on education or multicultural education as relevant to all pupils was an important message. Some schools in predominantly white areas had mistakenly thought that multicultural education was not applicable to their context or their pupils. The report stressed the need for *all* pupils (and I would add teachers) to understand diversity and to value it. The recommendation to integrate issues of diversity into the curriculum and to ensure that curriculum materials did not present cultural bias were important aspects of the report that served to indicate that a Eurocentric approach was not appropriate for the education of pupils who will be citizens of multicultural Britain in the twentieth and twenty-first century. Similarly, by raising the issue of racism, the Swann Report recognised the destructive and pervasive nature of individual and institutional racism. Swann (DES 1985:36) noted that 'for schools to allow racist attitudes to persist unchecked in fact constitutes a fundamental mis-education for their pupils'.

The report received a mixed reception. Some commended it, stating that at last there was an official recognition of the education of minority ethnic pupils within the context of schooling for all children, including white pupils, and a recognition of the damaging effects of racism within the education system; while others thought that the report was irrelevant to black people, being a superficial response designed to demonstrate that at an official level something was being done. Others thought that the report would go further and recommend the teaching of mother tongue in mainstream contexts. But the report indicated that this was the remit of the community rather than schools (Massey 1991). If, as stated, the Swann Report was truly a means for schools to work towards a pluralistic vision of society, then this could be considered a missed opportunity which has had the effect of devaluing pupils' mother tongues. With hindsight we can see that the official line represented by Swann has led to the demotion of pupils' mother tongues as a concern of parents and the community. The chance to raise the status of so-called community languages on a par with modern foreign languages was missed by Swann, which has had a lasting effect today. So while some schools with a viable number of pupils to offer GCSE Punjabi or Urdu willingly do so, others include French, German and even Japanese on the curriculum rather than the modern languages of Britain's minority ethnic population. The implicit message conveyed by this curricular omission to both teachers and pupils is that the languages of Europe and commerce are more important than the languages in your communities or prevalent in multilingual Britain. I know I would have liked to have studied GCSE Punjabi as part of my school timetable rather than spend Sundays trying to learn it at a community language class.

Massey (1991) notes that others were disappointed with the report because it did not offer a clear ideological steer, either towards multiculturalism or anti-racism, but seemed to fluctuate between the two. Others were angry by Lord Swann's stance that ' "race" was an invalid biological concept. His summary refused to acknowledge that "racism" was a valid, socially constructed concept which impinged directly on the lives of black people' (Massey 1991 : 20). In this way, critics of the Swann Report felt that the report did not acknowledge the barrier of racism as a significant negative factor in their lives and the systems which perpetuate racism seemed to remain unaddressed through the report. On reflection, while the criticisms are valid, it must not be forgotten that the report made some positive recommendations which served to shape future practice in some all-white schools.

The approach described as anti-racism arose from the criticisms levelled at multiculturalism, which was seen to be soft; it sought to persuade and lacked an analytical perspective in its consideration of racism. Also, multiculturalism was criticised as an approach articulated by white practitioners in response to the perceived 'problem' of black and minority ethnic pupils in schools. As stated earlier, it was seen as an approach in which white British culture was considered the norm. But black and minority ethnic educationalists defined the 'problem' in terms of the racism suffered by pupils within the education system. The anti-racist approach is one which has been articulated and developed by these black professionals who insist that before a society can be truly multicultural, as a matter of social justice, it must first expose and eliminate racism. In order to do this, educators needed to help pupils to understand the power relationships in society, the curriculum and in schools, and how those that hold power can shape the outcomes for black and minority ethnic people. Gaine (1995 : 43) notes two ways in which to develop anti-racist education:

> firstly to examine structures and practices, secondly to have a curriculum and a pedagogy which are liberating and transformational in the sense of making students critical of the linked inequalities which they experience.

Massey (1991) outlines how pressure groups such as NAME (National Anti-racist Movement in Education) sought to expose racism in schools through practices such as streaming or SEN procedures. Also, around the same time, in the early 1980s, research revealed discrimination in housing and employment; in 1981 a Home Office Report stated that Asians were 50 times more likely to be victims of racism. He clearly indicates that this evidence provided some LEAs with the opportunity to formulate policies based on the need for equality. But although this was the first time that policy was articulated in racialised terms, the approach was seen as a political and rather radical approach due to its identification of 'the roots of British racism, which lay in the economic systems of both the past and present' (ibid.:16). Anti-racism was seen as hard-edged, political, analytical and oppositional in its approach.

In the mid-1980s the polarisation of multiculturalism and anti-racism led to the formation of two factions within the field of race equality. This was seen as both a damaging, some would say an ideologically constructive, period. However, I did resent being asked, 'Are you a multiculturalist or an anti-racist?'. Why did the two approaches have to be diametrically opposed responses to the presence of black and minority ethnic people? Grinter (1985:7) argued that this internal factionalised debate was damaging to the establishment of social justice and argued for an anti-racist multiculturalism, noting that, 'multicultural and anti-racist education are essential to each other'. In fact, Gillborn (1990) states that one of the factors for moving on the multicultural/anti-racist debate were the recommendations in the Swann Report, which advocated a multicultural, anti-racist approach.

The Swann Report resulted in responses from a number of LEAs, various funded initiatives, such as education support grants, which helped to establish projects to promote issues of cultural diversity in mainly white schools. But Massey (1991:29) notes that many LEAs and schools did not respond and 'many did not bother'. In the 1990s, the terminology debate continued and the term anti-racism was ridiculed and denigrated by the popular press, but particularly by the New Right (Gaine 1995; Gillborn 1990). The entry of the debate into the public arena led to the labels of 'looney left' and the debasing of the anti-racist policies of some local councils. This served to scare other councils, who opted not to use the label of anti-racist in order to avoid similar attention from the right-wing popular press. This New Right thinking influenced the policies of the Thatcher government. The arguments of the New Right pivoted on the premise that links between achievement and equal opportunities are political and serve to undermine and attack white British society. The now abolished Inner London Education Authority (ILEA) – recognised by some as one of the leading local authorities in multicultural, anti-racist education – was subjected to unremitting attacks from New Right theorists and newspapers. The dominance of New Right thinking and policies effectively stemmed the tide of debate on terminology but significantly shaped policies such as the 1988 Education Reform Act and the content of the National Curriculum (Gaine 1995). In the 1990s proponents of race equality continued to search for suitable terms. For example, Hampshire LEA used the term 'intercultural education' which incorporates the European and global dimensions of diversity.

Race equality

At present we use the term race equality to reflect the language used in current legislation, the Race Relations Amendment Act 2000, important legislation that raised the issue of race equality in the field of education. The election of the Labour government in 1997 saw the introduction of this Act. Labour had indicated that they would amend the 1976 Race Relations Act, which provided protection against racial discrimination within employment, education, housing and the provision of goods and services. It outlawed the differential and discriminatory treatment on the basis of race, colour, nationality and ethnicity. At the time, this Act also distinguished between direct and indirect discrimination. However, the need for amendments to the Act became evident following the racist murder of Stephen Lawrence and the recommendations of the inquiry into his death. The Race Relations Amendment Act 2000 is intended to extend and strengthen the 1976 Race Relations Act; it is not intended to replace it (www.multiverse.ac.uk). The Race Relations Amendment Act places an enforceable general duty on all public authorities to:

■ promote race equality;

■ eliminate unlawful racial discrimination;

■ promote equality of opportunity; and

■ promote good relations between people of different racial groups.

The Amendment Act emphasises the responsibility of public bodies to tackle institutional racism; it stresses the importance of public authorities to provide services that are fair, accessible and non-discriminatory. The Act was passed in November 2000 and did not fully come into effect until May 2002.

The Amendment Act was welcomed since it clearly signalled the need for public bodies to promote race equality. Commentators believe that the Race Relations Amendment Act 2000 has a greater impact because it strengthens legislation to outlaw racial discrimination. The duty on authorities needs to be monitored to establish how well the Act has been implemented. For schools, this means that they need to have a clear race equality policy and monitor admissions, attainment and progress by ethnic group.

In a recent lecture at the Institute of Education, Professor David Gillborn (7 October 2005) stated that there was 'little compelling evidence that the Act was impacting on practice in schools'. He reported on a survey by the Commission for Racial Equality to establish the implementation of the Act and noted that only 50 per cent of schools had set clear goals for change and that schools were the least positive about race equality.

Activity 3.6: The school race equality policy

Find out if your school has a race equality policy. How is it monitored? What impact does it have?

How is the achievement and attainment of minority ethnic pupils monitored in your school? What actions are taken if certain groups do not show progress?

Schools in high- and low-diversity areas

You may well say, 'But I work in a mainly "white" school. What's this got to do with me?' In response to this, those who work in such schools need to be aware that they are in a powerful position to influence the attitudes and actions of pupils in their school. The Race Relations Amendment Act 2000 applies to all schools regardless of their location and the ethnic minority diversity within and outside of the school. All schools have a duty to promote race equality and eliminate racial discrimination. Let us examine the recent murder of Anthony Walker. His family moved to the mainly white Huyton area of Liverpool where racism is described as endemic and the supporters of the murders remain on the streets (Townsend 2005). In the BBC *Real Lives* programme screened on 2 December 2005, Anthony's sister remarked that they (herself and her siblings) were called names at school, but they just ignored it. The question has to be asked, 'Why did the school not act? Why did the children not have the confidence to report the abuse to the school? Jones (1999) notes how a trainee teacher remarks that a Muslim boy in her class was called names and received a 'lot of stick', but it appears she never did anything about it. Why not?

As people who work with children we are in powerful positions; our actions and inactions can influence the lives of the pupils in our care. We can combat racism or we can chose to ignore it, and in doing so allow the seeds of racism to take root, which later reach fruition perhaps in acts of violence or subtle racist acts. Both are equally damaging to the lives of minority ethnic pupils.

Looking forward – developing practice

How can we develop the school ethos and curriculum to reflect genuine commitment to race equality in our school? The starting point must be a statement of intent, a race equality policy, a clear policy on dealing with racial incidents, which can happen in schools in low-diversity areas, and then to have a powerful curriculum which acknowledges the multicultural nature of British society implemented by staff who understand issues of race equality. Blair and Bourne (1998) outlined the following strategies for successful multi-ethnic schools, but these strategies are applicable in other contexts. They suggest that these schools showed:

- successful leadership by the head teacher and governors on equal opportunities issues;
- they listened to parents and pupils;
- they created links between the school and the communities it served;
- they worked with the whole child;

- they had clear procedures for dealing with racist bullying and racial harassment;
- they had prevention strategies to limit the exclusion of pupils;
- they tackled underachievement through monitoring pupils' results by ethnicity and had high expectations of teachers and pupils; and
- they ensured that the curriculum reflected the pupils' cultural identities.

What can we do to ensure the school curriculum is responsive to cultural diversity?

The school curriculum needs to move beyond the celebration of different cultural or religious festivals. Let us celebrate Divali, Eid and Chinese New Year, but we need to empower children to appreciate cultural diversity, to be comfortable about this notion, to have the confidence to combat racism and not to be complicit in its perpetuation. If a child hears a racist joke in the playground, I would like to think that other children would not laugh at it, but have the confidence to say 'Hey, that's out of order!'. We need to examine the curriculum and develop a less Eurocentric perspective; we should allow the pupils to examine other perspectives; for example, to consider the origin of our numbers in mathematics; to examine how it might feel to be a native American being 'discovered' by Columbus; to integrate materials which provide pupils with a balanced perspective on slavery and on the contribution of soldiers from the Commonwealth in the two world wars; to examine society and the structures of society; and to identify social bias which may favour some groups. Indeed, Herman Ousley, a former chair of the Commission for Racial Equality, noted that the National Curriculum and classroom activity should address race equality and racism. This was echoed by Bishop Sentamu, who advised the Stephen Lawrence Inquiry, when he said, 'Education is still very much Anglo-Saxon in its approach . . . people wherever we went, including education officials, said we need to do more to reflect the changing face of Britain . . . the education system has not recognised that it's dealing with a multi-ethnic, multicultural society' (Pyke, in TES 5 March 1999).

In a letter in the TES (Anon, 5 March 1999) a trainee teacher in a multi-ethnic school wrote about how she was shocked that her own colleagues thought black pupils were stupid and used the term 'paki shop', but she felt unable to report these incidents to her teacher training college. The letter states, 'racism is widespread, it is institutionalised, it is insidious in its ignorance, and it needs to be challenged with sensitivity and intelligence, not just across the education system, but within society'. The writer is absolutely right, and educators have a large role to play in this process to help establish a just society.

Conclusion

It is not all doom and gloom; I am pleased to live and work in multicultural Britain. I believe that in terms of developments in race equality Britain leads the field with reference to other countries in Europe. On 1 December 2005 the killers of Anthony Walker were found guilty of his murder and sentenced to life imprisonment, yet later in the news on the same day, John Sentamu, the first black Archbishop of York, was installed in a joyous ceremony with African dancing. In one day we had news which revealed the negative face of our multi-cultural society, while later we saw a positive and more hopeful picture. Within the Church of England, an iconic symbol of the English establishment, the barriers preventing black people reaching high office were breached. As educators and people who work with children, we need to examine our own practice to determine how we can improve it to ensure that we promote race equality and eliminate racism.

Bibliography

Anon (1999) 'All of society has to tackle racism'. *Times Educational Supplement*, 5 March.

BBC TV (2005) *Real Story*, 2nd December.

Blair, M. and Bourne, J. (1998) *Making the Difference: Teaching and Learning Strategies in Successful Multi-ethnic Schools*. London: DfES.

Commission for Racial Equality (2000) *Learning for All: Standards for Racial Equality in Schools*. London: CRE.

Commission for Racial Equality (2002) *The Duty to Promote Race Equality: A Guide for Schools*. London: CRE.

Department of Education and Science (1985) *Education for All (The Swann Report)* London: HMSO.

Gaine, C. (1987) *No Problem Here*. London: Hutchinson.

Gaine, C. (1995) *Still No Problem Here*. Stoke-on-Trent: Trentham Books.

Gaine, C. (2005) *We're All White, Thanks: The Persisting Myth about 'White' Schools*. Stoke-on-Trent: Trentham Books.

Gaine, C. and George, R. (1999) *Gender, 'Race' and Class in Schooling: A New Introduction*. London: Falmer.

Gillborn, D. (1990) *'Race', Ethnicity and Education: Teaching and Learning in Multiethnic Schools*. London: Routledge/Falmer.

Gillborn, D. (2005) Year 1 EdD lecture at the Institute of Education, London, 7 October.

Gillborn, D. and Mirza, H. S. (2000) *Educational Inequality Mapping Race, Class and Gender: A Synthesis of Research Evidence*. London: Ofsted.

Gillborn, D. and Youdell, D. (2000) *Rationing Education Policy: Practice, Reform and Equity*. Buckingham: Open University Press.

Grinter, R. (1985) 'Bridging the gulf: the need for anti-racist multicultural education'. *Multicultural Teaching*, 3 (2).

Hall, S. (1992) 'New ethnicities: "race" ', in Donald, J. and Rattansi, A. (eds) *Culture and Difference*. London: Sage.

Hall, S. (2003) 'Implementing the duty to promote race equality: translating policy into practice'. *Race Equality Teaching*, 21(2), 11–15.

Jones, R. (1999). *Teaching Racism or Tackling It? Multicultural Stories from Beginning Teachers.* Stoke-on-Trent: Trentham Books.

Lawrence, D. (2005) Foreword, in Richardson, B. *Tell It Like It Is: How Our Schools Fail Black Children.* London: Bookmark Publications.

Macpherson, W. (1999) *The Stephen Lawrence Inquiry: Report of an Inquiry by Sir William Macpherson of Cluny.* London: Home Office (www.archive.official-documents.co.uk) (para. 6.4).

Massey, I. (1991) *More than Skin Deep.* London: Hodder and Stoughton.

Miles, R. (1982) *Racism and Migrant Labour.* London: Routledge and Kegan Paul.

Omi, M. and Winant (2004) 'On the theoretical status of the concept of race', in Ladson-Billings, G. and Gillborn, D. *The RoutledgeFalmer Reader in Multicultural Education.* Abingdon: RoutledgeFalmer, pp. 7–15.

Pyke, N. (1999) 'Teachers not racist, but the system is'. *Times Educational Supplement*, 5 March, p. 4.

Sebba, J. and Sachdev, D. (1997), in Fredrickson, N. and Cline, T. (2002) *Special Educational Needs: Inclusion and Diversity.* Buckingham: Open University Press.

Sivanandam, A. (1985) 'RAT and the degradation of the black struggle'. *Race and Class*, 26, 4.

Stone, M. (1981) *The Education of the Black Child in Britain: The Myth of Multi-racial Education.* London: Fontana.

Tizard, B. and Phoenix, A. (1993) *Black, White or Mixed Race? Race and Racism in the Lives of Young People of Mixed Parentage.* London: Routledge.

Townsend, M. (2005) 'Racism? It's endemic here'. *Observer*, 4 December, p.18.

Troyna, B. and Williams, J. (1986) *Racism, Education and the State.* London: Croom Helm.

Web links

www.bbc.co.uk

www.multiverse.ac.uk

www.ofsted.gov.uk

www.tes.co.uk

www.timesonline.co.uk

Children who have English as an additional language

Jen Gardner

Introduction

THE AIM OF this chapter is to provide practical advice for those working with children for whom English is an additional language (EAL) to ensure an inclusive, supportive learning environment for children with EAL. It aims to develop knowledge and understanding that will help the reader plan and prepare appropriate learning activities and make an effective contribution to selecting and preparing teaching resources to meet the diversity of pupils' needs and interests.

This chapter also identifies the importance of accurate assessments being made by those who are involved in the teaching and learning of children with EAL, assessments which truly reflect individual stages of development relating to the learner of English as an additional language. It seeks to explore the key factors likely to affect the way pupils who have EAL learn. It demonstrates ways in which professional values and practice can be developed in this area, including how to liaise effectively with parents and carers, recognising their roles in pupils' learning.

Readers of this text will bring to it very diverse levels of experience. Some will have worked in multicultural settings for a number of years, others will be just beginning to experience working with children who are learning English as an additional language as, for example, eastern European children arrive in areas where schools have not experienced working with minority ethnic groups before. All adults working to support teaching and learning in a classroom have exciting opportunities to be the people who make the difference in a child's life by using their knowledge, understanding and empathy to support EAL learners. While it is important to recognise that this work cannot be done in isolation and needs to be a shared response from all adults working within a whole-school ethos and teaching team, the contribution that can be made by each individual concerned is of significant importance.

Developing an additional language

After a few weeks in school, newly arrived children will seem to 'pick up' an additional language quite quickly. But spoken playground language is very different from the language that is associated with higher thinking skills such as hypothesising, evaluating, inferring, generalising, predicting or classifying, which is related to learning and the development of cognition, necessary for learning not only in numeracy, literacy and science but also in all areas of the curriculum. These are also the skills which children need to acquire to become communicators in English. For a child's potential in academic areas to be realised, teaching and learning in the classroom must develop these skills through 'ways in' to the curriculum that will provide opportunities to develop knowledge, understanding and confidence.

Before any consideration is given to teaching and learning strategies, there are some key factors to consider. Learning a language is a long process. It can take between five and seven years before children who enter school with no English achieve fluency in the sometimes abstract language associated with many curriculum areas (Cummins and Swain 1984). The development of English needs to be supported across the curriculum subjects, not just in literacy lessons.

The first priority for any adult working with children who have English as an additional language is to find out as much as they can about the child's first language(s). This is key to enabling children to feel 'safe, settled and valued' (DfES 2002). If a child comes into a classroom environment where other languages are already seen as valued, through environmental print labelling, welcome posters or the language being heard spoken, they will immediately feel more at ease. If their first language can be used as a greeting, so that all the children in the class can enjoy hearing another language, there is less sense of strangeness or awkwardness, because the language will be part of the classroom environment.

Children who have English as an additional language can contribute much to the rich tapestry of a classroom environment. A beginning teacher who had taken up her first teaching post in Haringey came towards me after graduation, her face 'lit up', saying, 'Guess what! I have eleven different languages in my classroom'. She rightly saw this as an exciting environment in which to be working.

Finding out about first languages

One of the most immediate resources for learning more about a child's first language can be older siblings or family members collecting children from school. They may be willing to write a greeting in their first language and explain the pronunciation. Local education authorities often provide, or can put you in touch with, a translation service. The internet has given us many more opportunities for translation, with sites that provide information about a particular language, or those which just provide translation in a number of languages. (Treat these with caution, however, as the translations are not always reliable, but can be used for single words.)

Some children will be proficient in more than one language and their existing knowledge should not be ignored. Children who have a fluency and command in their first language have developed concepts of how language works.

EAL learners who already know the sound system of another language and the principles of phonology can bring that awareness to bear when learning to read and write in English (DfEE 2002: 107). Children who have developed fluency in their first language are in a stronger position to learn English than those who have only just begun to learn their first language. This is a vulnerable group as they are in danger of losing their first language while struggling to learn a second and should be given every support both to learn English and maintain their first language.

What is clear from the research (Kenner, cited in Evans 2001) is that development of this first language poses no threat to learning a second language. Children should be encouraged to use their first languages, see their language in environmental print, in dual-language books, and to code switch when writing if they know a word in their first language but not in English. Research has shown that the use of a first language supports the development of a second langauge rather than being detrimental. Parents may also need to be reassured that the child's continuing use of their own language will not hinder their development in English.

Activity 4.1

Plan with the class teacher to invite parent/family helpers to write simple dual-language texts. These can be stories that have been written in the classroom by children, or the text for the literacy hour simplified or customised to reflect a child's own experience. Build up a good library of these texts.

A further key factor that affects the way children learn is found in their level of self-esteem. Educational performance is enhanced where children are encouraged to have a strong sense of self-identity and an awareness of value being given to their cultural identity, values and practices. This can involve something as simple as ensuring that you pronounce a name in the way that it should be said. If your name is Sheila, you would feel undervalued if you were consistently called Shilla and if no-one made an effort to discover that this was a wrong pronunciation. Some cultures have specific naming practices. Find out what these are. All adults working on a staff team have a responsibility to develop such knowledge.

Knowledge about language can be developed in such a way that all children in the class can take ownership of it and be involved.

Activity 4.2

Plan with the teaching team to involve all the children in the class in writing their own language profile. This could be as simple as: 'We had a holiday in Spain and learned "Hola" '; or: 'My auntie has married someone who was born in France and he says "Bonjour" '; etc. Ask the children to draw a picture of themselves for a display and mount it with languages from their profile printed around them.

Encourage bilingual children to write their names in their first language for the display. Adults working in the classroom might like to add their own language profile to the display. Expand this activity by asking children to recount, or by researching through family members, their own personal histories. Focus on things that are important to each child; their family, country of origin, etc.

Case study 4.1: Isolated minority ethnic children

Bengali twins, aged 5, arrived in an all-British, white school in west Sussex. They were silent and clung to each other. The children in the school had not had an opportunity to meet children from another culture. I was assigned to work with these children. I brought a large globe into the school and set up a display to show where Bangladesh was situated. I borrowed traditional clothing from a friend and added this to the display. All the children in the class were encouraged to bring the clothes they might wear to a special occasion. The Bengali children were amazed at the interest the children showed in learning how to put on Jasmine's sari.

I was able to gain permission from the home and the head teacher to take the children to a local farm. Here they were able to collect hen's eggs and see some of the farm animals. Back at school the children helped set up a display that reflected this outing. Their vocabulary and confidence began to build as they wanted to share this experience and were able to take ownership of the display.

The class were learning about the food we eat. Jasmine and Aziz helped to cook potato and cauliflower pakoras in the school kitchen. Their self-esteem and confidence visibly grew as they took a bowl of pakoras round the school, and everyone asked for more. A large basket was placed on the display. This contained small pots of spices such as turmeric and chilli powder. It made a wonderful palette of colours. Everyone learned how to give a greeting in Bengali and soon the children became popular members of the class. Both children were assigned a 'buddy' to help them settle into the group. Aziz was initiated into playground football. He entered into this with such energy and enjoyment that he was rapidly included in the team. They began to communicate and learn very quickly. In the classroom, their language developed to include vocabulary for describing, evaluating, classifying, comparing, predicting, sequencing, etc. This was achieved primarily because they felt safe, settled and valued. Lessons were planned with the class teacher to include as many visual clues as possible, together with opportunities for tactile and interactive experiences.

Additional factors that influence the way a child responds

Some children who come into school environments have been traumatised by war. They may have witnessed horrific scenes and may only be able to communicate what happened through drawing pictures. Take these drawings very seriously; they can give you a great deal of information about a child's experiences and fears. Traumatised children need to be able to communicate what has happened to them, often many times over, in whatever form they are able.

There are children who choose to remain silent for a period of time simply because they want to be sure that when they do speak they have 'got it right' and will not be ridiculed. Every individual is different and it is for this reason that we need to get to know children if they are to feel secure in a learning environment. You will be able to identify from children's positive body language and facial expression when participation in an activity, planned specifically to include them and enable inclusion, is enhancing self-esteem. This results in an increased level of self-identity which, in turn, encourages engagement in learning. You will also find that you are building successful relationships because you are treating pupils with consideration; and respecting their social, linguistic and ethnic backgrounds.

It is important for all those who support the teaching and learning to find out about a child's religion and beliefs. When I visited the home of the children described in the case study, I asked teenage boys in the house what they most wanted a teacher to be aware of and they unanimously said: 'Please tell them to find out about our religious beliefs and customs and especially about Ramadam and why we might seem tired during that festival. Teachers don't seem to understand and we have to keep explaining.' All adults working with children need to get to know about the aspects of a child's life that are of importance to both them and their families and demonstrate respect for their beliefs through knowledge and understanding.

Planning and expectations

A teacher needs to take hold of the documentation and add flair, creativity and inclusivity.

(Jasper 2005)

All those who are involved with the teaching and learning of children will be aware that a team approach needs to be developed between the adults involved, especially one where ideas and initiative are welcomed by colleagues. This is especially true in the area of the selection and preparation of resources to support learning. It is comparatively easy to work with an objective and these are found in the initial planning for the activity, but the way you interpret how the teaching and learning is to be delivered requires that *you* take hold of the documentation and add flair, creativity and inclusivity.

All children, including those for whom English is an additional language, should encounter an element of problem-solving if their learning is to be effective. They need to be able to build on prior knowledge, not be overloaded in terms of the number of objectives for any one lesson, be able to interact with others and be given time to complete tasks.

When you are planning your resources, keep these elements in mind. For example, worksheets might make an adult feel secure that the objectives are right there in front of the learner; all that needs to be done is for the blank spaces to be filled in and an area of learning has been covered. But in reality, worksheets rarely support learning. They can have a place *if* they generate problem-solving, questioning, interaction etc., but should otherwise be avoided.

This following section will explore a range of resources and strategies likely to facilitate effective learning.

Using puppets as a resource to enhance teaching and learning

- If you have used puppets in your teaching you will already have witnessed the positive effect they can have in the area of developing speaking and listening. A child who is reluctant to speak becomes animated with a puppet on their hand. They can also speak 'safely' in their first language.

- Puppets can be used as a vehicle to tell stories in a home language.

- Puppets can act as a catalyst to develop discussion on PSHE issues because it is the puppet who has concerns about a situation and this takes the focus away from a child; e.g. when a popular classroom puppet called George ripped his trousers and everyone teased him, children questioned him sensitively about how he felt.

- Puppets can go home with a child for a weekend and come back with stories about what they did during their visit.

- When it was George's birthday, children came to school in the clothes they might wear for a party and brought an example of food they might eat on such an occasion. In this multicultural environment, much learning took place about different cultures and celebrations.

- When George did not feel well it was a problem. The children discussed what he might need to make him feel better. They had pictures of possible items such as a blanket, a mug for a warm drink, a hot-water bottle and a thermometer, and could choose three items to give him. There were also some objects that he would not particularly need, in order to engender problem solving and justification through the discussion. Sentence-level work was motivated and causal connectives were learned in a meaningful context.

- Digital cameras facilitate the making of images of your puppet for different situations in the classroom, e.g. George helped to devise a class alphabet frieze with his own name and picture. He featured on a dual-language chart giving his own 'Tips for reading'.

Through activities such as these, working with puppets will enable EAL learners to participate in activities likely to involve problem-solving, discussion, questioning, prediction, hypothesis and to develop communication skills. This will, in turn, motivate purposeful reading and writing, speaking and listening.

Barrier games

The resources for barrier games can be made easily. Provide identical pictures such as a simple map of a treasure island. Children can either sit back-to-back or have a screen/barrier between them. Child A gives child B instructions as to where to go or what to find on the island. Child B marks with a pencil where these instructions have led on their map. Once the destination is reached, both children check for accuracy; discussion is developed and the roles can then be exchanged.

With younger children, two copies of a laminated sticker chart are useful. These can be purchased from bookstores or supermarkets. They feature scenes such as 'The Farmyard'. Removable stickers of sheep, chickens, tractors etc. are supplied. Child A might instruct child B by saying 'I am putting the tractor near the barn'. Child A copies the action. Once the stickers are used up, the boards can be compared to see how closely they match. Child B then can take a turn at giving instructions.

Through this activity, children are learning to give instructions, to listen carefully and to use prepositions, e.g. by the tractor, next to the gate, over the field. It provides visual, tactile and interactive support to the EAL learner and includes problem-solving, expressing a position, asking appropriate questions and, often, giving clarification. This encourages the speaker to think carefully about how things can be said in a different way using an alternative sentence structure.

Role play

Role play is an important feature of any early years setting. In a well set up role play area, they can retell stories or re-enact home situations, hospital visits etc., free from inhibitions caused by concern about whether they are getting the words 'right'. They can also play with children who share their first language and use this language together. They will act out situations they are likely to encounter in real life or make sense of experiences they have had.

Where planned and appropriate, non-participant observation or actual adult participation in the role play can be useful when assessing a child's understanding and development in English in a positive play environment.

In order to enhance children's participation and ability to retell in an early years classroom, activities can be devised where children help construct the role play area prior to a story retell. One example of this strategy is where bricks were supplied in the classroom and a small wall was built before Humpty Dumpty was brought out to sit on it. On another day, the bricks were used as house-building materials together with a heap of straw and a pile of sticks. Through this visual and tactile experience the children saw how easy it would be for the wolf to blow two of these houses down and the story of the three little pigs was more meaningful and readily retold as a result.

Role play is not confined to early years practice and can also be used in hot seating, a strategy often used in the literacy hour. The person in the hot seat becomes the character in focus and answers prepared questions devised by children in the class. Depending on the character, a simple wig or mask might be supplied to help get into role. This strategy is useful for EAL learners as they are helped to think about devising and answering How, Why and What questions.

The importance of rhyme and story

All children will bring a range of story experience with them when they arrive in school. This is largely dependent on what they have been exposed to preschool or at home. What we do know through research is that children who have heard and enjoyed nursery rhymes or texts with rhyming patterns are more likely to become fluent readers earlier. If you are working in an early years classroom you will have opportunities to talk with parents. Many children will have younger siblings at home and all the family will benefit from knowledge that you can share relating to developing fluency in reading (Goswami and Bryant 1990). Repetition is another important tool for developing phonological awareness; children enjoy repetition, whereas adults may become bored. If you can share with parents that they are really enabling their children if they ask them to climb that spout with Incy Wincy Spider 50 times over at bedtime, or read that same book again and again, they will have more enthusiasm for this as they will understand the positive benefits to learning that can result from their actions.

In common with all children, EAL learners may, or may not, have had experience of stories and rhyme. If they have, they will have already developed conceptions about how stories work and how language is patterned. All children will benefit from new or continuing experiences in the classroom to build phonological awareness through the sounds and rhythm of language.

When reading a rhyming text to children, pause at the second rhyme to give children an opportunity to say it before you. This develops listening skills and reinforces the sound pattern as well as providing enjoyment. Customise well-known rhymes or devise your own to enhance this enjoyment. Write these out with the children. Some EAL learners may be able to tell the group playground rhymes in their first language. These can be collected in a class anthology and enjoyed by everyone.

Teachers' medium-term planning will identify appropriate texts for delivering the literacy hour text-level objectives. How these are used when you are given responsibility for delivering the planning for EAL opens up exciting opportunities to develop a child's enjoyment of the text. Story sacks, for example, can be made up or purchased to supplement the texts. Many schools already have a good supply of these. They contain artefacts that relate to the story which provide visual, tactile experiences.

Ask children to draw the characters from the story. These can be coloured, laminated and attached to sticks to create a puppet to enable a retell. I have often worked with children whose writing skills do not reflect age-related expectations, but their drawings, stimulated by the story, reflect a more advanced understanding and use of imagination. Because children have drawn the characters, they take ownership, which gives them confidence to retell a story. I am constantly amazed by children's knowledge of story structure and the vocabulary they use if encouraged to retell using their laminated puppets. This in turn helps self-esteem to develop and enables inclusion for children who have felt 'set apart' from the able writers in the class. If they can retell their story orally in the plenary, they become part of the group. This can include use of first language where the child is not yet proficient in English. Children can learn a tremendous amount about different languages from each other.

A major responsibility and requirement for adults working with children is that they get to know an extensive range of children's literature. It is useful to keep a record of the books you have used or read with a short blurb about these for future reference. Your enthusiasm for a story, an illustrator or a particular author will be infectious and will engender interest and motivation among the children you are working with. I was in a classroom recently where a reception teacher hid a book behind her back. She said to the children with great emphasis, 'Guess what I have got for you today ... it's a new Ruth Browne book!'. The children gasped with delight. Her enthusiasm was truly infectious. You need to be familiar with stories from a range of cultures.

Older siblings and parents can be a tremendous resource. Some may feel confident to come into school to tell traditional stories; others may be willing to record a story in their first language.

Activity 4.3

- Research stories from different countries. Try to develop the confidence to tell a story yourself without a book. Telling a story means that you can use body language, facial expressions and gestures, maintaining eye contact and breathing life into the story. It also reflects value on literacy that is not written down.
- Access the website of the Society for Storytelling (www.sfs.org.uk) for stories with information about the authors, pictures and music.

Additional visual tactile resources

While recognising the advances made in technology in schools, magnetic boards are often still to be found among resources. These can be used as storyboards. Make pictures of houses, artefacts, animals etc. and characters in the story. Attach a magnet to the back of each one. As characters are introduced and events occur, they can be added and moved about the board. Resources like this can be made using velcro. If you set the scene first (orientation) children are much more likely to understand new words because they are in a context. Characters are introduced visually as a problem or event occurs. As the story develops, the characters can be moved on the board and the setting changed until the end of the story (resolution). If the board is left in place and the characters are left nearby, it will become a tool for retelling as the children retell from the teacher modelling.

Encourage children to draw simple story maps, e.g. to show the route Goldilocks takes when she leaves her house, walks through the wood and arrives at the three bears' cottage. These will guide future retellings of the story.

Interactive whiteboards can be used to promote these strategies. Short films can be made using artefacts and props to tell the story.

Building on prior knowledge and personal experience

Barrs and Cook have researched the study of literature and writing development at Key Stage 2. Their work highlights the support given to a pupil who has English as an additional language through the use of a text that has a clear pattern in its structure. The writer is able to respond because he recognises this pattern and is able to build his own writing in the same way. It also gives him an opportunity to write from personal experience (Barrs and Cook 2001 : 139). This work illustrates the importance of enabling children who are developing English by giving them a structure to work with and enabling them to draw on something they really know about already. They can take ownership of the writing and there is purpose behind it. Where they can experience success as a writer in a piece involving self-identity and self-esteem, engagement with learning will follow.

These are some examples of the ways children can be supported. While the focus of the activities would appear to be literacy based, the skills learned are generic. When making choices for a puppet, hypothesis and justification are involved, and when playing a barrier game, the language needed for instruction is developed for use in other situations, i.e. explaining how to make something, how to play a game in PE or a board game. Maths and computer games involve interactive problem-solving.

How, Why and What questions are to be found in science, e.g. how a boat floats and why it rains. Using strategies such as these will ensure that you are promoting and supporting the inclusion of EAL learners with activities likely to be interesting, and motivating learning, giving them access across the curriculum.

Activity 4.4

- To extend this learning, research the Primary National Strategy's Excellence and Enjoyment: Professional Development materials.
- Reflect on the way in which these materials are appropriate when planning for EAL learners.

Supporting readers

One of the most important roles you will have is when supporting developing readers. It is vital that all adults involved have sufficient knowledge and understanding about the way we learn to read in order to contribute effectively and with confidence.

Activity 4.5

Consider the following passage:

A Jollyup was turling a lysandit.
A Meekshap holid and grilond 'Drimko!' to the Jollyup. The Jollyup disked frollily.

What was the Jolyup doing?

What did the Meekshap say to the Jollyup? (adapted from Gibbons 1996:70)

There is no doubt that you were able to answer the questions even though you made little sense of the text. Why is this? It is because you have some knowledge of how language works. When we read, we use three major cueing systems: syntactic, semantic and graphophonic.

Syntactic

This relates to the grammar of a sentence. The reader predicts what might come next and whether it sounds right within the grammar of the sentence. The reader might skip ahead as they have predicted what is coming.

A beginning reader might read in a text 'the jumped dog'. They will then pause and think about whether this sounds right. It is important here for an adult not to see this pause as a needing to immediately help by correcting the reader. Given a few moments, the reader, having had time to assess whether this sounds right or not, and using prior knowledge of word order/tense change, will usually re-read it as 'the dog jumped'.

What are the implications for this when working with EAL learners?

It is more difficult for children who are learning English as they will not always have the same background knowledge to draw on. This is particularly noticeable in languages that are not based on an alphabetic system (e.g. Japanese, Mandarin).

Children are born with an implicit knowledge of grammar but not all language systems have the same grammatical structures. Children who have English as their first language might say, 'I rided my bike and I felded off my bike I did', because they are already aware that there is a past tense even though they do not hear adults talking like this. As they develop more awareness of language, and through effective teaching and learning, children acquire explicit knowledge about grammar. It needs to be recognised that syntactic knowledge will build over a longer period of time where children are developing knowledge of the structure of English grammar.

EAL learners need to be immersed in reading, together with peers, hearing adults modelling reading and being taught strategies. Sentence-level work in literacy-based lessons will enable EAL learners to develop grammatical knowledge. Plan to use visual, kinaesthetic strategies such as the human sentence resource as further support for EAL children (NLS: Activity Resource 1998).

Semantic

This relates to the meaning of the text. If someone reading in another room at home calls out to us 'What does [word] mean? If we do not know, we invariably say 'Read me the whole sentence'. This is because when we hear the words around the unknown word, we are more likely to be able to establish the meaning of the unknown word.

What are the implications for this when working with EAL learners?

The primary act of reading is when we read for meaning. It will enable EAL learners if specialist vocabulary is printed out and discussed with them before they are required to write or talk about a particular subject. This will be done in whole-class situations when a topic is introduced, but it will benefit EAL learners if they have additional support, much in the same way that a guided reading session is conducted, as it will enable reading for meaning.

To return to the example of the Jollyup, it was easy enough to answer the questions but the text was incomprehensible in terms of meaning. This is an important point to consider when asking children to complete comprehension texts. They may get all the answers right but it does not mean they have understood what they have read. For the semantic cueing system to work effectively the whole text needs to be present and words discussed in context. EAL learners can be helped by seeing pictures that represent the key words, e.g. if you are working on a topic about Roman soldiers, have a picture that represents key concepts in the text, e.g. a centurion. EAL learners need support to recognise the key words that carry most of the meaning.

If you have learned a second language to any level, you will remember that you could read some of the words but not others because they were not commonly used in speech. We do not, for example, discuss Roman soldiers on a regular basis. When attempting this in a second language, if we were to be shown a specialist word and a picture, discuss the morphology of the word and told how it sounds in conjunction with reading the whole text, we would be likely to read with a greater understanding.

Build and extend vocabulary with EAL learners whenever possible using pictures, diagrams, short film extracts, puppets, poetry and drama, as well as the printed word.

Recognise also the value of ICT, both in terms of developing speaking and listening when working in a group seated around a computer, and in terms of visual experiences for a vast range of topics. ICT also facilitates children being able to take ownership of their learning by making and creating their work on the screen.

Graphophonic

If you think of 'graph' being something to do with drawing and 'phono' to do with sound, you will understand that graphophonic is the shape of the letter or cluster that represents the written form and the phonic is the sound that is made when this is spoken.

What are the implications for this when working with EAL learners?

EAL learners will benefit from additional support to introduce or revise phonemes, digraphs, consonant clusters, blends etc. This learning should be approached through games and interactive visual strategies.

When a graphophonic cue is employed, the reader can predict what might come next. If a text says 'blue, orange and . . .', we could not be sure what was coming next. If we are given the first letter, y, we would guess yellow (Gibbons 1996). Similarly, if we see 'buttercups are y . . .', some readers can predict the word will be 'yellow' because they know about buttercups and they are drawing on a semantic and cultural understanding. They grew up with buttercups and probably played at holding them under chins to shine yellow. Always appreciate that children's cultural experiences may not be the same. They will have a cultural capital of their own to draw on and will develop new aspects of this. The gaps in knowledge will be filled if children are offered rich experiences. This highlights again the need to provide texts from a range of cultures. These provide opportunities for children to draw on their cultural capital and to share their special knowledge and experiences with others.

EAL learners who are of the age where the class is receiving specific phonic instruction, will benefit from the word-level work with their peers. Where older children are concerned, it is useful to plan in terms of stage rather than age-related achievement. Literacy continuums are a useful resource (First Steps 1999). Always keep in mind when planning that EAL learners need to be using resources that are appropriate to their age and those which are perfectly acceptable for younger learners need to be adapted and customised for older children.

Supporting shared reading

Medium-term planning in your school will have identified the texts to be used in whole-class shared reading sessions. Adults working to enable children's learning will need to discuss the objectives to be taught through the selected text in advance of the lesson. It will help EAL learners if they are familiar with the text prior to the shared reading, and you have worked on key words together. During the shared reading of a big book, sit near your EAL learners and give them encouragement to join in. Shared reading can promote strategies similar to apprenticeship reading (Waterland 1989). To explore this analogy, think of a young apprentice to a carpenter. The apprentice would not immediately be given a difficult lathe-turned wooden chair leg to make alone. The carpenter who has all the skills would work with the apprentice, gradually encouraging them to take more responsibility as they became more experienced, until eventually they could attempt this and be successful on their own. Similarly, an EAL learner you are supporting may only mouth the words at first, but they are learning from the fluent readers and will eventually be able to read without support.

Supporting guided reading

Ofsted inspection evidence identified that guided reading has not always been taught effectively. It recognises, however, that it is 'the best opportunity for pupils to improve their reading through direct teaching which focuses on their individual needs' (Ofsted 2002). Where this strategy is taught effectively, developing readers can become more proficient and fluent readers can be enabled to see beyond the words on the page, beginning to look at text in terms of inference.

Schools will have identified the texts they are going to be using for guided reading. For your professional development there are excellent resources such as Book Bands (Bickler *et al.* 2000) to consult.

In many classrooms a number of adults will work together to identify the objectives for a guided reading session. Individual targets can be planned for specific children in the guided reading group. It is helpful if you share the objectives for the session with the children and enable them to become familiar with the strategies they are developing. In this way they are able to identify the strategies, check that they are in fact employing them and enter into discussion about their own concepts. Through careful observation and open-ended questioning, assessments can be made that will determine areas of support and development the reader needs. These assessments should be shared with the class teacher and will inform future planning.

Supporting independent reading

Dual-language texts, customised texts (where characters and settings in stories are adapted to include familiar settings and people) and picture-books are good starting points for developing additional language readers. Select texts, where appropriate, that relate in some way to children's own experience. Texts with repetitive language or rhyme provide structured support and will be read with great enjoyment over and over again. Texts that employ rhyme provide security as the graphophonic cueing system can be employed effectively. Multimodal texts offer small chunks of text that do not overwhelm the reader and provide visual clues that are useful and enjoyable.

Monitoring and assessment

Adults working in the classroom to support the teaching and learning offer an invaluable support in terms of monitoring the progress of children they are working with. One of the most important aspects of working with EAL learners is to assess their actual level of ability.

In assessing a child's overall language ability every effort needs to be made to establish competence in a child's first language. Writing in a second language that can seem very stilted and without expression, when repeated in a first language and translated, can reveal a very different level of competence.

Case study 4.2

A Chinese child who wrote a retell of Goldilocks in English, presented quite stilted language with short-sentence structure and limited vocabulary. She then wrote this in Chinese and it was translated back into English. In the translation it could be seen that this writer had considerable knowledge about story language and the way narrative works. It also demonstrated her skill in writing Chinese characters. An assessment made using the first piece of writing would have reflected a much lower level of achievement (First Steps Tutor Training Course 2000).

Case study 4.3

A recently arrived EAL learner was given very simple addition in a numeracy lesson. Eventually he took the board marker and proceeded to show that he was capable of working out a logarithm. He did not have enough proficiency in English to explain his frustration to the teacher but was able to non-verbally demonstrate the level of work he was used to and capable of (First Steps 2000).

Children who have EAL are sometimes inappropriately grouped with children who have special educational needs because a more informed assessment of their actual level of ability has not been made. It is worth stating again here that no-one works in isolation in a classroom and assessments will be made with the whole teaching team, but your contribution should be informed. To evaluate pupils' progress you will need to have knowledge and understanding of a child's level of achievement and be able to monitor their responses to learning tasks and modify your approach accordingly, recognising when the learner needs to see information presented in a different way because they have not quite understood.

The formative assessments you make should be recorded systematically and will make a major contribution to the teacher's own records of pupils' progress. It will be useful to level work using attainment targets set out in the National Curriculum documentation. This is criteria-based assessment.

Activity 4.6

Download 'A Language in Common' (QCA) (examples of EAL learners' writing is shown across a range of writing forms).

Ethnic Minority Achievement Grant (EMAG) is a key source of additional funding to schools and local authorities for the support of minority ethnic pupils. Ofsted has found that teaching was most effective where there was close collaboration, planning and support between class teachers and EMAG staff. If you are working in a situation where a school has EMAG support, it will be a positive opportunity to plan and work together. EMAG teachers are usually peripatetic. There will be benefits for the whole team where professional expertise is shared, time is allocated to plan together and assessments information is discussed, making contributions from your own perspective.

Bilingual adults supporting teaching and learning

If you are bilingual and share the same language as EAL learners in the school, your help in acting as an interpreter and source of information about the language will be valued highly. Discuss with colleagues concerned concepts that are developed in the first language and how these can be transferred to learning English. If you are able to read the text for the literacy hour together with EAL learners and code switch between English and first language before the reading with the whole class, it will be very advantageous for them. Your contribution to the planning process and ability to assess the level of language skills of the children who share your first language will be invaluable in the assessment process.

You will also have an understanding of your ethnic group within the context of the area in which your school is set. If you are in school regularly, you will have developed a highly professional role with teaching staff and may be in a position to alert where there is potential for cultural misunderstanding in a text.

You will have an empathy with parents who share your first language together with a professional position of trust within the school, which can be a support to teachers, parents and children. If you are able to translate letters that are being sent to parents, your unique knowledge and skills will be welcomed.

If you are bilingual but there are no children who share your first language, you will still be in a position to be able to empathise with the needs and anxieties of EAL learners. Share language profile activities and let children in the class hear your first language. This is part of giving children a global perspective and taking away the 'strangeness' of encountering another language. As language teaching returns to the primary school, you may be able to make a contribution with your first language. You will have a rich experience of your first language structures and a cultural capital to contribute.

If you are in the role of interpreter during parent interview meetings, it will be important to remember to have eye contact with the parent and not focus your responses solely to the teacher.

Working with parents

The most successful schools I have encountered in terms of literacy scores for children who have English as an additional language are where the senior management and teaching team are committed to Family Literacy programmes. These facilitate parents feeling comfortable about coming in and participating in the life of the school community while developing their own language skills. In my capacity as a home link teacher, I was able to make home visits and these gave me an invaluable insight into a family's hopes, concerns and aspirations for their child, while offering me an opportunity to be welcomed into another culture, which I valued and enjoyed. These visits broke down barriers that might otherwise have existed between home and school and usually resulted in developing a sense of security for the children concerned. Many schools include preschool home visits in their early years policy. Even where parents are not fluent in English, this policy brings positive benefits to both school and home in terms of shared knowledge, understanding, empathy and fostering an environment of inclusion.

Parents who have a limited amount of English can sometimes be wrongly perceived as impolite. Their language is heard as a statement or command rather than a polite request because they do not have the range of vocabulary which enables them to say: 'I'm awfully sorry to bother you but I wonder if we could discuss the possibility of your setting some work for . . . today as we are attending a really important family wedding in another part of England and he will need to miss a couple of days of school'. Instead they might say, '[name] not here two days'. It is not their intention to be abrupt and a limited use of a language should never be a cause of negative relationships with school staff.

Parents who did not do well at school themselves are also often reluctant to participate in the life of the institution where their self-esteem was not high. Concerns such as these often mean that parents stay away. It does not mean that they are not interested; it means that schools need to offer opportunities to participate, which are taken up because they allay fears and enable parents to feel part of the school community. All those who work with children can make an invaluable contribution to building positive relationships, particularly through liaising sensitively and effectively with parents and carers, even where they are not fluent in English. Get to know which languages can be found in the school community and learn words of welcome greetings, thanks and goodbye. With increased knowledge and understanding, you will feel confident to share with parents ways in which their positive involvement in school life makes a difference to a child's achievement.

Most schools provide opportunities for parents to attend meetings to learn about current documentation and teaching methods. A teacher may welcome your contribution where you have been working closely with EAL learners.

Conclusion

This chapter reflects the way in which children need to feel safe, settled and valued if learning is to be a positive experience and explores ways to facilitate learning that is likely to promote this. It is recognised that learning is influenced by the subject knowledge of the adults working with EAL learners and the importance for those involved to have an understanding of the ways in which children learn. It considers ways of ensuring that children are assessed to their actual level in order that expectations are to a high level and the learners remain challenged and motivated. The value of parental involvement is recognised, as is the importance for all adults working to promote children's learning to be effective and professional members of a teaching and learning team. It reflects the way in which all those concerned can make a positive contribution to the teaching and learning of pupils who have English as an additional language.

Bibliography

Barrs, M. and Cook, V. (2001) *The Reader in the Writer*. London: Centre for Learning in Primary Education.

Bearne, E. (2002) *Making Progress in Writing*. London and New York: RoutledgeFalmer.

Bickler, S., Baker, S. and Hobsbaum (eds) (2000) *Book Bands for Guided Reading KS1* (2nd edn). London: Institute of Education Reading Recovery National Network.

Cummins, J. and Swain, M. (1984) *Bilingualism in Education: Aspects of Theory, Research and Practice*. London: Longman.

DfEE (2000) *Grammar for Writing*. London: DfEE.

DfES (2000) Excellence in Cities/Ethnic Minority Achievement Grant.

DfES (2002) *The National Literacy Strategy: Supporting Pupils Learning English as an Additional Language*. London: DfES.

DfES (2003) *Aiming High*. London: DfES.

DfES (2004) *Primary National Strategy: Professional Development Materials*. London: DfES.

Education Department of Western Australia (EDWA) (1999) *First Steps Developmental Continuum in Reading*. Melbourne: Rigby Heinemann.

Gibbons, P. (1996) *Learning to Learn in a Second Language*. NSW Australian Primary English Teaching Association.

Goswami, U. and Bryant, P. (1990) *Phonological Skills and Learning to Read*. London: Lawrence Erlbaum.

Hobsbaum, A., Gamble, N. and Reedy, D. (2002) *A Handbook for Teaching Guided Reading at Key Stage 2*. London: Institute of Education.

Jasper, L. (2005) Teachernet interview. Available from: www.teachernet.gov.uk.

Kenner, C., in Evans, J. (2001) *A Place to Start from: Encouraging Bilingual Children's Writing*. London: David Fulton Publishers.

Ofsted (2002) *Primary Subject Report: English*. HMI.

QCA (2000) 'A Language in Common: the assessment of English as an additional language' (QCA/00/584/P).

Teacher Training Agency (2000) *Raising the Attainment of Minority Ethnic Pupils*. London: TTA.

Tizard, J., Scholfield, W.N. and Hewison, J. (1982) 'Collaboration between teachers and parents in assisting children's reading'. *British Journal of Educational Psychology*, 52.

Waterland, L. (1989) *Apprenticeship in Action: Read with Me*. Stroud: Thimble Press.

Web links

www.teachernet.gov.uk

www.sfs.org.uk

Reviewing gender issues in the primary classroom

Barbara Thompson

Introduction

THE FOCUS ON gender and achievement in the classroom has shifted dramatically over the last 20 years. The language of educational inequality has changed from a concern, by some, with girls' disadvantage to a national focus on the underachievement of boys. The feminist research of the 1970s and 1980s focused largely on the marginalisation of girls in the classroom by teachers and by boys. Numerous commentators (Lobban 1975; Clarricoates 1978; Clarricoates 1980; Delamont 1980; Spender 1982; Lees 1983; Browne and France 1985) argued that classrooms were places for boys that happened to have girls in them. For example, Spender (1980), in a study of teacher time, discovered that, conversant with gender issues as she was, Spender herself spent far more time interacting with boys than girls. Stanworth (1981) discovered that teacher expectations were higher for boys than for for girls and Arnot and Weiner (1987:160) pointed out that: 'Because of their underlying beliefs about gender behaviour, teachers act out, unconsciously, a hidden curriculum in favour of the boys and to the detriment of girls'.

Furthermore, in a later study, feminist writers such as Measor and Sikes (1992) noted that:

> sex role socialization means that schools prepare each sex for quite different styles of life and places in life . . . in schools boys are orientated towards a lifetime of paid work and girls are orientated towards the home and child rearing, or to the kinds of job that are an extension of nurturing and home-making roles.

Although as early as the 1970s girls were outperforming boys at primary level, and slightly more girls than boys were achieving five or more O-levels, Francis and Skelton (2001:1–2) inform us that:

> because these often included low status, 'feminine' subjects such as home economics and so on, the pattern was not taken seriously. Boys were doing significantly better at subjects like maths and science, which were perceived as most important (by feminists, who saw these

subjects as leading to the most highly remunerated careers; and by the public at large, who perceived these 'hard', traditionally masculine subjects as having more status than feminine subjects such as languages).

However, from the mid-1990s to date, much of the concern related to gender issues and schooling is now focused on the perceived underachievement of boys. The increased educational achievement of girls, far from receiving public accolade, is seen, almost, to be an indicator that 'something is wrong'. There appears to be what Epstein *et al.* (1998) describe as a 'moral panic' engendered by the failure of some boys to achieve academically, whipped up by a media frenzy that somehow 'things are not as they should be'. A headline in the *Guardian* on the 26 August 1995 announced: 'Girls doing well while boys feel neglected', and Chris Woodhead, the then Chief Inspector of Schools, is reported to have said that the underachieving boy is one of the most disturbing problems facing the education system (*Times Magazine*, 30 March 1996). Epstein *et al.* (ibid: 3) refer to the comments of a feminist colleague who remarked that boys were 'not doing better than girls any more, like they should'!

In 1996 the Office for Standards in Education (Ofsted) and the Equal Opportunities Commission (EOC) published *The Gender Divide: Performance Differences Between Boys and Girls at School*. Jackson (1998:77) argues that: 'Although the book's foreword stressed that any national debate about education and gender must take account of both sexes', most responses to the booklet put the spotlight on boys' performance.

As a result of intense media interest and the attention of an inspectorate directed to boys' underachievement, millions of pounds of government money has been spent on developing strategies to remedy 'the problem of boys'. In many schools the curriculum has been adapted to be more 'boy-centred' and money has been spent on resources to persuade boys to attain academically, as the *Guardian* headline of 11 July 1996 announced: 'Schools urged to focus on low achieving boys'.

Anyone working in education needs to provide genuinely inclusive learning opportunities for both sexes. To do so they need to understand the shifts in debates about educational inequality from a concern with girls' disadvantage, raised, in the main, by feminist teachers and researchers, to the national outcry about boys' disadvantage. Related to this is the necessity to understand the changes in the theory of gender and education. An understanding of these issues is essential if those who work in schools are to make effective interventions to challenge gender inequalities, for both sexes, in the classroom. Therefore the next sections of this chapter are as follows:

- a brief historical overview of gender inequality and education;
- an overview of the key feminist research findings of the 1970s and 1980s and an exploration of what is meant by 'the hidden curriculum' in schools;
- a consideration of more recent research and an interrogation of current concerns related to gender inequalities, particularly boys' underachievement;

- an analysis of the changes in the theory about gender and education. This will explore sex role theory prevalent in the 1970s and 1980s and more recent gender relational theories which emerged in the 1990s and which place children at the centre of developing their own gender identity; and

- examples of good practice that should be observable in a school that is inclusive in terms of gender issues.

In order to develop your understanding of these issues, a series of questions and practical activities will be provided. These are designed for personal study and with a view to developing good practice.

Setting the scene: placing gender inequality within an historical framework

Despite particular periods in history, for example Anglo-Saxon and Elizabethan times, when the education of girls was given more credence than normal, in general the ideology of female educational provision has been that it should be both inferior to and different from that provided for men. As Kamm (1965:28) states:

> For the vast majority of girls of all classes, marriage was the real goal. If a girl stayed at home under her mother's eye, if she went to a village school, or boarded in a convent, or with a noble family, her prime consideration was to find a suitable husband.

Mary Wollstonecraft, in 1787, wrote *Thoughts on the Education of Daughters*, a plea for the reform of women's education. The existing system was, as she later stated in her *Vindication of the Rights of Women* (1929:3):

> a grand source of misery . . . [by which] women are rendered weak and wretched . . . strength and beauty are sacrificed to beauty . . . one course of this barren blooming I attribute to a false system of education [whereby] the civilised women of the present century . . . are only anxious to inspire love . . . where they ought . . . by their abilities and virtues to exact respect.

Wollstonecraft believed that the minds of women were enfeebled by 'false refinement', but she was writing at a time when the belief was that intelligence in a woman was an unattractive and even dangerous trait.

The nineteenth century saw a complex debate surrounding the nature of girls' education. Whereas some middle-class parents advocated the setting up of small private girls' schools, controversy raged over the wisdom of educating girls at all. Burstyn (1989:145) points out: 'The ideal to be produced by schools in the nineteenth century was one which rested in the prototype of the frail, protected woman of the middle classes'. Lewis (1984:81) describes the idealised notion of womanhood revealed by such writers as Ruskin and Coventry Patmore:

A woman's fundamental task was to create a haven of peace, beauty and security for their husbands and children. The home was to be a sanctuary in which the wife reigned as guardian 'angel' in the words of Patmore, or as a Queen in the imagery of Ruskin.

The curricula of elementary schools at this time were 'to fit girls' for life. Girls' education, of whatever class, whether undertaken by mother, school or governess, was rooted in the domestic. As adult life was sex segregated, it was only natural to devise an educational system that fitted children to that system (Arnot 1986).

Official educational policy reinforced a separate and sexist education, which for girls was centred on preparing them for wife and motherhood. For example, the Norwood Report (1943:127) argued: 'The grounds for including domestic subjects in the curricula are . . . firstly that knowledge of such subjects is necessary equipment for all girls as potential makers of homes'. The Newson Report (1948:37) also noted: 'For all girls . . . there is a group of interests relating to what many, perhaps most . . . would regard as their most important vocational concerns, marriage'. Whereas the Robbins Report of 1963 admitted to the suitability of career training for middle-class girls, as Deem (1981:136) states: 'For working class girls, the emphasis remained largely on the preparation for marriage and a family'.

The Plowden Report (Central Advisory Council for Education 1967) provided an emphasis on individualised learning and established 'child centred' approaches to education. Although focusing educational provision on the demands of the individual seems designed to establish equality of opportunity, it could be argued that child-centred approaches mean that more teacher time is given to those who are more dominant in the classroom, usually boys.

The passing of the Sex Discrimination Act in 1975 saw the enshrining of boys' and girls' entitlement to the same curriculum in law. It could be assumed, therefore, that gender discrimination in education was to be a thing of the past. However, as has been mentioned briefly in the introduction to this chapter, and will be explored in greater depth in the next section, this was far from the case.

Activity 5.1: How much have we changed in what we think?

Try interviewing some people to find out:

- How much do you think the ideology of marriage and motherhood continues to influence the life/educational choices of girls and boys today?

- Interview some older members of your family or friends about what influenced their educational opportunities and their choice of career.

- Repeat this exercise with younger people. What are the differences in their responses? Are there any similarities in what older and younger people say? Is there any sign of a lingering ideology of domesticity for some girls and women?

Key findings from the feminist research of the 1970s, 1980s and early 1990s

It is interesting to note that the Department of Education and Science (DES) was remarkably reluctant to include education in the 1975 Sex Discrimination Act and was resistant to the implementation of major changes in schools designed to eradicate gender inequality (Arnot 1987; Skelton and Francis 2003). The studies of the 1970s and 1980s revealed that gender discrimination operated in schools at many different levels indicating that education, at this time, was still a patriarchal institution dedicated to maintaining and reinforcing gender discriminatory practices, which upheld the *status quo*. For example, the role models that children observed in school were found to be clearly gender differentiated; women were more likely to teach younger children and have more pastoral responsibilities. Men, on the other hand, were found more often in the older age bands teaching technological subjects and more visible in administrative and curricular responsibilities (Acker 1983). David (1984:197) showed that the ethos of the school was dedicated to reinforcing notions of traditional male and female societal roles: 'The whole "hidden curriculum" of the school points to the differ-ent work of mothers and fathers . . . Mothers who take paid employment either have to find part-time work to suit school hours or make elaborate arrangements to cover childcare'.

Roland Meighan (1981) also argued that the classroom is a 'haunted' place, pervaded by the messages of the 'hidden curriculum'. This he defined as all the other things that are learnt during schooling in addition to the official curriculum, or the subjects studied. The hidden curriculum involves such things as teachers' attitudes, how much time they give to boys or girls, who does the monitors' jobs, i.e. boys carry PE equipment, girls water plants.

Delamont (1983) separated everyday life in school, where the hidden curriculum might operate, into five categories which are useful in helping us understand how gender stereotyping invaded the primary school, at least at that time. These are as follows:

The formal organisation of schools (i.e. cloakrooms, playgrounds, registers)

Cloakrooms and playgrounds are often sex-segregated. If children share a play-ground, it is interesting to observe who dominates the available space. The boys usually occupy most of the area playing such games as football or 'gang' games, while the girls skip or play with small balls or stand talking. In many local education authorities (LEAs) registers are divided into boys and girls. Record cards are similarly colour coded – pink for girls, blue for boys.

The staff is usually divided into traditional groups; males tend to be found in positions of authority, with women in subordinate roles. This happens even in primary schools, which are supposed to be a 'female domain'.

Management and discipline

Teachers frequently use gender to discipline children. For example, King (1978:68) refers to the following comment heard from a teacher: 'Oh, Philip is a little girl. He's in the wrong queue'. Girls also gain approval for being 'neat and tidy', 'docile' and 'sweet natured', while boys are complimented on being 'tough', 'brave' and 'strong'.

Content and strategies of teaching

This is the attitudes, values and beliefs of the teachers, and also the tools used for teaching. Lobban (1975) found that school reading schemes showed evidence of sex stereotyping. The roles shown for girls and women were: mum, granny, queen, princess, witch, teacher, shopkeeper and handywoman. Male roles, on the other hand, could be chosen from 33 occupations.

Studies show that teachers prefer to teach boys. Clarricoates (1980) and Serbin (1983) show that boys receive more teacher time than the girls and also different types of instructions.

Socialising and sociability

This includes personal appearance, clothing and interaction between teacher and pupil, and pupil and pupil. Girls are more likely to gain approval for wearing dresses rather than trousers and are often told, 'You've done enough fussing. I know you're all film stars' (Delamont 1983). Pupils themselves monitor their peers' behaviour. Girls or boys who behave in an inappropriate manner are either greeted with hostility or ignored.

Pupils' attitudes and behaviour

Kohlberg (1974) states that children from about the age of 6 are 'fully fledged chauvinists'. They have a certain idea about what is correct behaviour. Even primary school children will choose not to work in mixed groups, and by age 9 the two sexes may vigorously avoid each other.

Secondary school subject choices

One of the effects of the primary school hidden curriculum is the subject choices made by pupils at secondary school. Linked to this, is a likely differential in earning potential between men and women.

Resisting gender issues in education

Despite a growing bank of evidence that schools were permeated by gender discriminatory practices, there was a marked reluctance among many of its practitioners to engage with issues of inequality. As has already been noted, the DES was resistant to having education included in the 1975 Sex Discrimination Act and Spender (1981:156) described the mainstream of education as 'male controlled and almost impervious to feminism'. Furthermore, in her research into the attitudes of primary teachers, teacher trainers and teacher-training students towards gender issues, Thompson (1989) found that the predominant attitude of many was that of either complacency or hostility. Many of the teachers and teacher educators whom she observed and interviewed were complacent that gender inequality was not a concern in schools because child-centred education meant that everyone was treated 'as equal'. One of the teachers in Thompson's (ibid: 68) research commented, 'I don't see what all the fuss is about; we treat them all the same anyway'. Skelton (1989) also referred to the fact that a belief in child-centred methods caused 'gender blindness' in the PGCE students with whom she conducted her research. Other teachers and teacher educators in Thompson's (1989:74) research were found to be hostile to the idea that the issue of gender should have anything to do with the training of primary school teachers, as it was not an appropriate issue for training. One student had been refused permission by a member of college staff to undertake a special study on gender. Another student had had permission for a similar study refused by her teaching practice school. Her tutor had commented: 'Its very difficult in a public sector like education, which at its root is very resistant to change, very conservative . . . schools are sensitive to subjects like gender'.

Maguire (1993: 269) also believes that there is reluctance among many teachers and teacher trainers to engage with controversial issues and links this to the fact that many teacher educators come directly from schools. This means that they often bring with them particular values and beliefs linked to what it is to be a 'good teacher or, in their new role, a good tutor'. Maguire (ibid.) says that the job of a school teacher has been constructed in terms of 'professional concern with individual needs' and that this positions them into a sort of 'neutrality' which is at odds with 'hard-edged politico- economic consideration of structural inequality and its relation to schooling'.

Interventionist strategies

Despite a gender-blind or even hostile attitude towards gender from many primary practitioners, accounts provided by feminist teachers and researchers pointed out the role education seemed to play in reducing girls' self-confidence and covertly steering them away from traditionally masculine subjects such as mathematics and science. As Francis (2000:5) points out:

This issue particularly concerned some feminist teachers and researchers, especially because qualifications in these subjects are often necessary for access to prestigious and highly remunerated careers.

As a result of this concern, initiatives such as action research projects were set up to encourage girls' interest in non-gender stereotyped subjects. Action research is the kind of research that makes changes in a particular setting and then monitors the progress and effects of those changes. One of the most well-known examples of this type of initiative in the UK was the GIST (Girls into Science and Technology) project which was reported upon by Kelly (1985). At the same time, as Francis (ibid.: 5) informs us, boys were underachieving in languages, but relatively little interest was given to this, because of the low status of languages in the curriculum and the fact that languages were perceived to be a feminine subject (Walkerdine 1988).

Activity 5.2: Find out whether there is a 'hidden curriculum' operating in your school?

- Carry out some research in your school to find out if attitudes to gender have changed. Use Sarah Delamont's headings to find out whether there is still a hidden curriculum operating in the primary school where you are based today?
- What issues have changed since Delamont carried out her research?
- Are there any aspects of her 'hidden curriculum' that still operate today?
- Investigate the interactions between boys and girls and adults in the classroom. Are there any differences? Does it make any difference if the adult is a man or a woman?
- Observe how girls and boys relate to one another.
- Who are the dominant influences in the class?
- What is the attitude of the adults in your school towards gender inequality?

Coming up to date

The early work of feminists did much to raise awareness about the marginalisation of girls in schools and their underachievement in high-status, traditionally masculine subjects such as science and maths. Interventionist strategies such as GIST went some way to improving the situation for girls and some local education authorities (LEAs) set up working parties on gender inequality, albeit in a rather ad hoc way (Arnot et al. 1999; Francis 2000). However, the ethos of education in the UK was to change dramatically. The Conservative government of Margaret Thatcher, in 1979, was dedicated to reshaping public sector institutions which were perceived to be economically straitened and in decline. Grocott (1989:119) comments that with the arrival of Thatcherism in the UK:

came a great determination to do what was 'necessary' to rescue Great Britain from the perceived national decline for which the civil service was partly to blame. Reducing public expenditure, eliminating waste, rolling back the frontiers of the state, lifting the dead hand of bureaucracy, cutting the public payroll were the objects of a crusade.

As part of this crusade came the desire to reform and standardise education which was perceived to be in the hands of left-wing liberals, more concerned with issues of equality than standards. As Francis (2000 : 6) points out:

> equality of opportunity was not a priority . . . Indeed the Conservative administration led by Margaret Thatcher in the 1980s and by John Major in the early 1990s often made this lack of concern with equity issues explicit.

With this desire for reform and standardisation of education came the introduction of the National Curriculum in England and Wales in 1988, and at the same time market forces were introduced into schools and other educational institutions which were now forced into competition with each other. The National Curriculum did, however, compel boys and girls to take the same core curriculum subjects for the first time and, as part of a new drive to measure and audit performance, also introduced standardised tests at the end of key stages 1 and 2 (SATs). These initiatives led to the production and publication of league tables of GCSE results at secondary level, and test results at primary level, which meant, in turn, that both the general public and educationalists could interrogate performance. As a result of this, for the first time, the extent of girls' success was revealed. Francis (ibid: 7) comments:

> Girls have been performing increasingly well in terms of attainment at GCSE level and their achievements at this level now equal or excel those of boys in all subjects.

Failing boys: national crisis . . . fact or fiction?

The national outcry about 'failing boys' has been referred to in the introduction to this chapter. Like Epstein *et al.* (1998) I am not arguing that we should be unconcerned that boys do not appear to be performing as well as they should; however, what is of concern is that the achievement of girls has never been celebrated. In fact, as Francis (2000) points out:

> girls' improvements are often presented in the media as having been at the expense of boys. As Arnot *et al.* (1999) observe, the improved achievement of girls has been problematized, leading to the denigration, rather than praise, of teachers' success with girls.

Cohen (1998) also points out that low achievement of boys is often linked to external factors such female/feminist teachers, wrong curriculum, wrong resources or inappropriate assessment, whereas low attainment among girls is linked to lack of ability. Like Francis (*op. cit.*) I argue that because of the somewhat hysterical reaction from some sections of the media to 'failing boys', it is important to separate fact from fiction and place the 'problem of boys' in context.

The first thing to note is that concern about the failure of some boys to engage with academic work is nothing new. Cohen (ibid.:21) informs us that:

> In his 1693 educational treatise Some Thoughts Concerning Education John Locke too was addressing boys' underachievement. He was concerned by young gentlemen's failure to master Latin despite spending years studying it.

In 1923 the Board of Education stated: 'it is well known that most boys, especially at the period of adolescence, have a habit of healthy idleness' (p.120).

From the late nineteenth century Cohen (ibid.) argues that there was a concern with the finite limitations of the body and a concern with the notion of 'overstrain'. The Schools Inquiry Commission, The Taunton Commission, of 1868, was the first public assessment of the performance of boys and girls. It is interesting that the Board noted girls' greater eagerness to learn than boys', but framed its discussion not in terms of how boys would keep up with girls but in terms of girls' over-conscientiousness and the fear that they would overstrain themselves. Cohen (ibid: 27) argues that:

> The eager and achieving girl had become pathologized, while boys' underperformance was an expression of their 'traditionally' boyish ways . . . 'Overstrain' is thus a critical construct for a history of boys' underachievement, because it contributed to producing the underperformance of boys as an index of their mental health.

The question must therefore be asked, 'Why are we now so concerned with the underachievement of boys when for years there has been a covert acceptance that "boys will be boys" and "real boys don't work" '? (Epstein et al. 1998:96). Mahony (1998) links this current preoccupation within the broader context of the introduction of market forces into education and increased competition within a globalised economy. She refers to the comments of Anthea Millett, Chief Executive of the Teacher Training Agency, who said:

> everybody is now agreed that the top priority in education is the need to raise pupils' standards of learning . . . And there is a widespread awareness that, in a competitive world, constant progress is necessary just to maintain parity with other nations.

There are other issues to consider when considering the 'problem of boys'. The notion that 'all boys underachieve' has been challenged as overly simplistic by commentators such as Epstein et al. (1998), Lingard and Douglas (1999), Francis (2000) and Forster et al. (2001). Exam results indicate that, in fact, performance is improving for both boys and girls although boys' results are not improving as fast as those of girls. Furthermore, as Skelton and Francis (2003) argue, just as not all boys underachieve, neither do all girls succeed. The binary divide between boys and girls masks the differences between boys and boys and girls and girls. Skelton and Francis (ibid.: 5–6) state:

> Groups such as middle-class white boys, and Indian and Chinese boys continue to achieve highly. White working class, African Caribbean and Bangladeshi boys tend to under-achieve in the British education system . . . white working class girls underachieve compared to their middle-class counterparts too.

Another reason put forward for the underachievement of some boys is the criticism that primary schools have become overly feminised. As Skelton and Francis (ibid.: 6) argue, there is no evidence for this as primary schools have always been staffed by a greater proportion of women than men.

Skelton and Francis also argue that in fact the position of girls in primary schools has altered very little. They illustrate this argument with reference to adult, including teacher, perceptions of girls' abilities and behaviour in the classroom.

One of the lingering stereotypes about boys is that they are innately clever, but unwilling to work, whereas any success that girls have is frequently put down to hard work and diligence rather than brilliance. Skelton and Francis (2003 : 8) refer to some very able girls in Renold's (2000) study who were not seen by their teachers as clever but as 'bossy' and 'overconfident' and, in one case, 'not as clever as she thinks she is'. In contrast, boys in Maynard's (2002) study were regarded as having 'innate if untapped potential'. In terms of behaviour, Skelton (2002) found that girls who demonstrated behaviours which were not considered 'feminine' were described as 'pushy'. Reay (2001) found that teachers described girls who were misbehaving as, 'a bad influence' and 'spiteful little madams', whereas boys who exhibited the same types of behaviours were described as 'mucking about' (see Skelton and Francis 2003 : 9).

This leads us on to the issue of boys and laddishness. Commentators such as Epstein *et al.* (1998), Rapheal-Reed (1998), Francis (2000) and Warrington and Younger (2000) argue that boys' constructions of masculinity as 'macho', 'competitive' and 'laddish' lead to a gradual alienation from school, particularly among those boys who do not achieve academic success. Rather than winning kudos through working hard, these boys gain peer group approval by being 'hardest' and cheekiest to teachers. Epstein *et al.* (1998) also note the denigration of more feminised boys who do not match the dominant 'macho' discourse. Epstein (1998 : 103) says:

> In the primary school context, the worst thing a boy can be callled is a 'girl' and calling him more specifically homophobic names is closely related and generally applied to boys who seem feminized in some way. And it is certainly feminized to be seen to work in most schools, both primary and secondary.

It is clear that issues related to the perceived underachievement of some boys and the perceived success of some girls are by no means as clear and straightforward as they may, at first sight, appear. The statements advanced by some government organisations and reported by some sections of the media mask a situation which is infinitely more complex than that implied by headlines such as 'Girls doing well while boys feel neglected' (*Guardian*, 26 August 1995).

In an attempt to address the 'problem of boys' there is a danger of rushing head-long into simplistic and arguably ineffective 'solutions'. From my own experience of working with trainee teachers and teachers over a number of years, I have noticed an increasing number of trainees wanting to carry out studies on 'boys' under-achievement' with a view to 'doing something about it' but having no concept that the situation may be more complex than they at first thought. I have also heard head teachers making sweeping statements to the effect that 'all boys need kinaesthetic learning styles', and a female head teacher in despair because she was being put under pressure to replace her reading materials with ones that 'boys would find more appealing'. It would seem that, at least in some cases, consideration of girls' experience in the classroom is slipping once more off the agenda. I argue here that what is needed is a more considered and informed approach to the question of gen-der achievement. I also argue that what is needed is the use of strategies which seek to change the dominant discourses affecting boys' attitudes to learning away from those that reflect the position that 'it is not cool to be a boff'. A consideration of what these strategies might be will be discussed in the final section of this chapter.

Activity 5.3: Find out what those who work with children in your school think about the issue of 'failing boys'

- Listen to what those who work in your school say about girls and boys. Are there differences in the way in which they talk about, or behave towards, them?

- What do those who support the learning and teaching of children say about the question of 'failing boys' in your school?

- What sort of strategies have been introduced to help to remedy the situation? For example, have reading materials been changed in order to reflect an emphasis on more 'boy-friendly' materials? Is the emphasis on one or both genders?

Understanding the changes in gender and education theory

In order that those involved with primary education can provide a genuinely inclu-sive environment for both genders and avoid being persuaded to adopt simplistic 'solutions' related to boys' underachievement, it is important to understand some of the theory related to how change might come about.

Sex role theory and gender relational theory

As we have already seen, the DES was very resistant to including education in the 1975 Sex Discrimination Act. Because of this the Equal Opportunities Commission and some local education authorities promoted what may be termed 'gentler' equal opportunity approaches in schools, rather than the 'stronger' anti-sexist initiatives (Weiner 1985; Skelton and Francis 2003). These equal opportunities approaches relied heavily on sex role theories. Sex role theories are an extension of role theories where children observe the ways of the world around them and gain approval for behaving in appropriate ways and disapproval for behaving in inappropriate ways. As far as gender roles are concerned, Skelton and Francis (ibid.:12) inform us that sex role theories suggest that:

> young girls learn how to be a girl by receiving approval for feminine traits such as caring, gentleness and helpfulness, while young boys learn that they are expected to be boisterous, rough and energetic.

Sex role theories were useful in that they marked a shift away from seeing gender as something biological to something socially constructed. They formed the basis for many strategies designed to encourage children to develop along non-stereotyped lines and which are still evident in schools today. For example, activities based on sex role theories encourage girls and boys to become involved in activities which are stereotypically associated with the other gender. Yet while these activities have their place in the classroom, Skelton and Francis (ibid:13) argue that:

> these approaches have done little, if anything, to change the ways that boyhood or girlhood is perceived and judged by adults as well as acted out by children in the primary classroom.

Simply providing children with a variety of different activities, or with different images of males and females, and hoping they will, on their own, internalise these alternative images as desirable is not enough. This is shown in Davies's (1989) work with young children on alternative fairytales. These fairytales present children with, for example, images of assertive and resourceful princesses who are active in solving problems. However, the children in Davies's study did not 'hear' the alternative messages being presented because of their own constructions about the 'correct' way to be a prince or a princess. Rather than seeing the alternative assertive princesses as something acceptable, they saw them as being 'not proper princesses'.

Skelton and Francis (2003 : 14) believe that sex role theories see children as passive recipients of what society expects and also generalises in terms of stereotypes about girls and boys. On the other hand, gender relational theories place children at the centre of developing their own gender identities and argue that gender identity is situational and relational and affected by class, ethnicity, age and life experiences. For example, gender relational theories:

contest the notion of stereotyping and do not support generalized ideas that *all* girls are quiet, hardworking and good at writing any more than *all* boys are competitive, assertive and naturally good at science.

These theories argue that there are many femininities and many masculinities and all those who work with children need to intervene actively to help children to understand that there are many acceptable ways to be a girl, and many acceptable ways of being a boy. MacNaughton (2000:30) provides a useful example of the fact that children understand about what behaviours are 'correct' in order to be a 'proper' boy or a 'proper' girl. She uses the example of Tom who found a bottle of perfume and liked the smell. However, Tom said: 'Don't tell the other boys it's a perfume bottle. I'll tell them it's an after-shave bottle.' MacNaughton (2000:33) reminds that:

> Identity is formed and reformed in interaction with others. Reshaping children's gendered identities requires considerable child–child and child–adult interaction . . . One aim of this interaction is to expand children's ways of seeing and doing gender.

Skelton and Francis (2003: 15) believe that before teachers can develop gender-relational strategies for working with primary children, they need to examine their own preconceptions of gender as well as examining those of the children. They suggest that those who work with children in schools might raise their own awareness by asking the following sorts of questions:

Activity 5.4: Find out about your own preconceptions related to how boys and girls 'should' behave

Ask yourself:

- Do I expect children to behave differently according to their gender?
- Do I want children to behave differently?
- Do I think that there are ways of being a 'proper boy' or a 'proper girl'?
- How do I feel when children act differently to how, stereotypically, boys and girls 'should' behave?
- Do I think of boys and girls as being homogeneous groups?
- Do I attempt to challenge the ways in which boys and girls practise gender in the classroom?
- What messages about gender are being given in the curriculum materials that I use?
- Are the toys that children play with giving them messages about the 'correct' way of being a boy or a girl?

So far this chapter has sought to raise your awareness of gender issues and primary education in a number of ways. It has:

- discussed, briefly, some of the origins of gender discriminatory practices in the classroom from an historical perspective;

- explored some of the findings from the research, mainly from feminists, from the 1970s and 1980s which found that, in the main, girls were largely invisible in mixed-sex classrooms;

- interrogated the more recent shift from feminist concerns with girls' under-achievement to the national outcry and crusade related to 'failing boys'. It has also attempted to interrogate some of the 'myths' related to this issue; and

- explored the changes in the theory of gender and education from sex role theory to gender-relational theory.

It is now time to investigate some of the strategies that those who work in schools can employ to create a genuinely inclusive gender environment in their classroom and in the wider school.

Making a difference: strategies to promote a gender inclusive climate in primary education

Both MacNaughton (2000) and Skelton and Francis (2003) argue that, in order to promote gender equity in the classroom, teachers and other adults need to intervene directly in children's interactions and activities. MacNaughton (ibid.) refers to as what she calls some of the 'myths' that get in the way of adults working with children in promoting gender equity in early childhood education. One of these is that good early childhood practice endorses the fact that children should be 'free to choose' what and who they play with, and that will automatically lead to good gender equity practice. However MacNaughton (ibid.: 37) points out that free choice is only 'free' for some. Referring to her study of very young children, she says:

> many of the boys were involved constantly in a range of strategies to define play spaces as theirs. They physically prevented girls from entering some spaces, they expanded their play to force girls into smaller play spaces and they tried to establish storylines in their dramatic play that were full of aggression and noise.

One of the teachers in the study decided to intervene in order to prevent such sexist play from continuing, and Read *et al.* (1993: 88–9) makes some suggestions as to effective strategies that staff can use when making interventions with young children. She suggests:

- use short clear sentences to children;
- use positive not negative instructions;
- make directives effective by reinforcing them where necessary;
- define limits clearly and maintain them consistently;
- reorganise the room to remove traditional areas such as the home corner;
- provide detailed alternative storylines and ideas for children's play;
- participate in children's play in a specific role;
- direct children's play;
- directly challenge children when they are sexist; and
- talk to the children about how they understand gender and sexism.

Skelton and Francis (2003) argue that many of the tactics in use in many primary schools to promote equal opportunities can still be used as a background against which adults who work with children actively intervene to enable children to confront gender stereotypes. Clearly, children still need to be given non-sexist curriculum materials, but without direct adult intervention these may not be as effective as they could be. Skelton and Francis (2003:16–17) offer the following suggestions for adults in the classroom. Like MacNaughton (2000) they argue that adults should involve themselves in children's activities and say that they should be sure that they don't avoid particular spaces stereotypically associated with the opposite gender such as the home corner for female teachers and the construction area in the case of male teachers. Skelton and Francis (ibid.: 16–17) continue:

- Children should be presented with imaginative play opportunities where they might devise, explore and deconstruct gender images.
- Teachers should reflect on children's storylines to identify the ways in which they make sense of themselves and others and to find ways of weaving alternative storylines into children's play.
- Teachers should take the opportunity to discuss gender stereotypes and expectations with children directly, in classroom debate.
- When boys and girls or boys dominate a play area, they should be asked to question their reasons for doing so. For example, teachers might ask, 'Who can play with these toys?'.
- If 'girl only' time is set aside for play with construction toys then teachers need to become involved in helping children recognise their developing skills.

Activity 5.5: Make a difference . . . get involved!

- Observe children working and playing together. Note the sort of things they say to or about each other. If you hear gender-inappropriate remarks, be prepare to intervene and challenge what is being said.

- Plan a session in your teaching schedule which is designed to give children the opportunity to discuss gender issues.

I saw a PGCE primary trainee manage such a teaching session very effectively. She was talking to the children about preparations for Christmas and described a scene where she was setting up the Christmas lights. One of the boys said that 'that was a job for dads'. The trainee asked the rest of the children what they thought and they debated the issue for a long time, one of the other boys saying, 'Don't be daft, my mum always does the lights'. It was very interesting to see the children really thinking about gender issues and challenging each other's, and eventually their own, thinking.

Conclusion

To actively intervene and confront stereotypical thinking in both children and adults can be both time-consuming and challenging. However, as this chapter has argued, these strategies are much more effective than depending on strategies related solely to sex role theory. It is very powerful and rewarding to see children rethinking what they thought they knew about how to be 'proper' girls and boys. You may well feel unsure about 'interfering' with how children 'do gender'. Remember, your job is to promote a genuinely inclusive educational environment for all children, and the only way to do that is to try and help children adopt inclusive attitudes themselves.

Bibliography

Acker, S. (1983) 'Women and teaching: a semi-detached sociology of a semi-profession', in S. Walker and L. Barton (eds) *Gender, Class and Education*. London: Falmer Press.

Arnot, M. (1986), in V. Beechey and E. Whitelegg (eds) *Women in Britain Today*. Milton Keynes: Open University Press.

Arnot, M. (1987) 'Political lip-service or radical reform?' in M. Arnot and G. Weiner (eds) *Gender and the Politics of Schooling*. London: Unwin Hyman.

Arnot, M., David, M. and Weiner, G. (1999) *Closing the Gender Gap*, Cambridge: Polity Press.

Arnot, M. and Weiner, G. (1987) (eds) *Gender and the Politics of Schooling*. London: Unwin Hyman.

Board of Education (1923) *Report on the Differentiation of Curricula between the Sexes in Secondary Schools*. London: HMSO.

Browne, N. and France, P. (1985) 'Only cissies wear dresses: a look at sexist talk in the nursery', in G. Weiner (ed.) *Just a Bunch of Girls*. Milton Keynes: Open University Press.

Burstyn, J. (1989), in V. Beechey and E. Whitelegg (eds) *Women in Britain Today*. Milton Keynes: Open University Press.

Central Advisory Council for Education (England) (1967) *Children and Their Primary Schools (The Plowden Report)*. London: HMSO.

Clarricoates, K. (1978) 'Dinosaurs in the classroom: a re-examination of some aspects of the "hidden curriculum" in primary schools'. *Women's Studies International Quarterly*, 1(4), 353–64.

Clarricoates, K. (1980) 'The importance of being Ernest . . . Emma . . . Tom . . . Jane: the perception and categorisation of gender conformity and gender deviation in primary schools', in R. Deem (ed.) *Schooling for Women's Work*. London: Routledge & Kegan Paul.

Cohen, M. (1998) 'A habit of healthy idleness: boys' underachievement in historical perspective', in D. Epstein, J. Elwood, V. Hey and J. Maws (eds) *Failing Boys?* Buckingham: Open University Press.

David, M. (1984) 'Women, family and education', in *The World Yearbook of Education: Women and Education*. London: Kogan Page.

Davies, B. (1989) *Frogs and Snails and Feminist Tales*. Sydney: Allen and Unwin.

Deem, R. (1981) 'State policy and ideology in the education of women, 1944–1980'. *British Journal of Sociology of Education*, 2(2), 131–43.

Delamont, S. (1980) *Sex Roles and the School*. London: Methuen.

Delamont, S. (1983) 'The conservative school', in S. Walker and L. Barton (eds) *Gender, Class and Education*. London: Falmer Press.

Department of Education and Science (1975) *Sex Discrimination Act*. London: HMSO.

Epstein, D., Elwood, J., Hey, V. and Maw, J. (1998) *Failing Boys? Issues in Gender and Achievement*. Buckingham: Open University Press.

Forster, V., Kimmel, M. and Skelton, C. (2001) 'What about the boys? An overview of the debates', in W. Martino and B. Meyenn (eds) *What About the Boys?* Buckingham: Open University Press.

Francis, B. (2000) *Boys, Girls and Achievement: Addressing the Classroom Issues*. London: Routledge/Falmer.

Francis, B. and Skelton, C. (2001) *Investigating Gender*. Buckingham: Open University Press.

Grocott, M. (1989) 'Civil Service management', in I. Taylor and G. Popham (eds) *An Introduction to Public Sector Management*. London: Unwin Hyman.

Jackson, D. (1998) 'Breaking out of the binary trap: boys' underachievement, schooling and gender relations', in D. Epstein, J. Elwood, V. Hey and J. Maw (eds) *Failing Boys? Issues in Gender and Achievement*. Buckingham: Open University Press.

Kamm, J. (1965) *Hope Deferred: Girls' Education in English History*. London: Methuen.

Kelly, A. (1985) 'Changing schools and changing society: some reflections on the Girls into Science and Technology project', in M. Arnot (ed.) *Race and Gender: Equal Opportunities: Policies in Education*. Oxford: Pergamon.

King, R. (1978) *All Things Bright and Beautiful*. Chichester: Wiley.

Mrs Kingsley? (1868) *Report from the Commissioners, Schools Inquiry Commission* [Taunton Commission] 23 vols. London.

Kohlberg, L. (1974) 'Stages in the development of psychosexual concepts and attitudes', in A. Oakley, (1981) *The Division of Labour by Gender*. Milton Keynes: Open University Press (series details: E200, Block 6, Unit 25).

Lees, S. (1983) 'How boys slag girls off'. *New Society*, 66, (1091), 51–3.

Lewis, J. (1984) *Women in England 1870–1950: Sexual Divisions and Social Change*. Sussex: Wheatsheaf Books.

Lingard, B. and Douglas, P. (1999) *Men Engaging Feminisms*. Buckingham: Open University Press.

Lobban, G. (1975) 'Sex roles in reading schemes'. *Educational Review*, 27(3), 202–10.

MacNaughton, G. (2000) *Rethinking Gender in Early Childhood Education*. London: Paul Chapman Publishing.

Maguire, M. (1993) 'Women who teach teachers'. *Gender and Education*, 5(3), 269–81.

Mahony, P. (1998) 'Girls will be girls and boys will be first', in D. Epstein, J. Elwood, V. Hey, and J. Maw, (eds) *Failing Boys? Issues in Gender and Achievement*. Buckingham: Open University Press.

Maynard, T. (2002) *Exploring the Boys and Literacy Issue*. London: Routledge/Falmer.

Measor, L. and Sikes, P. (1992) *Gender and Schools*. London: Cassell.

Meighan, R. (1981) *A Sociology of Educating*. London: Holt, Rinehart and Winston.

Millett, A. (1996) Chief Executive's annual lecture. London: Teacher Training Agency.

Newson Report (1948) *The Education of Girls*. London: Faber and Faber.

Norwood Report (1943) *Report of the Committee of Secondary Schools Examination Council on Curriculum and Examinations in Secondary Schools*. London: Board of Education/HMSO.

Office for Standards in Education and Equal Opportunities Commission (1996) *The Gender Divide: Performance Differences between Boys and Girls at School*. London: HMSO.

Rapheal-Reed, L. (1998) 'Zero tolerance: gender performance and school failure', in D. Epstein, J. Elwood, V. Hey and J. Maw (eds). *Failing Boys? Issues in Gender and Achievement*. Buckingham: Open University Press.

Read, K., Gardner, P. and Mahler, B. (1993) *Early Childhood Programs: Human Relationships and Learning* (9th edn). London: Holt, Rinehart and Winston.

Reay, D. (2001) 'Spice girls, nice girls, girlies and tomboys: gender discourses, girls' cultures and femininities in the primary classroom'. *Gender and Education*, 14(4), 153–66.

Renold, E. (2000) ' "Square-girls", femininity and the negotiation of academic success in primary school'. *British Educational Research Journal*, 27(5), 577–88.

Robbins Report (1963) Committee on Higher Education. London: HMSO.

Serbin, L. (1983) 'The hidden curriculum: academic consequences of teacher expectations', in M. Marland (ed.) *Sex Differentiation and Schooling*. London: Heinemann.

Skelton, C. (1989) (ed.) *Whatever Happens to Little Women?* Milton Keynes: Open University Press.

Skelton, C. (2002) 'Constructing dominant masculinity and negotiating the male gaze'. *International Journal of Inclusive Education*, 6(1), 17–31.

Skelton, C. and Francis, B. (2003) (eds) *Boys and Girls in the Primary Classroom*. Buckingham: Open University Press.

Spender, D. (1980) *Man Made Language*. London: Routledge and Kegan Paul.

Spender, D. (1981) 'Education: the patriarchal paradigm and the response to feminism', in D. Spender (ed.) *Men's Studies Modified: The Impact of Feminism on the Academic Disciplines*. Oxford: Elsevier.

Spender, D. (1982) *Invisible Women: The Schooling Scandal*. London: Writers and Readers.

Stanworth, M. (1981) *Gender and Schooling*. London: Women's Research and Resources Centre Publications.

Thompson, B. (1989) 'Teacher attitudes: complacency and conflict', in C. Skelton (ed.) *Whatever Happens to Little Women?* Milton Keynes: Open University Press.

Walkerdine, V. (1988) *The Mastery of Reason*. London: Routledge.

Warrington, M. and Younger, M. (2000) 'The other side of the gender gap'. *Gender and Education*, 12(4), 493–507.

Weiner, G. (1985) *Just a Bunch of Girls*. Milton Keynes: Open University Press.

Wollstonecraft, M. (1787) *Thoughts on the Education of Daughters*. London: Joseph Johnson.

Wollstonecraft, M. (1929) *A Vindication of the Rights of Women*. London: Everyman's Library.

Yolton, J.W., Yolton, J.S. (eds) (1989, first published 1693) *Some Thoughts Concerning Education by John Locke*. Oxford: Clarendon Press.

Supporting children with autistic spectrum disorders in a mainstream classroom

Katharine Amaladoss

Everything is so busy at school and everyone else, all the kids and all the teachers, seem to have a purpose and I never have quite fathomed out what the purpose is. I know we are there to learn, but there seems to be so much more going on than that. It is like beginning a game without knowing any rules or passwords.

(Jackson 1998)

Introduction

THE UNDERSTANDING and awareness of autistic spectrum disorders has grown in recent years, and as a result, more children with ASD are being identified. Research by the National Autistic Society indicates that one in 80 primary learners have the condition. The likelihood is that most schools will have children with these needs in their classrooms, and therefore it is crucial for practitioners to understand how to best meet these children's social, personal and learning needs.

Children with autistic spectrum disorders are a diverse group. They face many challenges but in an informed, positive and supportive school these children can succeed. This chapter sets out to help you in this goal. It will provide you with an introduction to the current understanding of ASD and how children with this may present in the school context. I will give a brief explanation of the challenges that these children face in school. The chapter will explore in more detail, using research and examples of good practice, how the environment can be managed and learning facilitated. Finally, I will describe how the autistic child and their peers can be helped to understand autistic spectrum disorders.

What are autistic spectrum disorders?

Autistic spectrum disorders as a description was first used by Lorna Wing (1996). She used the term to explain that there were features in common but that they might present differently in different people. All children in the group are commonly affected by a triad of impairments (Wing 1988) which are:

Social communication

Children have difficulty in understanding verbal and non-verbal communication. These children find it difficult to make sense of gesture and nuances in conversation, e.g. when they are told to pull their socks up, they will pull their socks up. They may have a good vocabulary but cannot use this vocabulary to communicate with others. They may talk at another child/adult, not recognising when to stop and allow a response. They may not show any interest in others. They may find interacting with others so stressful that they try to block the other person out by putting their hands over their ears or at worst hitting them.

Social interaction

Children have difficulty in understanding social behaviour, e.g. playing with others, how to make friends and what should or should not be said, i.e. saying to their teacher 'Your trousers make you look fat!'. They may, in the classroom setting, find turn-taking difficult and take little or no interest in other people, being more interested in things. Those with the disorder explain how this feels; it might be like an alien on Earth, not understanding life and its conventions.

Flexibility and thought

Children have difficulty behaving and thinking in a flexible way, e.g. they will insist on doing something the same way, will resist new experiences and find change very stressful. They may develop a special interest or a hobby about, for example, Thomas the Tank Engine, cars or travelling in space. They might like to repeat a behaviour again and again, e.g. twiddling a pencil. They prefer to be in control of a situation and so will often resist change and other ideas/suggestions.

To understand vividly what these impairments mean to those affected it is very useful to read books written by this varied group.

Oliver Sacks, in the introduction to Temple Grandin's book *Thinking in Pictures* (1996) says: 'books which speak from real experience give us a bridge between the autistic world and ours'.

In the book *Martian in the Playground*, Clare Sainsbury (2000) vividly describes her experiences of being at school with Asperger syndrome:

> I am standing in a corner of the playground as usual, as far away from people who might bump into me or shout, gazing into the sky and absorbed in my own thoughts. I am eight

or nine years old and have begun to realize that I am different in some nameless but all pervasive way ... I think that I might be an alien who has been put on this planet by mistake. I hope that this is so because this means there might be other people out there in the universe like me.

In the highly successful fiction book by Mark Haddon, *The Incident of the Dog in the Night Time*, the boy narrates the problems he has:

- not liking being touched;
- not liking yellow things or brown things and refusing to touch yellow or brown things;
- saying things that other people think are rude; and
- getting cross when someone has moved the furniture.

(A list of good books written by young people and adults about their experiences can be found in the booklist.)

The intelligence of children with ASDs can range from those with above-average ability to those with significant learning difficulties. Asperger syndrome, or high-functioning autism, was first described by Hans Asperger in 1944. Children in this group have average or above-average abilities, good spoken language and do not have language delay. While their impairments may appear more subtle, this does not mean that the difficulties are mild; children can often have too much expected of them, because of their high level of ability in a particular area. Nevertheless, they will still require a great deal of support and the curriculum to be modified to their needs.

Diagnosis of ASD may often occur preschool, but this is not always the case. Schools can play a very important part in providing information for medical professionals to aid correct identification.

Meeting children's needs with autistic spectrum disorders

These are key factors to facilitate the child in the school:

Knowledge and understanding

If schools are to manage the learning environment and facilitate the child, they must understand and have knowledge of the condition and what to do. It is crucial that *all* staff, including dinner supervisors and office staff, in a school have a basic training in ASD so that the needs of the child can be supported throughout the school day. Meeting regularly with parents/carers and contacting medical/other professionals who have assessed/lived/worked with the child, enable staff to develop an understanding of the child as an individual rather than relying on generalisation. Ideally, considerable information gathering should occur before the child, with a diagnosis, starts school, so that from the first day the child feels welcomed and supported.

Case study 6.1: Starting school – example of good practice

Benjamin, aged 4, was given a Statement of Educational Needs and was due to start in reception in two terms. His mum was very anxious about his move from nursery school. The class teacher and SENCO met with his mother and was able to find out about his likes, e.g. Thomas the Tank Engine, and his dislikes, e.g. other children too close to him. The school organised two visits by the class teacher to his nursery and met with his key worker. The head teacher obtained the child's records and read them, giving key features to all staff. The SENCO then organised a meeting of all who would have regular contact with Benjamin, the class teacher, teaching assistants, SEN teacher and parents. At this meeting, a plan for transition was drawn up which included:

- sharing and discussing information in the statement;
- photographic book about nursery to bring to school;
- making a photographic visual timetable;
- agreeing manageable targets and expectations, e.g. sitting on a carpet square for the register;
- fixing a series of dates for Benjamin to visit and planning a gradual move from part-time to full-time education;
- setting a review for three weeks after his start at school.

His mum felt reassured and all school staff were pleased to have a shared understanding and plan.

Focus on the visual

Many adults with high-functioning ASD can describe how they 'think in pictures' (Grandin 1996). Therefore using visual strategies is a very important way to help children learn new concepts, e.g. pictures to act as prompts and having instructions to do something visually organised. Visual information enables the child to have a constant reference point, rather than having to try and take all the information in in one moment.

In the classroom, it will help if:

- shelves are labelled with pictures and words;
- the child is shown visually how things are done, e.g. where to sit and put things;
- there are visual clues to link an activity to a place;
- there are visual sequences, e.g. Story Strip, showing how to do an activity (this is particularly useful for PE) (see Figure 6.1);
- there is colour coding of children's work materials; and
- there is a visual timetable enabling children to understand and order time in their day (see Figure 6.2).

| I will get my P.E bag | I will take my school uniform off but not my underwear | I will put on my t-shirt, shorts and plimsolls |

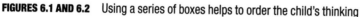

FIGURES 6.1 AND 6.2 Using a series of boxes helps to order the child's thinking

When choosing visual supports it is important to use pictures, symbols or photographs that the child understands. These picture schedules can be prepared either horizontally or vertically, can be attached to a board, a place mat or put in a pile or notebook. The visual prompts need to be developed with the child and referred to regularly. It is also important to show children what is not available. The international signal Ⓧ is good to use or an **X** over the picture, or remove that item from the timetable or schedule.

The PECS (Picture Exchange Communication System) was developed by Andi Bondy and Lori Frost (2001) for children who may not have any functional communication skills. The approach teaches the child to give a picture of a desired object to another person in exchange for that object. In this approach the child initiates the communication rather than responding to a prompt. This could be adapted in a mainstream classroom for children with very restricted speech.

Motivation

Keeping the child with ASD motivated to focus on the task is challenging, but these strategies can help:

- using the child's name before giving an instruction;

- using the child's own interests, their strengths and skills rather than spending all your time on what they can't do, e.g. with a young child, relating adding two numbers together as attaching coaches to Thomas the Tank Engine;

- being sensitive to the child's physical needs/dislikes, e.g. enough space/light and sound, not insisting on sand play if they do not like the feel of sand;

- finding a reward system that reinforces what the desired behaviour is and using it consistently;

- not overloading the child with instructions, instead breaking large tasks down into small parts, with rewards;

- making sure that there is a balance between doing more challenging tasks and less demanding/relaxing activities;

- gradually increasing the length of time for tasks;

- using ICT, such as Clicker, which enables text to be constructed more quickly and uses visual prompts;

- ensuring expectations are realistic and providing regular encouragement throughout, in a manner in which the child is comfortable; and

- on occasion allowing the child time to learn alone, without always having to collaborate with others which can make the learning even more difficult.

Structure

By using such strategies as visual timetables, the learning can be organised to support the child's need for routines. Being clear and consistent is supportive to all learners in the classroom but will be essential for the child with an autistic spectrum disorder. Organising the classroom into different areas for different tasks, with some space that is free from distraction may help. The TEACHH approach developed by Mesibov (1988) focuses on the organisation of the classroom, timetabling and teaching methods and so makes the learning world more predictable. In this way children find school less confusing and will behave more positively. More information on this approach can be found in the book list.

Despite putting structures, visual timetables and clear routines into the school day to support the child, change happens all the time. Children with ASD need preparation for any changes, explaining in clear, precise language what will happen next. This can help the child be less upset and avoid aggressive behaviour.

Social stories and comic strip conversations

Social stories is a technique developed by Carol Gray (1994a) in the USA. A social story is written about a particular social situation that a child finds difficult. The social story will describe and provide social cues, giving the child information about what to do, why and what the likely outcome will be. The stories include:

- **descriptive sentences** where situations happen, who is involved and why;
- **perspective sentences** which describe the feelings of others in a given situation;
- **directive sentences**, telling the child what he/she is expected to say and do; and
- **control sentences**, which help the child remember what to do.

It is best if the child is included in the writing of the story as then they can suggest what will help them remember and include their particular interest. Children sometimes like drawing pictures to go with their stories, or photos or symbols can be included.

Case study 6.2: Social stories – having a hair cut

My hair grows long. It goes down in my eyes. My dad's hair grows long and my mum's hair grows long.

We need to get our hair cut with scissors.

I go with my sister to get our hair cut with scissors at the hairdressers. I watch my sister have her hair cut. I sit on the chair and wait, and look at my Thomas the Tank Engine book.

Mum says, 'James it's your turn'.

I look at me in the mirror. I see the lady with the scissors. The lady cuts my hair with scissors and I sit still and quietly.

When the lady stops cutting my hair she says 'Well done'.

I get off the chair. I say thank you to the lady.

I leave the hairdressers with my sister and mum.

I am happy when the lady cuts my hair with scissors.

Carol Gray has produced examples in her book *My Social Stories* (2002) which give clear guidance. Children can carry these little stories with them. Ideally, they should be used regularly at school and home if the social situation is to be addressed successfully. Many children then feel able to cope in social situations, where previously they did not understand what to do.

Activity 6.1: Making a social story

Soon after Mona (aged 5) started at school, it became clear that she did not understand the routine of lunchtime, found it distressing and would sometimes try and escape from the lunch hall, causing anxiety and upset to staff and children.

Make a social story about lunchtime routines that would help Mona if she were at your school.

For some children **comic strip conversations** can be helpful. These also illustrate social situations but include thoughts/feelings as well as what is said (Gray 1994b). They develop out of a conversation between the child and facilitative adult. There are eight symbols for basic conversation concepts, e.g. for listening, talking, loud and quiet and others introduced by the child.

In these conversations, using stick people and speech/thought bubbles, children can be facilitated to think about what was happening, what was said by the child and others, what they thought when they said or did something and what others thought and said. Sometimes colour can be used to express emotions, e.g. happy words ('I like riding my bike' [green]; If you say that I'll push you over' [red]).

The facilitating adult encourages the child to think about solutions to the situation. This may not always be possible with some children, but this process will still help the adult to understand more fully the situation from the child's viewpoint.

Circle of friends

This was a technique devised in Canada for developing a support network around an individual who was socially isolated (Newton *et al.* 1996) and can be used with children on the autistic spectrum. It needs a confident, enthusiastic adult to facilitate the group, plus the child and his/her carer's support. Initially, the child to be supported is not in the class and a discussion is had to share the child's strengths and difficulties. The children in the class are invited to empathise and reflect on their own experience of friendship. At the end, volunteers to be in the circle of friends for the child are asked for. The adult then chooses from these, the group including some children who have good social skills and others more vulnerable (up to 6–8 children). This is followed by a meeting with the circle of friends who tell the child all the positive things about them and why they want to be in the circle of friends. The adult facilitates conversations about how the children might support and what actions to take. The group then meets weekly.

The group and child need to agree when the group will end and this needs to be planned carefully, so that the child is not left feeling unsupported. The circle can always be restarted if the need arises. There is evidence that this approach has achieved success. It enables children to be proactive in 'looking out for' and 'supporting the child' rather than this being solely an adult responsibility.

Peers' and the child's understanding of autistic spectrum disorder

Many books written by children/adults with ASD reflecting on their lives testify to the relief of knowing the explanation for their differences. Facilitating this understanding needs to be handled with great sensitivity so that it is manageable. It is also not a single conversation and will be a process over time involving parents, professionals and schools. Knowing when is difficult, but from my own experience in a primary school, it is when the child starts to recognise that they are different and

Table 6.1 Ordering a child's thinking

1	2	3	4
Draw where you are and who is with you	Draw what you are doing and what others did	Draw what you said and what others said (using speech bubbles for each person)	Draw what you thought when you said that and what others thought (use thought bubbles for each)

thinks there are things wrong with them, or they feel helpless to sort things out. A number of books written for children can help families and schools in this task (see booklist). It can also be helpful to do some work with their class of peers, who may then be able to be more supportive in the classroom and playground.

Carol Gray (1993) explains how using the concept of the Sixth Sense can improve pupils' understanding of ASD and show them how they could support a peer with it. First, the class are enabled to discuss the five senses – sight, hearing, smell, taste and touch – and that sometimes people have difficulties with these. The children are then encouraged to talk about ways to try and help people with these difficulties. The sixth sense is then described as our social sense, an ability to know what other people know and how other people feel. Impairment in this area will make it difficult to know what to do or say, e.g. would it be easy or difficult to take turns if you didn't know what others were thinking, or would it be easy or difficult to understand why people do things? It is then explained that child X has difficulty with these sorts of things. Finally, the child's peers are asked to suggest ways that they could help. The following is an example of how this was used in a school.

Case study 6.3: The sixth sense used with a class of eight-year-olds

Ashwin had a diagnosis of autistic spectrum disorder with associated dyslexia and dyspraxia and had a statement of SEN. He had daily TA support in class, as an individual and in groups, and twice-weekly withdrawal with a named teaching assistant.

He had recently moved to Year 3 and was experiencing acute problems with peers, most particularly at playtimes/unstructured times. He was regularly screaming and then withdrawing, locking himself in the toilet because the experience was too overwhelming. It became clear that he found it very difficult to play with others, especially if the game was without fixed routines or if children changed the rules.

In the classroom, he believed others were unkind and his carers thought that this was because the children did not really understand his difficulties. The SENCO contacted the local LEA Complex Social Communication Team for support, who, after meeting with carers, SENCO and class teacher/TA, agreed to work with children in his class on understanding child Y's condition through Sixth Sense material developed by Carol Gray.

His peers began to understand that Ashwin had difficulties with his social sense and needed their help. They developed strategies to support him in the playground/classroom, e.g. being clear about rules before the game and sticking to them, allowing him time out if he felt overwhelmed.

As a result Ashwin had more successful playtimes and over time developed a group of supportive friends.

Recognising emotions

Children on the autistic spectrum will often not naturally be able to read/use body language appropriately or understand and express feelings. They will often laugh at others' difficulties, draw attention to physical characteristics that can cause hurt, e.g. 'You've got big ears and a spot on your nose', and their own facial expressions may not show how they really feel. Children need to be supported to learn the variety of feelings, gestures, social behaviours and how they are linked.

This is often best done by an adult narrating or drawing the child's attention to an experience of emotion when they, or others, are experiencing it, e.g. happy to see Mummy at the end of day; Jack is angry because you tore up his picture (Jordan 2001). Sometimes watching clips of favourite videos or soaps can be used with sound switched off to discuss people's emotions and how they might be feeling. With some children, photos of real situations in school may be a good starting point to discuss behaviours and feelings and their consequences and corresponding feelings.

Making choices

It is important to be clear about choices in situations and their consequences, e.g. 'You have a choice, if you get changed for PE now, you can have five minutes at playtime on the computer, and if you do not, you will not be able to use the computer at playtime today'. By doing this, children are given clear expectations and boundaries to take some responsibility for their own actions/behaviours.

Managing unstructured times/playtimes/lunchtimes

These are often the most difficult times, as in the hurly-burly of activity the normal rules/controls that support are often missing; it can feel like a nightmare. It is in these unstructured play and social times that the child may feel most aware of their difference and inability to cope, not knowing how to make and keep friends, join and play a game.

It is then that the child may hover on edges, pace around the perimeter of the playground, find it soothing to make their own noises, follow lines painted on the playground, run wildly or simply not want to go out or be there at all. Children need to be taught how they can manage an unstructured time, make friends and play games.

An adult (dinner supervisor or teaching assistant) can model how to play the game by involving themselves in it, prompting with phrases like 'Whose turn is it now?', and model good things to say and do.

The child will need to be supported to practise being involved in a game, perhaps in a more controlled setting, e.g. a few children with a teaching assistant in the playground before a playtime. The child may need to be reassured that their turn will come and by encouragement in the game/activity, e.g. 'Let's see if we can . . .'. It is probably best to start with games that are co-operative rather then competitive. When it is felt right to try and support a child in a competitive game, learning a phrase like 'You win some, you lose some' could be taught. They will need to be taught where to stand, what to do and what might happen and to ask if they are not sure. The game/activity needs to be broken down into manageable chunks, with not everything expected at once. These elements will need to be rehearsed time and again, and possibly reinforced with a social story.

Activity 6.2: Support in unstructured times

EITHER:

Think of a child that you work with who would benefit from greater support in unstructured times. Decide on one or two strategies that you believe would help. Plan how you will enable these strategies to be developed;

OR:

The dinner supervisors are not managing Yasmin well at lunchtimes. You are regularly being called from your lunch break to sort out his rages. There appears to be a lack of understanding of his needs. Following a discussion with SENCO and class teacher, it has been agreed that it would be helpful to have a training session for dinner staff. You are asked to provide strategies. Make a list of what you might suggest/share.

Anger management

Children in the autistic spectrum will often express anger, e.g. when they cannot understand a situation, the normal routines are broken without warning, they are not allowed to do what they want to, there is too much social/sensory information for them to process or it is expected too quickly. Hopefully, these occasions will be less if the previous strategies are being employed in schools and staff have a clear understanding of the child's needs, but it would be unusual if schools did not experience problems without bouts of anger/aggression by the child. The following strategies can help:

- a mood diary kept by a supportive teaching assistant can help to determine cycles, and triggers which can then indicate what needs to be done and when;

- rewarding times when the child does not get angry and exercises self-control can help;

- teaching the child to check out a situation before responding and how/where to ask for help when difficult situations occur may avoid the need to get angry;

- providing a quiet place to go to calm down and agreeing a signal with the child to indicate need for this space.

The school community and their roles in the management of autistic spectrum disorders

A child with ASD will be registered on the school's SEN register and the school must respond within the framework of the SEN Code of Practice (2001). The SENCO will need to co-ordinate the professional advice and family views and be strategically responsible for the overview of the child's needs and corresponding provision. The SENCO should, wherever possible, facilitate regular multi-professional meetings for health and education to ensure everyone is aware of all the child's needs. An individual education plan will need to be drawn up with clear, measurable targets. Developing this with the relevant staff, parents/carers and the child will be likely to lead to greater success in achievement of targets set. These should be set and reviewed regularly (not usually longer than a term) and parents should be offered regular opportunities to discuss progress and strategies. They will need reassurance and evidence that their child's needs are being met. It is also important that the child and his/her family know the named person to speak to when they are concerned.

There is now evidence to suggest the type of teaching style that is likely to be most effective in a school (Jordan and Peeters 1999). It includes being able to cope with giving and not having thanks, keeping calm, being attracted to difference, being willing to adapt styles of communication and interaction and always feeling there is more to know. This information may help a SENCO support the teacher in the classroom and identify the most suitable teaching assistants to support the child in regular 1:1 and small-group activities. The teaching assistant, while employing the strategies agreed and with the teacher delivering the programme, needs to be like 'a parrot on the shoulder', explaining the school day. In this way the teaching assistant can make the experience of being in school less of a puzzle or a mysterious game, or an experience to be viewed, but not understood. Their role is key and cannot be underestimated, but they must work within a school environment and with teachers who are proactive in creating an appropriate learning environment, and who are not just reactive when problems occur. All support staff, dinner supervisors, office team and welfare will also need to be aware of their roles and be given training, as it is often out of the classroom, at playtime and lunchtimes that most support is needed. In my experience it is also crucial to have a head teacher who clearly values the gifts of these children, and a school ethos and culture of care and support for all, where difference is celebrated.

Conclusion

Children on the autistic spectrum are 'a bright thread in the tapestry of life' (Attwood 1998). Despite their difficulties they will all have special gifts, and if they have Asperger syndrome they may have very good memories, extensive vocabulary and an excellent knowledge of a particular subject. They will exhibit in different ways and so schools need to select strategies of provision that best meet the individual's needs. This task is for the whole school community, with the support of other professionals, the parent/carers and the voice or behaviour messages of the child. The child on the autistic spectrum can succeed if there is a programme of provision that includes strategies to develop the child's knowledge, understanding and skills and which enhances their self-esteem within a supportive environment.

The task will often be challenging and frustrating. There is no magic answer or recipe for success, but I hope that this chapter will provide professionals with guidance and suggestions for further reading that will enable you to make a positive difference to these children's lives.

Acknowledgement

West Sussex Complex Social Communication Team based at Centenary House Worthing, West Sussex.

Bibliography

Attwood, T. (1998) *Asperger's Syndrome*. London: Jessica Kingsley Publishers.

Bondy, A.S. and Frost, L.A. (2001) *A Picture's Worth: PECS and other Visual Communications: Strategies in Autism*. Bethseda, MD: Woodbine House.

DfES (2001) Special Educational Needs Code of Practice. London: DfES.

Grandin, T. (1996) *Thinking in Pictures: And Other Reports from My Life with Autism*. London: Vintage.

Gray, C. (1993) *The Sixth Sense: Taming the Recess Jungle*. Arlington, TX: Future Horizons.

Gray, C. (1994a) *The Social Storybook*. Arlington, TX: Future Horizons.

Gray, C. (1994b) *Comic Strip Conversations*. Arlington, TX: Future Horizons.

Gray, C. and White, A.L. (2002) *My Social Stories Book*. London: Jessica Kingsley Publishers.

Haddon, M. (2003) *The Curious Incident of the Dog in the Night Time*. London: Vintage.

Jackson, L. (1998) *Freaks, Geeks and Asperger's Syndrome: A User Guide to Adolescence*. London: Jessica Kingsley Publishers.

Jordan, R. (2001) *Autism with Severe Learning Difficulties*. London: Souvenir Press.

Jordan, R. and Peeters, T. (1999) 'What makes a good practitioner in the field of autism?', in G. Jones (ed.) *Good Autism Practice: The First in a Collection of Papers Written for Those Working and Living with Children and Adults with Autism*. Birmingham University School of Education.

Mesibov, G. (ed.) (1998) *Diagnosis and Assessment in Autism*. New York: Plenum Press.

Newton, C., Taylor, G. and Wilson, D. (1996) 'Circles of friends: an inclusive approach to meeting emotional and behavioual needs'. *Educational Psychology in Practice*, 11(4).

Sainsbury, C. (2000) *Martian in the Playground*. London: The Book Factory.

Wing, L. (1988) 'The continuum of autistic characteristics', in E. Schopler and G. Mesibov (eds) *Diagnosis and Assessment in Autism*. New York: Plenum Press.

Wing, L. (1996) *The Autistic Spectrum*. London: Constable.

Web links

Autistic Spectrum Disorders: Good Practice Guidance (2002) (www.teachernet.gov.uk/management/sen)

National Autistic Society (www.nas.org.uk)

Social Stories (www.thegraycenter.org)

Further reading

Attwood, T. (1998) *Asperger's Syndrome*. London: Jessica Kingsley Publishers.

Barratt, P., Border, J., Joy, H. *et al.* (2000) *Developing Pupils' Social Communication Skills: Practical Resources*. London: David Fulton Publishers.

Cumine, V., Leach, J. and Stevenson, G. (1998) *Asperger's Syndrome: A Practical Guide for Teachers*. London: David Fulton Publishers.

Cumine, V., Leach, J. and Stevenson, G. (2000) *Autism in the Early Years*. London: David Fulton Publishers.

Hardy, C., Ogden, J., Newman, J. and Cooper, S. (2002) *Autism and ICT*. London: David Fulton Publishers.

Jones, G. (2002) *Educational Provision for Children with Autism and Asperger Syndrome: Meeting Their Needs*. London: David Fulton Publishes.

Jordan, R. and Powell, S. (1995) *Understanding and Teaching Children with Autism*. Chichester: Wiley.

Jordan, R. and Powell, S. (2000) *Autism and Learning*. London: David Fulton Publishers.

Leicester City Council/National Autistic Society (1998) *Asperger Syndrome: Practical Strategies in the Classroom*. London: The National Autistic Society.

Mesibov, G. and Howley, M. (2003) *Assessing the Curriculum for Pupils with Autistic Spectrum Disorders*. London: David Fulton Publishers.

Smith-Myles, B., Tapscott Cook, K. and Miller, N. (2000) *Asperger Syndrome and Sensory Issues*. Shawnee Mission, Kansas: Autism Asperger Publishing Co.

QCA for Wales (ACCAC) (2000) *Guidance on the National Curriculum and Autistic Spectrum Disorder*. Thames Ditton, Surrey: ACCAC Publications.

Smith Myles, B. and Southwick, J. (1999) *Asperger Syndrome and Difficult Moments*. Shawnee Mission, Kansas: Autism Asperger Publishing Co.

Vermeulen, P. (2000) *I am Special*. London: Jessica Kingsley Publishers.

Whitaker, P. with Joy, H., Harley, J. and Edwards, D. (2001) *Challenging Behaviour and Autism: Making Sense – Making Progress*. London: National Autistic Society.

Wing, L. (1996) *The Autistic Spectrum: A Guide for Parents and Professionals*. London: Constable.

Supporting social skills activities

Csoti, M. (2001) *Social Awareness Skills for Children*. London: Jessica Kingsley Publishers.

Kelly, A. (1996) *Talk About*. Bicester: Speechmark Publishing.

Schroeder, A. (1996) *Socially Speaking*. Wisbech: LDA.

From a personal perspective

Gerland, G. (1996) *A Real Person Life on the Outside*. London: Souvenir Press.

Grandin, T. (1996) *Thinking in Pictures*. London: Vintage.

Holliday Willey, L. (1999) *Pretending to Be Normal – Living with Aspergers Syndrome*. London: Jessica Kingsley Publishers.

Jackson, L. (2002) *Freaks, Geeks and Asperger's Syndrome: A User Guide to Adolescence*. London: Jessica Kingsley Publishers.

Sainsbury C. (2000) *Martian in the Playground*. London: The Book Factory.

Williams, D. (1992) *Nobody, Nowhere*. New York: Doubleday.

Williams, D. (1995) *Somebody, Somewhere*. New York: Doubleday.

Williams, D. (1998) *Autism and Inside – Our Approach*. London: Jessica Kingsley Publishers.

Books for children

Hoopman, K. (1988) *Blue Bottle Mystery: An Asperger Adventure*. London: Jessica Kingsley Publishers.

Hoopman, K. (1988) *Lisa and the Lacemaker: An Asperger Adventure*. London: Jessica Kingsley Publishers.

Hoopman, K. (1988) *Of Mice and Aliens: An Asperger Adventure*. London: Jessica Kingsley Publishers.

Ogaz, N. (2002) *Buster and Amazing Daisy: Adventures with Asperger Syndrome*. London: Jessica Kingsley Publishers.

Wever, C. (1998) *Full of Beans*. Concord West, NSW: Shrink-Rap Press.

Physical and sensory disability

Sue Gilbert

Introduction

RECENT LEGISLATION, INCLUDING the Disability Discrimination Act 1995 (DDA), has identified challenges for many mainstream schools. Since the introduction of the DDA schools have been admitting children with disabilities not previously met in mainstream schools. Invariably, many of these children will have extra support, which puts an emphasis on teamwork for all involved with their education and care. The DDA covers all aspects of school life, including extra-curricular activities and school visits. This chapter seeks to provide a sound level of understanding of current legislation and requirements and a consideration of how physical and sensory disabilities impact on the child's experiences in school. Ways of offering structured support within the classroom will be discussed, including the use of information and communication technology (ICT). The benefits of positive relationships and clear communication with parents in the learning process are also examined.

Background to the issues

Before considering how children with physical and sensory disabilities may be supported in schools to benefit from an inclusive education, it is important to consider the background to the issues and so develop a sound level of knowledge of the current legislation and requirements.

> From September 2002, schools will be required not to treat disabled pupils less favourably for a reason relating to their disability and to take reasonable steps to ensure that they are not placed at substantial disadvantage to those who are not disabled.
>
> (www.opsi.gov.uk)

The Disability Discrimination Act 1995, as amended by the Special Educational Needs and Disability Act 2001, makes it unlawful for schools and LEAs to discriminate against disabled pupils for a reason relating to their disability, without justification. The Disability Discrimination Act 1995 defines a disabled person as someone who has: 'A physical or mental impairment which has a substantial and long term adverse effect on his or her ability to carry out normal day to day activities' (www.opsi.gov.uk/acts/acts1995).

There is a common view that the definition of a disability refers to a small number of pupils in our schools. However, a report from the Cabinet Office (2005), *Improving the Chances of Disabled People*, draws on estimates suggesting that 11 million adults and 770,000 children in the UK are disabled, equivalent to 24 per cent of the adult population and 7 per cent of all children (www.teachernet.gov.uk). We now need to consider this definition further, to understand the different constituents contained within it. Such consideration will explain the large number of children who fall within the definition of disability.

Disability Rights Code of Practice

In order to disseminate information for those involved in supporting disabled pupils in schools, a Disability Rights Code of Practice for schools, prepared by the Disability Rights Commission, explains the new anti-discrimination duties to schools covering every aspect of life. There are close links between this Code and the SEN Code of Practice (2001). They are designed to complement each other. The principle behind the legislation is that, wherever possible, disabled people should have the same opportunities as non-disabled people in their access to education.

It is important to understand the range of activities covered in all aspects of school life. The following list, although not exhaustive, is taken from the Code:

- preparation for entry to the school;
- the curriculum;
- teaching and learning;
- classroom organisation;
- timetabling;
- grouping of pupils;
- homework;
- access to school facilities;
- activities to supplement the curriculum, e.g. a drama group visiting the school;
- school sports;
- school policies;
- breaks and lunchtimes;
- the serving of school meals;

- interaction with peers;
- assessment and exam arrangements;
- school discipline and sanctions;
- exclusion procedures
- school clubs and activities;
- school trips;
- the school's arrangements for working with other agencies;
- preparation of pupils for the next phase of education.

(www.drc-gb.org)

The Code of Practice covers all schools and local education authorities in England and Wales, and all schools and education authorities in Scotland. Young children aged 16 and over are included if still in school. The Code gives valuable guidance on how to avoid discrimination against disabled pupils, and as such is essential reading for all those concerned with education. Further use concerns advice to disabled pupils and their parents and carers on how to interpret the law, and provides details of action that can be taken if a pupil has been discriminated against.

There are two main key duties contained in the Code; these are:

- not to treat disabled pupils less favourably; and
- to take reasonable steps to avoid putting disabled pupils at a substantial disadvantage.

(www.drc-gb.org)

The planning duties in Sections 28D and 28E of the Act require LEAs to produce accessibility strategies, and schools to develop accessibility plans to improve access for disabled pupils. There are three elements to this work:

- improvements in access to the curriculum;
- physical improvements to increase access to education and associated services; and
- improvements in the provision of information in a range of formats for disabled pupils.

(www.drc-gb.org)

Schools were required to produce their first accessibility plans by April 2003. These plans are inspected by the Office for Standards in Education (Ofsted). The Ofsted report, *Special Educational Needs and Disability* (2004), states that:

In four out of ten schools visited there was satisfactory planning for improved access to premises, particularly when this could be achieved with relatively small adaptations. A few schools had planned for increased access to the curriculum. In one school the disability access plan included wide-ranging changes to the curriculum to ensure what the school called 'presence, participation and achievement'.

However, over half the schools visited had no disability access plans and, of those plans that did exist, the majority focused only on accommodation.

... in too many cases the plans were merely paper exercises to fulfil a statutory responsibility rather than demonstrating a clear commitment to improving access.

Too often, accommodation remains a major barrier to the full inclusion of pupils with physical and sensory difficulties.

(ibid.:22)

Schools should not wait until a disabled pupil has been admitted before making reasonable adjustments to their provision. These adjustments involve schools in reviewing their policies, practices and procedures on a regular basis to ensure against discrimination. By 2005, reasonable physical adjustments must be made in schools to accommodate pupils with disabilities.

Activity 7.1: Investigate progress on your school's accessibility plan

1. Improvements in access to the curriculum

In your discussions with colleagues who work with children, and the SENCO, and through reading the school's plan, make notes on the following points:

- What are the school's priorities in terms of improved access to the curriculum?
- Is the school able to offer disabled pupils access to the wider curriculum, i.e. after-school clubs, sporting and cultural activities?
- How have teaching strategies been adjusted to meet individual needs?
- What INSET support is available to staff to improve their practice?
- Does the school have links with different phases and sectors of education, i.e. special schools/units for mutual support to enhance the curriculum?
- What links does the school have with specialist advisers to develop the curriculum for children with disabilities?

2. Improvements to the physical environment

In your discussions with colleagues who work with children, and the SENCO, and through reading the school's plan, make notes on the following:

- What recent improvements have been made to the school and its grounds to increase the accessibility for pupils with disability?

- Take a walk around your school and playground and note accessibility and possible hazards for disabled children.

- Which issues of access and potential hazards could be quickly overcome and which need a more long-term solution?

3. Access to written information

In your discussions with colleagues who work with children, and the SENCO, and through reading the school's plan, make notes on the following:

- Are written texts interpreted through supporting adults?

- Is voice recognition software available and used frequently?

- Does the LEA provide specialist guidance on converting written texts into alternative formats? Does your school use this service?

Physical and mental impairment

The DDA definition of physical and mental impairment is given below. Physical impairment includes sensory impairment, such as those affecting sight or hearing.

> There is a wide spectrum of sensory, multi-sensory and physical difficulties. The sensory range extends from profound and permanent deafness through to lesser levels of loss . . . Physical impairments may arise from physical, neurological or metabolic causes that only require appropriate access to educational facilities and equipment; others may lead to more complex learning and social needs; a few children will have multi-sensory difficulties, some with associated physical difficulties.
>
> (Disability Rights Code of Practice:88)

Mental impairment includes learning difficulties and an impairment resulting from, or consisting of, a mental illness. Such a definition covers a wide range of impairments, including hidden impairments such as learning difficulties and dyslexia.

Long-term adverse effect, for the purposes of the DDA, is described as 12 months or more. This means that some conditions commonly found in school, such as broken limbs, are ruled out of this provision. However, it is hoped that knowledge gained from working with these children would inform practice with regard to those covered by the Act and vice versa.

A substantial adverse effect, according to the Disability Rights Code of Practice for Schools, is:

> Something more than a minor or trivial effect. The requirement that an effect must be substantial reflects the general understanding of a disability as a limitation going beyond the normal differences in ability which might exist among people.
>
> (Appendix 1 : 77)

When considering normal day-to-day activities, the Code makes reference to those activities which are carried out on a 'fairly regular and frequent basis'. To help decide if an impairment affects day-to-day activities, broad categories of capacity are listed in the DDA. These are:

- mobility;
- manual dexterity;
- physical co-ordination;
- continence;
- ability to lift, carry or otherwise move everyday objects;
- speech, hearing or eyesight;
- memory or ability to concentrate, learn or understand; and
- perception of the risk of physical danger.

(www.teachernet.gov.uk/wholeschool/sen/schools)

Normal activities can be defined as those that most people carry out on a regular basis.

Pupils with severe disfigurements are automatically covered by the DDA; they do not have to prove that their impairment has an adverse effect on their ability to carry out daily activities. This is clearly an impairment which requires both understanding of the condition and practical support strategies which Frances (2004) states can be difficult to find as so few children are affected:

Working with people with facial disfigurement in particular and visible difference in general is full of strange surprises. What you think you should do, out of kindness and good intentions to help a pupil who looks different, may not improve things at all. Something you think you should not do because, for instance, you don't want to increase the self-consciousness of the affected child, may turn out to be the most effective intervention of all.

(ibid.:4)

Medical conditions include those that are likely to change and develop over time, e.g. muscular dystrophy. The DDA specifically brings people with cancer, multiple sclerosis and HIV infection within the definition of disabled people. For the purpose of the DDA, if a child is receiving treatment for an impairment, schools must consider the child's condition as though she were not receiving any treatment. Thus a child who is receiving treatment for diabetes has to be considered as though no treatment is received. The only exception to this is in the case of pupils who wear glasses, to correct a relatively minor sight defect. As we have seen above, the key to understanding disability lies with the long-term effect on a child's ability to carry out normal everyday activities.

Ensuring disabled children are included

The National Curriculum inclusion statement emphasises:

'Schools have a responsibility to provide a broad and balanced curriculum for all pupils.' This statutory inclusion statement on providing effective learning opportunities for all pupils outlines how those who work with children can modify, as necessary, the National Curriculum programmes of study to provide all pupils with relevant and appropriately challenging work at each key stage. It sets out three principles that are essential to developing a more inclusive curriculum:

A Setting suitable learning challenges

B Responding to pupils' diverse learning needs

C Overcoming potential barriers to learning and assessment for individuals and groups of pupils. (DfEE/QCA 1999:30)

The following key features of effective practice which help schools' efforts to be inclusive are taken from Ofsted's 2004 report *Special Educational Needs and Disability*:

a climate of acceptance of all pupils, including those who have distinctive needs; the availability of suitable teaching and personal support; sensitive allocation to teaching groups and careful modification of the curriculum, timetables and social arrangements; assessment, recording and reporting procedures which can embrace and express adequately the progress of pupils who make only small gains in learning and personal development; widespread awareness among staff of the particular needs of pupils with significant special needs and an understanding of meeting them in the classroom and elsewhere; the availability of appropriate materials and teaching aids; and involving parents as fully as possible in decision making.

1. A climate of acceptance of all pupils, including those who have distinctive needs (Ofsted 2004:19)

Further findings from the Ofsted report (2003) states that the inclusive ethos for learning is important, creating effective learning environments where contributions from all children are valued and grouping ensures that pupils with SEN work with other pupils.

It is through this inclusive ethos that all children feel secure and able to contribute, and in this way stereotypical views are challenged and pupils can learn to view differences in others in a positive way.

December 2005 was an important time for the millions of disabled people, as it marks the start of new rights under the DDA, and the International Day of Disabled People occurs as an annual event. However, the current figures are stark in relation to the opportunities offered to adults with disabilities. In a joint publication between the *Guardian* newspaper and the Department for Work and Pensions, *Extending*

Boundaries (2 December 2005), only 50 per cent of disabled people of working age are in employment, compared with 81 per cent non-disabled, and they earn 30 per cent less when they are working. The fact that disabled people are twice as likely to have no qualifications is of clear concern to all involved in the education of pupils with disabilities. Educating all pupils in disability issues and equality will help both the disabled and non-disabled child respect each other. This work should be seen as part of the schools' programme of inclusion issues, aimed at driving out prejudice and stereotyping. It could be incorporated in either the citizenship curriculum or PSCHE. From 2006 schools will have a statutory obligation to promote positive attitudes towards disability.

Activity 7.2

In this activity you are asked to consider the ways in which children and adults with disabilities are portrayed in your school. While doing this work, consider not just the number of times disability is shown, but the quality and nature of the portrayal.
Look at the long-term and medium-term plans for your class or group.

- Consider the opportunities for inviting in disabled adults who are experts in their field.
- Review the books available to the children. Do they show positive images of children and adults with disabilities?

Consult your literacy curriculum manager/LEA adviser for booklists recommended for showing positive images.

- Could you use a book with younger children which uses images of difference and isolation in order to develop empathy and an understanding of other people's feelings and emotions?
- Investigate the web for positive images. Can you incorporate these into illustrations on worksheets, posters and displays?
- Consider how you could use images of successful disabled athletes and sports people, could these be used within the PE curriculum and on displays on sports noticeboards?
- Use your LEA adviser to investigate local charities that specialise in education and training on disability issues for children and adults. Disability Equality in Education runs such a network of trainers.

The Ofsted report *Special Educational Needs in the Mainstream* also cites successful schools as having clear policies and procedures which have developed over time and where development of an understanding of inclusion had led to raising of standards for all pupils. They believed that the idea that teaching should take into account individual needs and learning styles as had value for all pupils. An article on the website (www.equalitytraining.co.uk) states that:

The crucial understanding is that the child is not expected to change. The starting point is that the child is valued; there is no difference to the approach to all the children in the setting – they are all different, each one is central to the decisions made for their individual learning and development. (www.equalitytraining.co.uk)

Thus inclusion is seen as part of the overall improvement of the school that encourages all children to achieve to their full potential.

Case study 7.1

Chloe arrived in the nursery class at the age of four. She had no contact with preschool provision prior to this point. The only details of her possible impairment, gained from her parents, detailed short-sightedness in one eye. Chloe's inability to cope with the routines in the nursery class stood her apart from her peers in her early days at nursery, which led to a diagnosis of extreme loss of sight. The school responded by considering provision which would support her individual learning, while at the same time guiding the direction of learning of the whole class. This was felt to be an important issue with inclusion, that good practice for a child with a disability contained elements of good practice for all.

An early activity was based on the story *Not Now, Bernard*. All the children wrote an individual version of the story, incorporating their name in the title. Thus, for Chloe, *Not, Now Chloe*. All the stories were written up using a computer. For Chloe, the text was written in a font suitable for her needs.

Another strategy involved a learning support assistant (LSA) working closely with Chloe during a carpet session. The LSA would whisper a description of what the teacher was doing/looking at in order to guide her in the direction of the focus to allow her to take part fully in the session.

The reception class had a strong play-based philosophy. In the outside play areas Chloe's target was to feel safe in a familiar environment. Initially, she would hurt herself or others during free play in the nursery garden, as she was not able to see dangers. The LSA began a detailed and gradual exploration of the play space with Chloe continually by her side until her confidence developed and she was able to understand where dangers occurred and how to cope with them. Alongside this growth in confidence came a reduction in the incidents of hurting other children.

In order to set high expectations for children with disabilities, there is a need to look beyond the diagnosis, to consider the individual needs of the child. 'The issue about the diagnosis of a syndrome is that it is a simplification . . . every child with the same medical diagnosis does not have the same educational needs (Fox 2003 : 25). It is important to consider how a child's particular difficulty may be overcome, whether this results from accessing the curriculum, or in terms of mobility.

2. The availability of suitable teaching and personal support (Ofsted 2004:19)

If children with disabilities are to be seen as individuals with their own needs, it is important that these needs should be discussed with the child. For them to succeed in the school system it is important that they become independent learners. In recent years there has been a move to employ teaching assistants to work closely with children with disabilities, and schools have become dependent on this level of resourcing. Although there are many positive sides to this work – Ofsted (2004) found 'Support by teaching assistants can be vital' – it was noticed that pupils had too few opportunities to work independently and that the focus was often on how pupils with disabilities could be kept engaged, rather than on advancing learning.

Activity 7.3

Carry out an evaluation of your work with a pupil with a disability over the past two weeks. Consider the opportunities you had to advance cognitive development. How did this compare with advancing social skills?

Now consider the plans covering the next two weeks. Identify the learning outcomes and plan an evaluation sheet that will focus on giving feedback on academic learning.

Examine the Individual Education Plan (IEP) for a child with a disability. Does it contain targets for further academic learning? If not, begin to consider the inclusion of such targets at the next review.

Next, look at the weekly plan to be followed by a pupil with a disability. Is there a focus on developing the pupil's independence? Could specific targets for this be incorporated into the lesson plans alongside intended learning outcomes?

Consider the organisation of the support given to an individual pupil. Is the child involved as part of a group so that it is possible, when appropriate, for the LSA to distance themselves physically from the child to encourage independence?

3. Sensitive allocation to teaching groups and careful modification of the curriculum, timetables and social arrangements (Ofsted 2004:19)

Grouping is another aspect of planning which merits particular consideration for pupils with disabilities. There is a danger that a pupil with multiple disabilities will find themselves isolated from their peers, as there may not be other children with similar needs. This may also have an impact, discussed above, on the disabled pupil's need for independence in their learning and may need planning modifications to facilitate inclusion.

In order to access fully certain curriculum areas, e.g. PE, a child with a disability may need one-to-one support from an LSA. In cases where the LSA is not employed full-time, timetables may need altering. In many primary schools the core curriculum is taught in the mornings, usually with LSA support, and the foundation curriculum in the afternoons. Adaptations to this pattern may be necessary in order to provide an inclusive curriculum for all.

4. Assessment, recording and reporting procedures which can embrace and express adequately the progress of pupils who make only small gains in learning and personal development (Ofsted 2004 :19)

Given the number of teaching assistants who work supporting pupils with disabilities, Ofsted (ibid.) found systems for receiving feedback on their work to teachers to be weak in many cases, often focusing on what the children had achieved rather than the discussion of the next stage in their learning. The recent government initiative in creating the award for Higher Level Teaching Assistant (HLTA) status has led to the creation of a set of standards for HLTAs.

Two of these standards are:

- Monitoring pupils' participation and progress, providing feedback to teachers and giving constructive support to pupils as they learn;
- Contributing to maintaining and analysing records of pupils' progress.

(TTA 2004 : 41)

In order for candidates to gain the HLTA award there is also a requirement that they should be able to 'contribute effectively to teachers' planning and preparation of lessons' (ibid.). The practical application of these standards in the classroom should enable support staff to be involved in the full cycle of assessment, recording and planning, thus raising the quality of feedback.

Activity 7.4: How do LSAs and others who work in supporting children communicate a pupil's progress?

- Is time allocated for this and does the feedback discuss the processes a pupil went through as well as the end-product and the amount of scaffolding required to achieve this? How could the feedback be improved?
- Is there dedicated time for the support staff to discuss the next steps necessary to advance learning, as well as give feedback?
- If not, consider if there are timetabling issues to address.

5. Widespread awareness among staff of the particular needs of pupils with significant special needs and an understanding of meeting them in classrooms and elsewhere (Ofsted 2004:19)

The Ofsted report, *Special Educational Needs and Disability,* found that:

> Even in better practice there was often insufficient attention paid to the involvement of pupils in decisions about the nature of support they would receive or reviewing that support and the progress they make as a result of it.

(p.20)

If we are to consider that fostering independence in their learning and everyday life is vital for pupils with a disability, then we need to listen to the opinions of the children we teach. We need to provide opportunities for them to tell us about their experiences in school, when they need help or not and which part of a learning task presents difficulties and requires assistance. When supporting the pupil with disabilities, we should concentrate, above all, on supporting them to achieve the higher cognitive skills such as exploring ideas, questioning and challenging, problem-solving and reviewing progress, rather than repetitive tasks to achieve a lower-level motor skill which may not be achieved to a fully functioning standard.

Case study 7.2

The Council for Disabled Children in their CDC Digest (Summer 2005, Issue 7) reported on a joint project led by Barnardo's (Somerset Inclusion Project) and supported by the LEA and Parent Partnership in which children with additional educational needs are reporting on how their learning needs are being met in primary and secondary schools.
Key questions children are being asked are:

- What do they enjoy learning and doing?
- What helps them learn?
- What stops them learning?
- What else would make a difference?
- What makes them feel happy and confident in school?

The article outlines how very young children, children with learning difficulties and those with communication difficulties need creative individual approaches, so the Inclusion Team are using puppets, symbols, signing, drawing, playing games and singing songs to find out what the children want to say.

The results will be published in a format that is user-friendly for the children and their schools, and will influence LEA policy.

Activity 7.5

In the light of the above case study, consider how you might gain feedback from pupils with a disability on a given task.

- Will the feedback involve any of the resources outlined above?
- Most importantly, what will happen to this data? For example, how will it influence support for a named child?
- This may involve resource/equipment implications, timetabling changes or a change in procedure whereby the pupil directs the help needed.
- Will more in-service training be needed? If so, how will this be provided?

Importantly, if we are to be truly inclusive in our practice, the voices of the children must be seen to influence our policy and practice, as in the case studies above.

Planning

In order for children to make progress, suitable learning challenges need to be set (NCC Inclusion). This involves a clear understanding of what pupils already know (subject knowledge) as well as planning to remove barriers to learning, to create a suitable learning environment.

Case study 7.3

The following example of good practice is taken from the Ofsted report *Special Educational Needs and Disability* (2004):

For example, in one inclusive school, a checklist was used during planning sessions to make sure that all the factors which could prevent pupils being included effectively were considered. The list included:

- consideration of the most appropriate grouping arrangement;
- the support required for information and communication technology (ICT);
- multi-sensory resources for each part of the lesson;
- personal targets incorporated into the learning objectives;
- opportunities for independent learning embedded in the planning;
- the next step in learning clearly spelled out.

(ibid.:15)

The following activity asks for reflection in considering the role of all in the planning process.

Activity 7.6

In the light of the good practice shown above, and working in your role to support teaching and learning, consider the involvement of all the staff team in the planning process, in order to maximise the effectiveness of learning support.

When are the short-term plans available for learning support assistants?

In terms of individual children, is the above information passed on, or is it the role of the LSA to adapt plans? If so, does this give them time to discuss these plans, prepare resources and adapt these to the needs of the pupils as outlined above?

How could the timing be improved to facilitate this increased role in planning to meet the needs of named individual pupils, including planning for the next steps in learning?

Are there timetabling implications? If so, how could they be overcome to enhance the learning opportunities for disabled pupils?

Meeting the need elsewhere

The recent legislation surrounding the Every Child Matters programme (DfES 2005) provides extended day provision for all children, and children with disabilities or special educational needs must be able to access all the new services. The government has stated that children's centres and extended school provision will be based on principles of inclusion. The Council for Disabled Children (www.ncb.org.uk/cdc) is involved with a project funded by the Department for Education and Skills to look at the current barriers to access that face disabled children and to provide materials to ensure the barriers are overcome. The project will cover the full range of extended provision and will involve working with a number of LEAs. Draft materials will be available by March 2006.

6. The availability of appropriate materials and teaching aids (Ofsted 2004:19)

Children with disabilities can benefit from a wide range of access resources in order to achieve their full potential. One of the most powerful aids to learning is the use of information and communication technology (ICT). The following statement is taken from the Becta website:

ICT can support learners with physical disabilities by enabling them to access the curriculum alongside their peers. It is particularly helpful for learners who find it difficult to record their school work using conventional methods. (www.ictadvice.org.uk).

However, it would be a mistake to think that ICT is limited to helping those pupils who have problems with mobility. Children who have difficulties with verbal communication, gross and fine motor skills and children who are visually or hearing impaired can all be helped.

In choosing when and how to use ICT, it is important that the views and feelings of the pupils are taken into account. For example, the aim of using ICT is to facilitate inclusion but care should be taken that the technology does not isolate the child from others in the group or class. This can be overcome in some cases by pupils working collaboratively and by all children having access to ICT to enhance their work.

Both parents and those who work with the children in school should be involved in decisions relating to ICT provision and it is possible to get an ICT assessment completed, identifying software, training and support. This may be carried out by the LEA Support Service.

In order for ICT equipment to be used successfully it is important that it is arranged so that the pupil can use it with ease. The height of the keyboard and screen should be considered and the use of a copy holder or angled work surface can also aid use. A wrist support placed in front of the keyboard and arm rests on a computer table can facilitate access.

Alternative input devices worth considering include:

- a computer with Braille keyboard;
- alternative keyboards with large keys;
- tracker ball, touch pads and joystick to replace the mouse;
- a concept keyboard – the keys can represent words, phrases and whole sentences; and
- speech recognition software.

ICT to support pupils with hearing impairments

The use of the interactive whiteboard to model learning is ideal for hearing impaired children because they can see what is happening without the need to hear. Care should be taken over seating arrangements so that the pupils are directly facing the whiteboard and have access to any adults signing.

Visual cues aid the learner. These can be produced using images from the computer and through the use of a digital camera for a more personalised approach.

ICT to support pupils with visual impairments

A word processor can be used to create text using larger, bolder and wider-spaced fonts to help with reading. Using the 'accessibility options' and the 'control panel' settings on the computer can help by increasing font size for word processing. The use of a talk facility, such as that provided with Textease, can help children with checking their work.

7. Involving parents as fully as possible in decision-making, keeping them well informed about their child's progress and giving them as much practical support as possible (Ofsted 2004:19)

The *Report for the Education of Disabled Children* (DES 1978) became known as the Warnock Report, named after the chair of the committee, Mary Warnock. It was influential in many aspects of provision for children with disabilities; among these was the belief in the need for greater parental involvement. Since that time, schools have been providing more extensive information for parents and carers in line with the requirements of government legislation. However, the many and varied agencies involved in the support of the child with disabilities has made holistic feedback to parents and carers difficult. In 2005 the government's Every Child Matters agenda – 'Extended schools: access to opportunities and services for all – a prospectus', stated:

Bringing services together makes it easier for universal services like schools to work with the specialist or targeted services that some children need so that problems are spotted early and handled effectively.

(DfES 2005:6)

Alongside this co-operation there is a requirement for schools to consult with parents and the local community about the extended day provision:

Consultation, particularly with families and the community, should not be a one-off exercise. It should be carried out regularly to obtain feedback to ensure what is being provided continues to be what is needed.

(ibid.:17)

The location of a range of services in schools, bringing together educational support workers and health (including, by 2010, a school nurse for each cluster or group of primary schools) and social care services should reduce bureaucracy for parents with disabled children.

When considering communication with parents, the starting point should be an acknowledgement of their expertise in understanding the complex needs of their children. It is this expertise which should allow all involved in education to accept parents as full partners in their child's education. However, at this point it is important to reflect on the notion of partnership. Frederickson and Cline (2002:18) state that 'professionals and LEAs have generally been slow to embrace partnership insofar as it requires active sharing of information and control'.

However, the SEN Code of Practice states that:

Parents should be fully involved in the school-based response for their child and understand the purpose of any intervention or programme of action, and be told about the parent partnership service when SEN are identified.

(www.opsi.gov.uk)

In order to reinforce partnership, the DDA includes the right of parental appeal:

> If a parent considers that a responsible body has discriminated against their child, they can make a claim of unlawful discrimination.
>
> (www.opsi.gov.uk/acts/acts1995)

Not only do parents and carers understand their child's disability, they can also see through the diagnosed condition and recognise the child's individual needs, for example their cultural background, interests, abilities and emotions.

In *Working With Parents as Partners in SEN*, Gascoigne (1995: 46) states:

> parents have a unique view of their child's difficulties and long-term prospects. They can offer much more than a regurgitated developmental history. If they are only ever asked for information about the age at which their child first walked, talked or rode a bicycle, the qualitative elements of their perception will be lost. When parents are involved in an appropriate way, the extra dimension can fundamentally change everyone's view of the child and his or her potential for achievement.

Parents will also know strategies that they or their children have put in place to compensate for their disability. This background information is vital if schools are to develop learning begun in the home and should, in turn, lead to an exchange of knowledge allowing the progress made in school to be consolidated in the home.

Activity 7.7

Consider the initial enquiry made about the admission of a child with a disability to your school.

How does the school initially demonstrate its inclusion policy to prospective parents?

How quickly does the school respond to a request for information and does the response include a named person, e.g. the special educational needs co-ordinator (SENCO) for the parent to contact?

Are the parents and child invited for a visit that is planned in such a way as to encourage the admission?

Consider ways in which the school could further improve its admission procedures.

Now investigate the processes your school has in place to report on achievement to parents and carers.

Consider who is authorised to communicate with parents. If this involves only the class, those who work with children and/or the SENCO, could there be benefits to the partnership if a TA working with the child was also allowed to communicate?

How often are parents given feedback?

Are they given positive feedback as well as being alerted when there are difficulties?

How is feedback given? Is there a mix of written and face-to-face communication. Is electronic communication considered?

What are the processes for a parent to report to the school, and how clear are the lines of communication?

Finally, investigate the views of parents and carers on the school's arrangements in order to improve communication.

Conclusion

Children with physical and sensory disabilities have the right not just to an inclusive education, but also one in which their aspirations can be raised so that they are able to fulfil their potential in all aspects of life. In order for this to be achieved, schools need to put effective support procedures in place, listen to the voices of the children with disabilities and work effectively with parents and carers to build on their unique knowledge and experiences. Alongside this practice, our schools should be seen to provide training in equality and disability issues so that all children, disabled and non-disabled, are able to recognise the contributions that each can make to society.

Bibliography

Beveridge, S. (2005) *Children, Families and Schools: Developing Partnerships for Inclusive Education*. London: Routledge/Falmer.

DfEE/QCA (1999) *The National Curriculum Handbook for Primary teachers in England*. London: HMSO.

DfES (2001) Special Educational Needs Code of Practice. London: DfES.

DfES (2005) *Every Child Matters: Extended Schools: Access to opportunities and services for all: a prospectus*. London: DfES.

Fox, M. (2003) *Including Children 3–11 with Physical Disabilities*. London: David Fulton Publishers.

Frances, J. (2004) *Educating Children with Facial Disfigurement: Creating Inclusive School Communities*. London: RoutledgeFalmer.

Frederickson, N. and Cline, T. (2002) *Special Educational Needs, Inclusion and Diversity*. Buckingham: Open University Press.

Gascoigne, E. (ed.) (1995) *Working with Parents as Partners in SEN*. London: David Fulton Publishers.

Ofsted (2003) *Special Educational Needs in the Mainstream* (HMI 511). London: Ofsted.

Ofsted (2004) *Special Educational Needs and Disability* (HMI 2276). London: Ofsted.

Qualifications and Curriculum Authority (QCA) (2004) *Inclusive Learning* London: QCA.

Stainback, S. and Stainback, W. (1996) *Inclusion: A Guide for Educators*. Baltimore, MD: Paul H. Brookes Publishing Co.

TTA (2004) *Meeting the Professional Standards for the Award of Higher Level Teaching Assistant Status: Guidance to the Standards*. London: Teacher Training Agency.

Wilson, R. (2003) *Special Educational Needs in the Early Years*. London and New York: RoutledgeFalmer.

Wolfendale, S. (ed.) (1997) *Working with Parents of SEN Children After the Code of Practice*. London: David Fulton Publishers.

Web links

http://www.direct.gov.uk/DisabledPeople/EducationAndTraining/Schools/fs/en

http://www.drc-gb.org

http://www.equalitytraining.co.uk

http://www.ictadvice.org.uk

http://www.ncb.org.uk/cdc (Summer 2005 issue)

http://www.opsi.gov.uk (1995 and 2001 Acts)

http://www.strategy.gov.uk/work_areas/disability/

http://www.teachernet.gov.uk/wholeschool/sen/schools/accessibility

Gifted and talented

Gianna Knowles

Many schools now use the *Excellence in Cities* definition of these words. The *gifted* are those with high ability in one or more academic subject, and the *talented* are those with high ability in sport, music, visual arts and/or performing arts. Schools are encouraged to identify the top 5–10% of each year group as gifted or talented, regardless of the general level of ability within the school.

Children may also have abilities, such as advanced social skills and leadership qualities, that fall outside the given definitions. These should also be recognised and provided for.

(www.teachernet.gov.uk/teachinginengland/detail.cfm?id=402)

Introduction

THIS CHAPTER EXPLORES what it means when we say a child is gifted or talented. It discusses a range of research to provide a guide for what behaviours gifted and talented children might display. The chapter also explores carefully the current DfES definition of giftedness and talentedness since it defines the terms in a way that differs from other authors in the field, which can cause confusion. The last part of the chapter discusses what constitutes barriers to learning for these children. In some ways it seems at odds with the very term 'gifted' or 'talented' that such children should experience any barriers to learning. Indeed, far too often they have been seen as the 'lucky' ones. It can seem unfair that while some children struggle for years to try to gain some proficiency in reading, writing or basic mathematics, gifted children have no problem competently completing work that is well in advance of what children of their age are normally able to achieve; or where some children struggle to make any meaningful marks on paper, a talented child can draw objects that look extraordinarily true to life. However, for too long the attitude of giving tasks to gifted and talented children to complete and letting them 'get on with it', simply because they can, has prevailed. Research has shown that where children do not have their giftedness or talentedness recognised and planned for, such neglect can lead to children failing to reach their potential, often becoming bored and disaffected, and in the saddest cases becoming so disruptive that they are excluded, or so bored that they simply refuse to attend school.

What do we mean by gifted and talented?

Before exploring who the gifted and talented children might be and how best they can be supported in schools, what may be meant by gifted and talented needs to be explored. It is particularly important to spend some time discussing this as the definition currently being used by the Department for Education and Skills (DfES), cited above, is sometimes at variance with other educationalists' discussion and understanding of the terms 'gifted' and 'talented'. Many books on the subject of gifted and talented do not make a distinction between the two. Authors will use the terms interchangeably. Therefore we need to explore how 'gifted' may be different from 'talented', and if there is any overlap in those characteristics which may denote giftedness, or talentedness. Further to this, it is also necessary to spend some time exploring what may be meant by two other terms often used when writing about gifted and talented children – 'intelligence' and 'creativity'. The next few sections of this chapter will explore definitions of intelligence, creativity, giftedness and talentedness, to ensure a frame of reference against which supporting gifted and talented children in schools can be explored.

Intelligence

Currently, the concept of intelligence held by most western psychologists is that it involves 'the ability to carry out abstract problem solving' (Gardner *et al.* 1996:2). The ability to think in terms of abstract ideas and concepts involves the aptitude to grasp relationships and patterns, particularly where such relationships and patterns cannot be detected by other methods, for example through the senses. The senses can be used to see colours and hear music, but abstract thinking is needed to solve the abstract and logical reasoning problems, such as those below.

1   Insert the word that completes the first word and begins the second:
    PRACT(. . .)BERG

2   Find the odd word out:
    BLOW
    NOPOS
    LETAP
    DHATUMB

3   Insert the missing word:
    ORBIT(RILE)WHEEL
    ARSON( )STEMS

4   Insert the missing number:

196(25)324

329( )137

5   What is the next number in the series?

18   10   6   4   ?

(Eysenck 1966:25)

Being able to solve problems in the example above tests only a part of what the brain is capable of; in this instance abstract thinking and logical reasoning. At the present time, in western societies, the ability to carry out such tasks is often used as a measure of intelligence, sometimes being measured and tested through specific tests that award an individual an intelligence quotient, or IQ score. However, in terms of thinking about an inclusive school and an inclusive society, it is important to consider that abstract and logical reasoning ability are only part of a child's capabilities, although they are abilities that, at present, are highly regarded in the west. That is, the notion that abstract and logical reasoning abilities are the only abilities that denote intelligence may be a cultural convention, not a fact. Different concepts of intelligence exist between different psychologists and different cultures.

> Many American parents believe innate mental abilities account for their children's intellectual performance. In contrast, many parents in Japan and other parts of Asia are more likely than their American counterparts to believe that hard work (or lack thereof) accounts for intellectual performance.

(Gardner et al. 1996:6)

Industrialised western cultures, of which Britain is one, tend to associate intelligence with the ability to solve problems quickly, or take on board and remember knowledge easily. However, in more traditional, less industrialised cultures, patient and sensible behaviours that are deliberately in line with social norms are often seen as markers of intelligence: 'In Zimbabwe, the Mashona tribe's word for intelligence, *ngware*, is applied to a person who exercises prudence and caution, especially in social interaction' (ibid.:7).

The needs of different cultures vary and change over time. In a society like Britain, whose wealth and success is dependent on those who can rapidly assimilate and process information and perform certain problem-solving tasks quickly and efficiently, the detection of such potential problem-solvers is important. Similarly, the identification and cultivation, through the school system, of such abilities will be paramount. However, alongside other attributes of intelligence, many societies recognise well-developed social skills as a mark of intelligence (Gardner et al. 1996:2), and this is mirrored in the DfES definition of gifted and talented above. Again, the ability to work with others, to motivate and lead teams of colleagues, is an important skill in a society like Britain.

Since the 1980s there have been challenges to the cultural notion that only the ability to be proficient at abstract problem-solving denotes intelligence. The strongest challenge has come from Howard Gardner in his work on multiple intelligences (Gardner 1993). Gardner argues that in our day-to-day life, in the workplace and beyond, we meet many individuals, children and adults alike, who are attaining high levels of competence in many challenging fields, and he states: 'A moment's reflection reveals that each of these individuals . . . should, by any reasonable definition of the term, be viewed as exhibiting intelligent behaviour' (ibid.:4).

In *Frames of Mind* (1993:8), Gardner argues for the existence of several *relatively autonomous* human intellectual competences, which he refers to as *intelligences*. That is, humans possess 'one or more basic information-processing operations' designed to deal with specific kinds of input (ibid.:63). We might recognise particular input as belonging to an area of experience we can name as a conventional curriculum subject, for example music or a bodily kinesthetic area such as dance or football. In most people, one such intelligence will be more pronounced than the others. Although these intelligences are not mutually exclusive, specific intelligences can be linked one to another and supplement or balance one another to enable one to 'carry out more complex, culturally relevant tasks' (ibid.:67).

What is evident from this discussion about intelligence is that everyone is intelligent, that is they posses the capacities outlined. When working in an educational setting with children, we need to consider carefully, when discussing intelligence, what aspect of intelligence we may be considering at any one time and in what quantities. We may be basing our measure of intelligence on the traditional western notion of abstract thinking and logical problem-solving which may blind us to the other intelligences, as discussed by Gardner, that children possess. When we think of intelligence as related to gifted and talented children, again it is usually abstract thinking and logical reasoning abilities that are used to determine giftedness or talentedness. Indeed, this is the case with the DfES definition of gifted and talented. And the marker of a gifted and talented child is that they possess the capacity to reason in an abstract logical way, and can do so more efficiently than other children of a similar age, or faster and with greater effect than may be the norm for a child of that age. However, while this form of intelligence, measured in this way, is a very good tool for beginning to assess giftedness, or talentedness, as we have seen, what may denote intelligence may be more complex than has traditionally been understood in western schools. Therefore the concern is that some children will be labelled gifted or talented who may not be, and may not be able to cope with the label, while other children who are gifted or talented may be missed. This is a concern Porter (1999:14) expresses: 'If we focus on a particular intelligence domain we may be excluding individuals who truly are gifted'.

Activity 8.1: Does your school's SEN policy make reference to gifted and talented children?

- What provision does the school's SEN or inclusion policy make for gifted or talented children?
- Do you see the policy working in practice?
- In the planning for learning activities, how are the gifted or talented children planned for?

Creativity

Many writers on intelligence and giftedness and talentedness believe that beyond a certain threshold of intellectual ability there is an additional skill called 'creativity'. 'These researchers believe that creativity is the vital and defining characteristic of giftedness' (ibid.:27).

Porter defines 'creative' children as those who posses the following four abilities:

- fluency, which enables them to generate many ideas;
- flexibility, which allows them to change thought patterns;
- originality, which is the ability to produce an unexpected idea; and
- elaboration, which is the ability to extend ideas, perceive detail and assess consequences.

(ibid.)

These defining attributes of creativity are shared by many educational researchers. For example:

> Creativity can be described as combining the following five characteristics: using the imagination; a fashioning process; pursuing purpose; seeking originality; and judging values.

(Wilson 2005:18)

Particularly, it would seem, creativity is evidenced by an ability to generate something new, or innovative, often through interaction with others' ideas, or current knowledge and understanding. It is about reflecting on what is known, or exists already, and being able to create new or novel links between ideas, or in finding solutions to problems (ibid.). However, the wider use of the term 'creativity' is often linked to the notion that for someone to have a creative idea, or for something to be original, it must be entirely new and novel in the social domain (Porter 1999:28); something that is 'a new invention', the vacuum cleaner that does not require a bag, for example.

However, in the classroom, children will be being very creative, but not necessarily constantly *inventing* new things. To view creativity in this way is to focus only on the measurable output, or product, of the creative process. As Porter states:

> the social judgement of the worth of a product may not accurately reflect the creativity of the thought processes involved in its discovery or invention, and may simply reflect the product's timeliness (ibid.).

Ebert maintains that all thinking is creative: 'if you have never had that particular thought before, then thinking it for the first time is creative – for you'. This is not necessarily helpful in distinguishing gifted and talented children from their peers, since all children will have thoughts and ideas that are new to them. It might well be, therefore, that creativity, as intelligence, is one of a range of factors we need to consider when thinking about giftedness and talentedness. Just as a final note, however, where researchers disagree on how creativity may be used to determine giftedness and talentedness, what they do agree on is that creative thinking is not reflected in conventional intelligence tests, since these measure only particular ways of thinking and conventional knowledge, rather than the generation of new or original ideas (Porter 1999 : 28).

Who is gifted and who is talented?

> Gifted young children are those who have the capacity to learn at a pace and level of complexity that is significantly advanced of their age peers in any domain or domains that are valued in and promoted by their sociocultural group.
>
> (ibid.:33)

Porter's statement above reflects the view of many writers and researchers in this area of education in terms of what it is to be described as gifted, and it is a concept already touched on above. Also, it is important to stress again that most writers and researchers in this area do not make a distinction between gifted and talented, using the two terms interchangeably (ibid.). However, giftedness is usually seen as the *potential* a child may posses in any particular subject or area of human activity; it is characterised by the child's ability to learn in that area faster than its peer group. Talent is seen as the *realisation* of that giftedness; in effect, the performance of that giftedness (ibid.; Sternberg and Davidson 2005). This is slightly different to the definition used above by the DfES. Therefore, let us explore further the broad range of how giftedness and talentedness is discussed, and then look specifically at the government definition.

> Giftedness is an age-specific term that refers to the potential of young persons who are judged to have demonstrated rapid learning compared with their peers. The judgement is made on the basis of some normative standard.
>
> (ibid.:54)

Key indicators of giftedness:

- display of advanced cognitive (thinking) skills that are shown in how they acquire, recall and use their knowledge;
- certain characteristic intellectual styles;
- knowledge acquisition hastened by advanced speech and language skills and early mobility (learnt to walk at an early age); and
- advanced social skills compared with age peers.

(Porter 1999 : 52)

Activity 8.2: Recognising gifted and talented children in the early years

As you have been reading this you may have particular children in mind that you believe may be gifted. Observe them over a number of lessons and look for the characteristics listed below.

Children in the early years:

- are more advanced than their peer group in terms of mobility and range of vocabulary;
- are able to reason about why they should/should not be allowed to do something;
- are able to empathise with another's thoughts and feelings and articulate their own feelings;
- can adapt the materials around them to 'create' new games or otherwise use materials in novel ways;
- read early and are in advance of their peer group in terms of completing the learning activities they are given;
- may find it hard to settle to finding one particular friend, or become frustrated with other children who cannot 'keep up' with their ideas and interests;
- are able to talk with insight and detail, recalling a range of factual information about something that engages their interest;
- will want to talk to adults and ask questions, sometimes about things seemingly unrelated to what is happening around them, perhaps as a result of something they have encountered outside the EY setting and want to talk about;
- show an awareness of the world around them and will continue to ask questions about something until they are satisfied with the answer (see the case study below).

Case study 8.1

When Somy was 4 she was with her family on a trip round the local cathedral. Family friends were visiting and the excursion was part of the local sightseeing tour. The cathedral used to be a priory and some of the features from the days of the priors still remained, particularly the cloisters.

Somy was obviously very interested in the buildings and the different objects and artefacts in the cathedral and asked many questions about what they were for, and how old they were. However, she was very interested in what had happened to the priors. Somy's mother had been answering Somy's barrage of questions for over an hour and was getting tired of providing information, so, with some exasperation, she gave an adult account of Henry VIII's reformation of the Church and the dissolution of the monasteries. Finally, Somy stopped asking questions. Somy's mother felt slight guilty at overwhelming her daughter with information for the sake of some respite. However, that evening, Somy repeated, almost verbatim, to the family friends the account of the reformation and dissolution of the monasteries she had heard earlier. The account Somy gave more than merely repeated her mother's information; it indicated she had been thinking over what she had been told and used the opportunity of talking to the friends to consolidate what she had learnt.

Activity 8.3

As you have been reading this you may have particular children in mind that you believe may be gifted. Observe them over a number of lessons and look for the characteristics listed below.

Children in the primary years:

- are more advanced than their peer group in terms of range of vocabulary;
- are able to provide a logically reasoned and structured argument about why they should/should not be allowed to do something, or in response to an activity they have been set;
- are able to empathise with another's thoughts and feelings and articulate their own feelings, and may be upset and worried by events that they have picked up from the news or other media;
- can adapt the materials around them to 'create' new games or otherwise use materials in novel ways;
- read early and are in advance of their peer group in terms of completing the learning activities they are given;
- become disaffected because they are bored by the work they are given, since it is below their level of ability and does not motivate or interest them;

- may find it hard to settle to finding one particular friend, or become frustrated with other children who cannot 'keep up' with their ideas and interests;

- are able to talk with insight and detail, recalling a range of factual information about something that engages their interest;

- will want to talk to adults and ask questions, sometimes about things seemingly unrelated to what is happening around them, perhaps as a result of something they have encountered outside school, or which is a particular interest of theirs;

- show an awareness of the world around them and will continue to ask questions about something until they are satisfied with the answer.

Cognitive (thinking) skills

This chapter has already introduced the idea of thinking skills in relation to the discussion about intelligence. This section explores what is meant by thinking skills and abstract and logical reasoning. Then, through a more detailed analysis of the terms, it helps the reader distinguish between intelligent behaviour and giftedness or talentedness. Cognition refers to our ability to process information; it is essentially our brain's capacity to acquire, store, retrieve and apply knowledge. In gifted children it would seem that their cognitive abilities are more efficient or better able to undertake these activities than is usually the case with children of a corresponding age.

Cognition: knowledge acquisition, storage, retrieval and application

Knowledge base

Academically gifted children have wider and deeper knowledge than average learners, despite the two having experienced similar learning opportunities.

Knowledge acquisition

It may be the case that gifted children are faster at acquiring knowledge and more efficient at storing and retrieving it. In this way a child becomes increasingly more competent in a particular subject area, because of this ability to acquire and recall knowledge with such efficiency.

Knowledge application

Having acquired a more broad and deeper knowledge base than is usual for children of a similar age, gifted children are able to apply it to abstract and complicated subjects, for example time.

(Porter 1999:57)

Metacognition

Where cognition refers to activities our brain undertakes as a matter of course in dealing with information, metacognition is the conscious ability to monitor those processes; that is the monitoring of thinking, at the same time as doing the thinking.

What is metacognition?

When going round a supermarket you may take a shopping list which you have compiled because you have thought about what you need, or what you intend to cook over the next week. You may simply buy what you usually buy plus anything that catches your eye and looks interesting. Or – and this is where metacognition comes in – you may be shopping and planning your meals at the same time. At the cognitive level you are using your knowledge of food sold in the particular shop you are in, the foods and foodstuffs you have at home, those you have run out of and those you usually buy. That is, you are recalling your stored knowledge about food and your cooking habits and applying it to this shop. If you are planning your meals at the same time, you are using your metacognitive abilities to 'think about thinking-about' the shopping. You are planning the meals, focusing on appropriate foods to buy, evaluating which items will be best and probably ensuring that, overall, the items you buy will provide for a healthy, balanced diet and be within your budget. And, if you have thought it through well, there may also be a few treats.

Metacognition in gifted children

Metacognition in gifted children is:

- the ability to focus;
- the ability to define the particular nature of the task and select the information and skills which are needed to complete the task, including the use of metamemory to scan for relevant information and possible, already stored, solutions;
- the ability to apply knowledge or previously tried solutions in an innovative way;
- the ability to synthesise information, that is take information from a range of perhaps seemingly unrelated sources and work it together to find a solution (which may involve, or appear to be, creativity);
- elaboration and development of ideas;
- evaluation – to test whether the solution to the problem is viable, or possible.

(Porter 1999:57)

Testing as a measure of giftedness

High performance in tests does not mean gifted.

(Sternberg and Davidson 2005 : 55)

Regard this as a health warning about using particular types of test as the only measure of intelligence. Similarly, this is a warning about using only a correlation between performance outcomes in tests as the only measure of ability. To look at the results a child scores in any particular test is to start with the outcomes first, and if they are unusually above average for what is expected for that age range, the temptation is to trace that outcome back to 'gifted' ability. However, tests are very particular in what they measure. For example, a times table test measures, at its most basic level, recall and memory of a particular set of facts. That the facts are, in this context, mathematical is not relevant. Most children are able to memorise information in this way and can repeat something they have remembered, and often 'do well' in a test.

As we have seen above, it is important to also observe how a child uses the stored information. In this instance, how does the child use their knowledge of tables to solve mathematical problems? Or, what knowledge do they use? For example, when presented with a maths problem that requires solving through using and applying number, are they able to determine the various elements of the problem, select the most appropriate computation method(s) that can be used and evaluate whether they are likely to have reached the correct solution? Often, a child gifted in the area of maths will know the answer without needing to 'work it out'; indeed, will find it tiresome and frustrating to have to 'show' how they achieved their answer. They may not even be able to articulate something that they simply know to be the case. Similarly, most children are able to 'read' – that is verbalise the print on a page – but the level at which children are able to comprehend and make sense of what they have read will vary considerably.

Giftedness may not always be obviously linked to curriculum subjects. As such it may fall within a domain, or field of knowledge, skills and understanding, or it may cross a number of aspects, some of which appear in a range of subjects. Analytical reasoning, for example, may be a feature of a range of subjects, or, given the curriculum as it may be presented in schools, may not appear in any subject. Each subject, as it appears in the National Curriculum, has its own *body of knowledge*, areas of *understanding* it covers, *rules* that apply within it, and *skills*.

Historical knowledge, understanding, rules and skills as described in the National Curriculum:

- **knowledge** of events, people and changes in the past, that is historical facts that can be learnt and remembered, about such things as British history, Romans, Anglo-Saxons and Vikings;

- **understanding,** particularly *chronological* understanding of how these events affect people and changes in the past – and into the present, for example, how we are still today influenced by the Romans;

- **rules** about how information is organised and communicated in a way that is specific to history, for example using dates and historical vocabulary to describe periods studied; and

- **skills** specific to history, which are to do with interpretation and enquiry.

(DfES 1999 : 105)

Again we can see many children will be able to remember and recall historical knowledge, but it is quite a different ability to have understanding of how the people and events recalled affected the course of events. Conversely, a child who is able to reason analytically may not be able to recall a list of historical facts, but presented with a range of information about the Romans will be able to analyse their impact on any given locality. Tests measuring historical knowledge will allow the first child to achieve well, but not the second and, similarly, a test that asks for analytical reasoning will benefit only the second child. As we have already seen, measuring ability purely by asking children to recall knowledge will only provide part of the picture of a child's ability and potential. Asking a child to apply other cognitive or metacognitive processes to a subject-based task will provide a more accurate measure of a child's ability. The child who is gifted in history is the one who has, for their age, compared with their peers, an above-average insight into those aspects of the subject that are specific only to history; for example, an understanding of chronology and the ability to organise and communicate information in a way that is specific to history; for example, using dates and historical vocabulary. As Dr Christine Carpenter from the University of Cambridge states:

> History is an unusual discipline. Its core is hard fact that you cannot get away from and have to learn to master. At the same time you have to be deductive, perceptive and imaginative in the use of that fact.

(ibid.:103)

In this way, if we only use the outcomes of test scores as a measure of giftedness we might be missing some gifted children. The school curriculum has a limited number of subjects and, at present, can be confining in the way it allows children to express themselves within those subjects. The child who is gifted in analytical reasoning and argument – who may be gifted in terms of philosophy, for example – may not have the opportunity to develop or express this aspect of their abilities. Similarly, those children who are creative or emotionally gifted may not, because of the curriculum they are presented with, have the opportunity to demonstrate or pursue their particular area of giftedness. Not all these areas of possible giftedness are taught or tested, and therefore some children's giftedness may not be recognised by the school. Similarly, a child who's area of giftedness lies outside the school's curriculum and testing regime may actually not perform well in those subjects and tests they are expected to undertake. From a child's point of view this will cause frustration and possible loss of self-esteem that they are not recognised for what they can do, and regarded as normal, or underachieve because they are measured only in what they are expected to do.

The DfES definition of giftedness is helpful, up to a point. It helps schools identify children who have 'high ability in one or more academic subjects', but the downside of this definition, as we have seen, is that it determines giftedness in a way that is often dependent on the outcome of test results, or predicting how well a child might achieve in the National Curriculum end-of-key-stage tests. The other problem with this definition of giftedness is that it is no predictor of potential, other than in particular curriculum tests used by the British education system. It is no indicator of how a child's ability in any particular subject or field might develop later in life.

What is talented?

Let us revisit the DfES definition from the start of this chapter:

> The gifted are those with high ability in one or more academic subjects, and the talented are those with high ability in sport, music, visual arts and/or performing arts.
>
> (www.teachernet.gov.uk)

Many writers, writing about giftedness and talentedness and about performance, do not limit themselves to meaning 'performance' in the way suggested by the DfES. The DfES definition of 'talented' relates to those children who demonstrate a high ability in areas that seem to have a physical performance element, i.e. dancing, playing a sport, playing or composing music or producing a piece of art. It could be argued that a gifted mathematician is recognised because of his/her performance in maths.

Therefore, the DfES defines giftedness as being specific to academic subjects (although it is also tied to both potential and performance in those subjects), while those children who are talented are said to be so when their unusually proficient outputs are related to performance endeavours. However, all the attributes we have explored in relation to giftedness would seem to apply to talentedness. What is dissimilar is that we are considering a different area of skills, knowledge and understanding. Therefore, a child may be talented if they meet the criteria below.

A talented child is one who is:

- able to perform at a level above what might be expected for a child of their age;
- able to understand the knowledge base of the area of endeavour faster than might be expected for a child of their age;

- able to be creative and innovative in the area of endeavour; and

- able to demonstrate skills in the area at a level higher than might be expected for a child of their age.

As discussed above, we have seen how one of the markers for identifying a gifted child is that they possess the capacity to reason in an abstract logical way, and can do so more efficiently than other children of a similar age, or faster and with greater effect than may be the norm for a child of that age. We have also seen how the focus of what is thought of as intelligence is dependent on the presence of these attributes, particularly as they relate to specific academic curriculum subjects. However, it is possible to argue that a talented musician possesses a faster and above-average ability, in terms of what is usually expected for their peer group, to reason in an abstract way – but musically; as does a talented dancer, or a child who is good at art or sports. To perform any act requires the application of skills, knowledge and understanding and to perform it unusually well, that is to be talented in that performance, is to have the above-average ability to think in abstract terms and apply skills, knowledge and understanding creatively. As a child gifted in mathematics can solve mathematical problems, sometimes without being able to articulate how, so a talented dancer may be able to interpret, through physical movement, an idea or concept, without being able to explain how. One of the greatest services Gardner's work on multiple intelligences has done for the gifted and talented debate is to change, particularly in the west, the notion that some abilities are of greater value than others; that is that a child who is gifted in an academic subject is more special than a child who is talented in a performance-based subject. Through Gardner's work it is increasingly apparent that *intelligence* can be manifest in any number of ways; and it is only when the potential of a talented dancer is spotted, developed and encouraged that the potential can be realised; as with a child who, early on, demonstrates a giftedness in maths. It is not possible to score goals in football, or netball, or to produce an outstanding piece of art without being able to think in an abstract way – to see the possibilities of the application of known skills, knowledge and understanding and to apply them in a novel or creative way.

Let us revisit Porter's definition of 'creative' and look at how it might apply to talentedness. For Porter, creativity is manifest through:

- fluency, which enables talented children to generate many ideas, or actions;

- flexibility, which allows them to change thought patterns although these might not be of the conventional, abstract logical variety;

- originality, which is the ability to produce an unexpected idea or action; and

- elaboration, which is the ability to extend ideas, perceive detail and assess consequences.

(Porter 1999:27)

One would be hard-pressed to argue that talented children do not exhibit the indicators listed above. And again, just as we have seen how many children who may be gifted are not being recognised because their giftedness is not detected through the conventional measures we use in school, so many talented children are being missed because the area of endeavour in which they excel is not a regular or rigorous aspect of the conventional school curriculum. If many talented footballers and dancers had not joined clubs and classes outside school it is unlikely that their talent would ever have been realised. But to press the point, if some gifted children go undetected in schools, then how many more talented children are failing to be detected because the current focus of the curriculum on literacy and numeracy marginalises dance, drama, many aspects of PE, and music. As Cross and Coleman, in Sternberg and Davidson (2005), state:

> Some talents are developed entirely outside of school, whereas others are developed in schools to a considerable extent. Some talents are in domains that schools have key roles in developing, others may have no direct relationship to a school's curriculum.
>
> (Sternberg and Davidson 2005 : 52)

One of the solutions to this problem may come through the development of extended schools; that is where provision is being made for cultural and sporting activities to be available to children after the conventional school day, there is a better opportunity for recognising and developing the potential of talented children.

Barriers to learning

At the beginning of the chapter is a list, drawn up by Porter (1999), of key indicators for determining a gifted child. In addition to those indicators are two further indicators:

- While gifted children's social skills tend to be advanced compared with age peers, sometimes they will become frustrated with age mates, as they may be unable to play at the level the gifted child is able to. This can lead to the gifted child resorting to solitary play and, in some cases, becoming friendless and isolated and leaning to bullying.

- Perhaps surprisingly, gifted children can sometimes appear to be emotionally immature. This may indeed disguise their giftedness (Porter 1999 : 52).

- A gifted child's highly attuned nervous system contributes both to advanced learning and an increase in their emotional sensitivity. Again, this may disguise their giftedness.

(ibid.:26).

In light of the discussion above about talentedness, the remainder of this chapter will discuss the above key indicators as if they apply to gifted and talentedness. That is, where gifted children experience some of the factors suggested by Porter, so, too, do talented children. However, Porter's list is of possible indicators; not all gifted or talented children will display all of the indicators above.

Emotional immaturity and sensitivity

It may well be that these two factors are linked. The gifted child is able to take on board and understand more information than is usually the case for children of the same age. For example, a child picks up knowledge and information from a whole range of day-to-day contacts. Information may be collected incidentally from such sources as the television, overheard news reports, adult conversations or conversations between older children, newspapers, magazines, etc. Sometimes the child will pick up information which is distressing to them as they are able to understand the content of the information but are too young to be able to put it into a context of life experience that enables them to manage it. It may also be the case that they are unable to discuss it with their age peers. Although friends often are a source of comfort, because they do not process the same information at the same level, they dismiss the event more readily than the gifted child. Because the gifted child may feel overwhelmed and confused by some of the information they are trying to deal with they may seek constant reassurance from adults and appear over-sensitive or clingy. Porter discusses the work of Jackson and Butterfield (Porter 1999) and Roeper (ibid.) in this area, stating that while the ability to gain and retain knowledge is usually thought of as advantageous, 'it can propel gifted children into examining abstract issues before they have the emotional maturity to cope' (Porter 1999:54).

Case study 8.2

Eddie is now 12. He could walk at 10 months and displayed highly developed speech and reasoning powers at the age of three. For example, as a three-year-old, in discussions he would say: 'I want to make three points: point one . . .', and he would explain his first argument; 'point two . . .', he would explain the second reason, 'and point three . . .'.

As a young child he was not interested in learning to read; however, he was very able in work with numbers at an early age.

'As they progress pass the toddler years, many – but not all – begin to read, write or use numbers in advanced ways, which again helps them to acquire knowledge that is ordinarily considered to be advanced for their years' (Porter 1999:54).

At age 4, Eddie could tell the time. Until this point Eddie had never slept through the night. But once he made the connection between numbers on a digital clock and their temporal connection to denoting what the time was, with a digital clock by his bedside he would sleep through the night. He had made a connection between something he understood – using numbers to measure, in this instance time, and the convention of staying asleep throughout the night. Therefore, when he awoke during the night, as he did on the first night, he knew by looking at the clock that it was not yet time to get up. This gave him a sense of control over the length of the night, how long he had been asleep and how much longer he was expected to sleep. This sense of control also provided the security to, on the next night and subsequent nights, sleep through.

At age 6 he initiated a discussion about infinity, having worked out for himself that if you begin counting from 1 along the number sequence 1, 2, 3, 4 etc., there will always be one more number, and you could go on forever.

However, throughout nursery and school he has found it difficult to find age peers to form close friendships with. He has friends with whom he enjoys practical activities – football, riding his bike and playing at game consoles – but often turns to adults for company and conversation. He has always found it difficult to deal with the 'robust' nature of school life, the day-to-day knocks and slights which children can, unwittingly, perpetrate on one another. He can appear over-sensitive to comments made by other children or adults, and it sometimes means he will not engage in an activity he enjoys as he is wary of what others might say.

He will always refer to adults if he wishes to talk over anything he has learnt at school or picked up from the television. Where the information may cause him distress he can become seemingly morbidly obsessive or emotionally very dependent and 'clingy' towards trusted adults. For example, watching news reports about such events as those in New York on 11 September 2001, and the subsequent war with Iraq, made him very upset. As a gifted child he could understand the import of what he was seeing, but did not have the experience in terms of age to put it into a context. Therefore he became very insecure and in need of a trusted adult's presence.

Similarly, talented children may be able to perform in such a way that the adults around them fail to support children in coping with their talent. A talented child may react in a way markedly different to their peer group when exploring a work of art, a piece of music or being involved in dance. Children may become very involved in the experience, and if the cause of this is not recognised, such children can be labelled as being 'over-sensitive', 'highly strung' or 'dreamers'. In the same way, children who possess a particular sporting talent may become bored and frustrated at working with children who do not match their level of performance. In the worst cases, where a school does not recognise a child's gift or talent and embrace it within its inclusive ethos, children who are markedly different from their peer group, because they are gifted or talented, can become isolated from the group and, in some instances, become the victim of bullying.

Assumptions about children's home backgrounds can lead to schools failing to recognise children who are gifted or talented

Some studies into giftedness in children, particularly in identifying giftedness in young children, have found that a preponderance of those children identified by schools as being gifted come from home backgrounds that can be described as middle-class. (Porter 1999 : 53). Two things may be happening here: the first factor to consider is that some children come from home backgrounds that are aware of, and engage with, the norms and conventions of society that have traditionally been those recognised, prized and rewarded by schools; for example:

- punctual and regular attendance at school;
- the ability to converse articulately in the language in which learning is conducted – in this instance, English;
- parents who are interested in the child's schooling, attend parents' meetings and ensure homework is completed; and
- parents who read with children at home, regulate bedtimes, ensure a healthy, balanced diet, monitor television watching and playing of electronic games, etc.

Where young children are already socialised into behaviours recognised by school, it may be more straightforward for a school to identify giftedness. A young child who comes to school from a home background that is less able to provide these conditions, or a child who may have limited understanding in the language the learning is conducted in, or a background knowledge of the culture the subjects are derived from, may present difficulties which mask their giftedness. That is, if the first factor is to do with what is happening at home, the second factor is to do with what is being expected by the school. That the school does not recognise giftedness in some children, because of behaviours they are bringing from home and the seeming difficulty they are having with the school environment, means the school is not identifying giftedness in terms of ability to learn at a faster rate than age peers or potential to perform above the average for their age, but by how well adjusted to school life they are. The school, through the content of the tasks it presents, may also be making assumptions about the cultural background of the child and assume prior knowledge and understanding which the child does not possess. For example, not all cultures contain the fantasy creatures, fairies or dragons. Therefore, if a child who has not grown up being read stories about fairies and dragons, or seen them portrayed on television, is asked to write a story containing such creatures, he/she may appear to be achieving at a level lower that might be expected for their age.

Activity 8.4: What abilities do learning activities actually explore?

When working with children in a lesson that requires recall of information, rather than using skills to process information given, note those children who struggle with the activity. Is it because they just do not have that background knowledge, or because they genuinely cannot engage with the subject?

Gifted and talented and the non-conventional subject curriculum

Children may also have abilities, such as advanced social skills and leadership qualities, that fall outside the given definitions. These should also be recognised and provided for.

(www.teachernet.gov.uk)

The domains in which giftedness are recognised are reflective of society's values and are subject to historical influences.

(Sternberg and Davidson 2005:62)

One of the problems of giftedness, from the child's point of view, is that the child's particular area of giftedness may not be easily identifiable as a curriculum subject and therefore not recognised or planned for by the school. This is because teaching and learning within schools is generally arranged around specific curriculum subjects. It may also be that the way the curriculum is taught may not enable all children to learn. If giftedness or talentedness has not been identified, and the learning activities are not appropriately planned for children, then at some point they will become bored. It is likely that prolonged exposure to a curriculum that is a barrier to a child's learning may result in the child becoming withdrawn or, at the other extreme, exhibiting unwanted behaviours.

Activity 8.5

In the next PE lesson you support, note how the children who are particularly talented in this area are planned for and supported in the session. Is there specific planning to ensure their needs are met, that is are they given challenges and activities to work on that extend their current level of performance?

Activity 8.6

In the next art lesson you support, note how the children who are particularly talented in this area are planned for and supported in the session. Is there specific planning to ensure their needs are met, that is are they given challenges and activities to work on that extend their current level of performance?

Activity 8.7

In the lessons you support, how are the gifted children provided with challenges and learning experiences that stretch them?

Are they simply expected to do 'more of the same' or have appropriate extension activities been planned for them?

In the first section of this chapter, in discussing what constitutes giftedness, it is suggested that the gifted child is faster at acquiring information and better at storing it than their age peers.

Some children may be gifted in areas outside conventional curriculum subjects, for example PSCHE; and, just as children gifted in terms of mathematical understanding need challenge, so, too, do children gifted in this area. Many schools are good at recognising giftedness in traditional curriculum subject areas and providing for these children; however, providing for a child who has an above-average understanding in terms of non-conventional curriculum subjects can be more challenging. Just as children develop knowledge and understanding of English and mathematics, so, too, they can be seen to pass through stages of development in terms of their moral understanding. It is the educationalist Kohlberg who has done most research in this area. Kohlberg was a contemporary of Jean Piaget and studied how human beings progress through stages in terms of their moral development.

The problems arise when a child is able to grasp notions out of step with those of his/her peers. For example, a child who is gifted in this area may be at stage 3, whereas his or her peers may be at stage 1 or 2. The gifted child will understand notions of sharing, while the children around him will not. The gifted child may experience other children egocentrically grabbing at desired objects, and become upset and frustrated because they can understand how to share, indeed *why* sharing is important; but he/she may be in a peer group who only share when an adult in control tells them to. These experiences may leave the gifted child feeling isolated from their friends and let down by the adults who seem to be indulging the 'naughty' children who are grabbing. In its most extreme form this can cause the gifted child to become isolated from their peer group, withdrawn and depressed, or go to the other extreme of disruptive behaviour.

If the school does not identify giftedness in such a non-conventional curriculum subject area, the problems for both the child and the school may become exacerbated, as the child gets older. Continuing our discussion of moral development, according to Kohlberg, those aspects of having reached knowledge and understanding at stage 5 include the following characteristics:

- being aware that there is a variety of values and opinions, often relative to a given group;

TABLE 8.1 Development of moral understanding (Taken from Reimer *et al. Promoting Moral Growth: From Piaget to Kohlberg*, 2nd edn 1990. Reprinted by permission of Waveland Press Inc., Long Grove, IL. All rights reserved)

Level and stage	Social perspective of stage
Level I: pre-conventional Stage 1:	■ Egocentric point of view ■ Does not consider the interests of others ■ Does not relate two points of view ■ Actions considered by physical effect on others, not psychological ■ Confusion of authority's perspective with one's own
Stage 2:	■ Concrete, individualistic perspective ■ Aware that everybody has interests to pursue and that these can conflict ■ Correct is relative (in the concrete, individualistic sense)
Level II: conventional Stage 3:	■ Perspective of the individual in relationships with other individuals ■ Understands 'Golden Rule' – what it is like to be in the other person's shoes
Stage 4:	■ Differentiates societal point of view from interpersonal agreement or motives
Level III: post-conventional, or principled Stage 5: social contract or utility and individual rights. Pre-adolescent/adolescent	■ Considers moral and legal points of view ■ Recognises that they sometimes conflict and finds it difficult to integrate them

■ although there are some overarching values, liberty, justice, etc.

(Reimer *et al.* 1990)

The following case study is an example of the frustrations suffered by children with a highly developed moral sense, clearly out of synchronisation with those around them.

Case study 8.3: Gifted children and moral development

This case study is part of a discussion between an adult researcher and a group of Y7 girls and boys. The children are part of the school's Junior Governor scheme. They are elected to be junior governors by their classmates and represent the student voice in junior governor meetings. The main speaker in the discussion below is a gifted Y7 girl. Throughout the following conversation she leads the discussion and is the child grappling with the problem presented to her by the lunchtime supervisors.

'We have like a lunchtime meeting with the dinner ladies. Like Y4 or Y5 we think we should have more tennis balls, and we think we should have sweets in our lunch boxes – something like that. So we've all thought about different things.

'And since we've been meeting, if there is a problem at lunchtime the dinner ladies always ask the junior governors about it; like someone had a Twix in their lunch box and the dinner lady comes up to me and says, "As a junior governor you should know to sort it out", and I felt a bit embarrassed.'

'So you were put on the spot because you didn't know it had happened, but then you were supposed to do something about it?'

[This is met with general agreement.]

'The really weird thing is, though, you're allowed lunch boxes with biscuits in, but you're not allowed chocolate. You're allowed one stick of Twix, but not two, because it's from the shop.' [Some children have lunch boxes made up by an outside company. These sometimes contain a one-finger Twix. This seems acceptable to the lunchtime supervisors, but not a lunch brought from home containing a two-finger Twix.]

'There was a girl who had a bottle of Pepsi or Coke and the dinner lady chucked it down the sink. I think it's just unfair to chuck it down the sink – it's like 90p wasted; because they're quite expensive.'

[General discussion ensues about making packed lunches: who makes them at home and, therefore, has control over what goes in them; concern that, as children, they might be blamed at school for something the lunch box contained, yet they have no control over it.]

'So what happened after the business about the chocolate and the Coke?'

'Well, we found out later that she wasn't allowed to have chocolate or Coke. But we hadn't really been informed about it. If we'd been informed then it would have been fair, we'd know where we stand.'

'So what happened after that? Did one of the teachers say to you "OK, we're now saying that you must not have chocolate"? Or did people just begin to realise?'

'Well some teachers give you sweets; not all, just some. Our teacher gives them at the end of Friday, so it's better. But some teachers give sherbet lemons like at maths. And they eat them during lunch.'

Throughout this conversation we can see how the children, particularly the girl mentioned above, are trying to grapple with a complex situation. They are expected to do something to sort out a problem they know nothing about and have no control over. They are also able to see that it is difficult to enforce one rule in a situation where there are so many variables. The situation is further complicated by the lack of consistency in the way the school attempts to enforce a policy on chocolate and sweets; indeed they know that some teachers will, deliberately or inadvertently, undermine the apparent school policy by giving out sweets. That these children can explore the layers of control and the complexity of the issues raised indicates that they would seem to be operating at a high level of moral development.

Conclusion: a different sort of differentiation

Borland, in Sternberg and Davidson, writes:

> along with my colleagues in the gifted-education field, I believe that high-achieving or high-ability students are among those who are the most ill-served when curriculum and instruction are not differentiated.
>
> (Sternberg and Davidson 2005:2)

Cross and Coleman agree with this statement, adding that:

> having a group with unrealized potential is unacceptable because students are supposed to perform near their potential. The typical reply to this situation is to assert that the child has some problem that is inhibiting his or her development.
>
> (Sternberg and Davidson 2005:56).

With regard to ensuring an inclusive curriculum that meets the needs of gifted and talented children, schools must guard against the pitfalls described by Cross and Coleman below:

> Environments that are unresponsive to rapid learning have inadequate resources relevant to a domain and provide no models for development and inhibit advanced development. Impoverished environments have the most pervasive negative effect . . . some contexts promote the development of the individual more than others.
>
> (Sternberg and Davidson 2005:60).

This chapter has examined what is meant by giftedness and talentedness and it has sought to explore what barriers to learning and achievement a gifted or talented child might encounter. Gifted and talented children possess incredible potential, but as Sternberg and Davidson state, unless the context is there for a child to thrive, the giftedness or talentedness may never be realised, and, to date, there has been an ongoing concern in the field of gifted and talented education about the underachievement of such children (ibid.:60). Many schools now have procedures for identifying gifted and talented children and have enrichment programmes which can help children to realise their potential. However, while most schools have become very effective in providing for children who have difficulties grappling with learning at the level deemed the norm for their age, many schools still have a long way to go to provide an effective curriculum differentiated to meet the needs of the gifted and talented.

Bibliography

Blackburn, S. (2001) *Being Good*. Oxford: Oxford University Press.

Brugman, D. (2003) 'The teaching and measurement of moral judgement development'. *Journal of Moral Education*, 32(2), 195–203.

DfES (1999) *The National Curriculum Handbook for Primary School Teachers*. London: HMSO.

Eyre, D. and McClure, L. (2001) *Curriculum Provision for the Gifted and Talented in the Primary School*. London: David Fulton Publishers.

Eysenck, H. J. (1966) *Check Your Own IQ*. London: Penguin.

Gardner, H. (1993) *Frames of Mind*. London: Fontana Press.

Gardner, H., Kornhaber, M. and Wake, W. (1996) *Intelligence Multiple Perspectives*. Fort Worth, TX: Harcourt Brace.

Gross, U. M. (2005) *Exceptionally Gifted Children* (2nd edn). London: Routledge/Falmer.

Harrop, A. and Holmes, M. (1993) 'Teachers' perception of their pupils' views on rewards'. *Journal of Pastoral Care*, March, 215–27.

Higgins, C. (2003) 'MacIntyre's moral theory and the possibility of an aretaic ethics of teaching'. *Journal of Philosophy of Education*, 37(2), 279–92.

Hinman, L. (2003) *Ethics: A Pluralist Approach to Moral Theory* (3rd edn). New York: Thompson/Wadsworth.

MacCarchan, B. (http://tigger.uic.edu/~lnucci/MoralEd/articles/nuccimoraldev.html)

Nucci, L., in H. J Walberg and G. D. Haertel (1997) 'Moral development and character formation'. *Psychology and Educational Practice*, 127–57.

Porter, L. (1999) *Gifted Young Children: A Guide for Teachers and Parents*. Buckingham: Open University Press.

Reimer, J., Pritchard, D., Paolitto, D. and Hersh, H. R. (1990) *Promoting Moral Growth from Piaget to Kohlberg* (2nd edn). Prospect Heights, IL: Waveland Press.

Sternberg, R. J. and Davidson, J. E. (2005) *Conceptions of Giftedness* (2nd edn). Cambridge: Cambridge University Press.

Wilson, A. (2005) *Creativity in Primary Education*. Exeter: Learning Matters.

Winstanley, C. (2004) *Too Clever by Half*. Stoke-on-Trent: Trentham Books.

Web links

www.teachernet.gov.uk/teachinginengland/detail.cfm?id=402

Learning styles: overcoming barriers to learning

Gianna Knowles

Introduction

SO FAR, THIS book has examined the variety of intellectual, cultural, social and linguistic backgrounds that individual children might bring to the learning environment. The different chapters have explored a variety of factors that, if not considered and managed appropriately, may unwittingly lead to those managing the learning environment to place unnecessary barriers in the way of a child's learning. In particular, the book has raised issues with regard to learning needs that must be considered in relation to: the cultural and ethnic backgrounds of children; the challenges of teaching children for whom English is an additional language; managing the learning for children who have a special educational need; how a child's gender impacts on its learning; and the learning needs of children who are gifted or talented.

Planning learning activities and managing the learning environment is a challenge in itself. The thought of also needing to consider the range of different learning needs individual children bring to the classroom can seem daunting. However, while so far this book has explored the differences *between* children, this chapter looks at children's learning from the standpoint of what unites them all, that is the learning styles they share. Children may speak different languages, approach life from differing cultural or gender perspectives and learn at different rates, but all human beings can be encouraged to learn if learning activities are presented in ways that meet their learning styles. That is, if a learning activity is planned with consideration given to the variety of ways that will best suit individual learners – and we all share learning styles while not necessarily sharing cultures – it is more likely that learning will take place. A literacy lesson that is planned with consideration of a range of learning styles, and taught in a way that allows all children's learning styles to be triggered, will help all children become more proficient in English, whether it is their main language or not. Therefore, the aim of this chapter is to explore supporting inclusive practice through consideration of learning styles.

Assuming knowledge and understanding

Before discussing how approaching teaching and learning through thinking about children's learning styles can support developing inclusive practice, a note of warning must be sounded: learning takes place in a *context*; the learner makes sense of the new learning they are engaged in in relation to the skills, knowledge and understanding they already have. If those that are supporting the child's learning make assumptions about the skills, knowledge and understanding they believe the child has, or make the value judgements about what they *ought* to know, then however carefully the lesson has been planned, with consideration of different learning styles, the child will not learn as effectively as they might. The following case study will explain this concept more fully.

Case study 9.1: The importance of monitoring and assessing a child's prior skills, knowledge and understanding

Krisjanis is in Year 3. He has just joined his new school having moved to the south coast of England from Latvia. He is about to embark on a history topic about the Romans in Britain. Krisjanis has studied history before and he knows that it is about researching the past. His understanding of chronology is what would be expected from a child in Y3. He has learnt about Latvian history and has a Y3 knowledge and understanding of Latvia's recent struggle for independence, first from the Russian empire and then from the USSR. However, he has little or no knowledge of the Romans, since although Latvia was known to the Romans, Latvia as such never formed part of the Roman Empire.

The skills and understanding that are specific to the subject of history are universal; historical skills and understanding apply to whatever history is being studied, anywhere in the world. The National Curriculum recognises this, containing in the history programme of study the requirements that children learn about chronology, how events in the past have an impact on the future and how to find out about the past from a range of sources (DfES/QCA 1999:104).

Although children learn these universal historical skills through the National Curriculum, much of the content of history in the National Curriculum at key stages 1 and 2 is British history; that is historical skills and understanding are most often taught through studying British history; and most children who have been brought up in Britain bring to their study of history at school some knowledge and understanding of Romans, Vikings, Henry VIII, Elizabeth I and the First and Second World Wars, since much historical knowledge is deeply woven into mainstream British life and is variously portrayed through books, stories, films and other media. Therefore, many children, who have been brought up in Britain, whatever their background, will recognise, for example, a picture of a Roman soldier when they see one. The child who is new to this aspect of British history and has never heard of the Romans before will be beginning their learning at a different place to the child who has some knowledge.

In this way, when Krisjanis first started learning about the Romans, those working with him thought he was less able in history than his peer group. Even taking into account English being an additional language for him, he still seemed unable to engage at all in the lessons. In thinking through why Krisjanis seemed to be struggling, the class teacher and teaching assistant began to realise that they had approached planning and teaching the work based on the assumption that the children had already undertaken some work on the Romans in KS1, and that most children who have grown up in Britain have picked up some knowledge about the Romans from the media. Having realised that the Romans meant nothing to Krisjanis, they changed the way tasks were presented to him and he began to demonstrate that he did indeed possess appropriate historical skills and understanding for his age range.

For example, in a lesson about the Romans Krisjanis was asked to compare a picture of a Roman wearing a toga with a picture of someone dressed in contemporary western clothes. He achieved well in this task as, while he had no prior knowledge of the Romans, he was able to compare and contrast the two styles of dress and make deductions; that is, use his historical skills. However, when he was asked to draw pictures of the things the Romans brought to Britain, without being provided with appropriate information, he failed to achieve the task.

Activity 9.1

When working with children in a lesson that requires recall of information, rather than using skills to process information given, note those children who struggle with the activity. Is it because they just do not have that background knowledge or because they genuinely cannot engage with the subject?

Good practices in teaching and learning support enable all to learn

In 2003 Ofsted published *Yes He Can*, a report that comments on the factors contributing to the success that some schools are having in enabling boys to write well (Ofsted 2003:1). The report was written as a result of visiting and inspecting seven primary schools and eight secondary schools. What is particularly important about the report is that the schools that were visited were chosen because the difference in performance in writing between the girls and the boys was significantly smaller than that found in other schools, and also the schools had good results overall. 'This was to avoid selecting schools where the gap was smaller than usual because of poor performance by girls' (ibid.). That is to say, the schools were selected because *all* children were writing well, although the interest of the inspectors was on those aspects of teaching and learning support that were enabling boys to write well. Therefore, in studying the main findings of *Yes He Can*, it is possible to gain some idea about what will enable all children to achieve.

Case study 9.2: Factors contributing to children writing well

- There is a culture in the school and classroom where all children's intellectual, cultural and aesthetic accomplishments are valued.
- In terms of written work, value is placed on:
    1 the use of a range of writing styles and approaches – for example report writing, recount and instructions – and not only narrative (stories);
    2 the ability to write succinctly as well as descriptively is valued;
    3 the ability to write logically is valued as much as the ability to write expressively.
- Feedback is prompt and indicates clearly what has been done well and what can be improved.
- Pupils are often given a choice as to the content of their writing, even if the form or genre is prescribed.
- Writing tasks are purposeful and written for real audiences, through 'publishing' and displaying writing.
- Writing tasks are tackled in stages, with feedback or review at each stage of planning and drafting.

(ibid.:3)

Perhaps one of the most significant aspects of the findings of this report is that it keeps coming back to the fact that children achieve best in schools where it is the children themselves and their efforts that are valued. In the case of writing, as seen above, children do well when consideration is given to how they naturally prefer to write; there is a purpose to the writing; those who are supporting their learning help them structure and plan their writing and give practical feedback – that is they help the child be successful in the endeavour; and when the writing is finished it is celebrated by being shared with others. As the report comments:

> Many boys in particular seem to need to know that someone is watching over and caring about their efforts, to be able to see a clear purpose for their work, and to experience tangible progress in order to maintain motivation.
>
> (ibid.:5)

Further factors that contributed to the success of the children's achievement were adults supporting and directing the learning and teachers showing interest and enthusiasm for the tasks. In particular, boys did well in schools where there existed powerful male role models (ibid.:7). In schools where no male teachers were employed, fathers, grandfathers or other significant male figures were invited into the school to support learning activities. Indeed, all the primary schools inspected for the report had a strong partnership with parents (ibid.:8).

However, good teaching of basic skills was a contributing factor to success (ibid.:9), that is, ensuring children have the tools to enable them to achieve. In the case of writing, this is a good handwriting style (or access to a word processor where handwriting is difficult), knowledge and understanding about phonics and spelling rules, and knowledge and understanding of grammar rules.

Children wrote well where the schools had established a positive whole-school approach to reading, again supported by a strong home–school partnership. However, the reading culture was successful in these schools as, again, it was recognised that children, like adults, have a wide-ranging interest in the material they like to read. Not all children like reading fiction; some prefer to read information material, often linked to hobbies and interests (ibid.:12). Again we see children succeeding where they are motivated by having their interests considered. However, as with all successful learning, those doing the teaching are providing a 'balance . . . between support and challenge' (ibid.:17).

Activity 9.2: How are children in your school motivated to write?

Use the checklist below as a guide to enable you to think about how your school motivates children to write and provides support to enable them to be successful in their writing.

Is reading and writing valued in your school? Is there a culture of enthusiasm for reading and writing? Do adults provide good role models for children in these areas of the curriculum? Is there a strong home–school partnership that fosters the children's interest?

Are children's efforts valued? Is their work collated into book form that can be shared with others? Is it displayed?

Are only certain genres of writing or particular qualities in writing encouraged? Are children given broad enough scope to exercise choice as writers? Are qualities of succinctness, humour and depth of thought valued, as well as elaboration, detail and length?

Are writing tasks clearly structured with good-quality feedback given promptly?

Does writing have a purpose and an audience, or is it simply a response to the need to 'do some writing today'?

Intelligence and learning

Multiple intelligences

Chapter 8 discussed the notion that, traditionally, only particular forms of behaviour have been recognised as intelligence, and that society has only prized and rewarded these behaviours. Consequently, schools have focused their teaching and teaching methods on this notion of intelligence. In the main, the form of intelligence that has been most recognised is that which enables the child to reason in an abstract and logical way and, often, to use this ability to solve problems, sometimes producing new and innovative solutions to problems. However, Howard Gardner's work on multiple intelligences has challenged this notion of what we might regard as intelligence and how we ought to structure learning activities for children. Gardner's work stemmed from his concern that, particularly in the industrialised 'western' societies, the notion of intelligence is based on the assumption that:

> it is a single, general capacity that every human being possesses to a greater or lesser extent; and that, however defined, it can be measured by standardized verbal instruments, such as short-answer, paper-and-pencil tests.
>
> (Gardner 1993:xiii)

In Gardner's view, simply looking around at the different abilities children and adults have and display, particularly in the everyday tasks and functions they perform, refutes the notion that intelligence is only that which can be measured by a very particular form of test (ibid.:xiv). Gardner suggests it is 'necessary to include a far wider and more universal set of competences than has ordinarily been considered' (ibid.). Initially, Gardner suggested there may be seven 'candidates' that might be described as intelligences: linguistic and logical-mathematical intelligences; musical intelligence; spatial intelligence; bodily-kinaesthetic intelligence; and two forms of personal intelligence, one directed towards other persons (interpersonal intelligence) and one directed at the self (intrapersonal intelligence) (ibid.). Although Gardner states that 'there will never be a master list of three, seven or three hundred intelligences which can be endorsed by investigators' (ibid.:59), the important thing is: 'Central to my notion of intelligence is the existence of one or more basic information-processing operations or mechanisms, which can deal with specific kinds of input' (ibid.:63). That is to say, our capacity to deal with situations that require logical reasoning or mathematical ability will be dealt with by our logical-mathematical intelligence, but our capacity to respond to a ball being thrown at us will be dealt with by our kinaesthetic intelligence.

For a range of capacities to qualify as an intelligence Gardner states that 'it should have an identifiable developmental history' (ibid.:64). What he means by this is that our kinaesthetic intelligence has a path of development, just as our linguistic intelligence does. As babies we are born with the capacity to learn to communicate with others through talk, although initially we cannot distinguish between sounds and recognise them as words that carry meaning in any particular language. As we develop, and our capacity for linguistic competence develops, so we become more proficient at distinguishing particular sounds, attributing meaning to those sounds and then making choices about using the sounds ourselves. However, our developing capacity to talk and communicate successfully needs to be scaffolded by an expert, or a range of experts, who can use language successfully themselves and can teach us the next stage in our development. This developmental path, as with any developmental path for each of the intelligences, has its own innate trajectory which can be recognised as 'normal' development. Most children will follow the normal path of development, although some children will appear to be behind what is expected for their age and some will be more proficient than is expected for their peer group. That is, we may recognise some children as having a special need in any given area of development, and some children as being gifted or talented in a particular set of competences. Gardner also suggests that we all possess the seven intelligences, as described, but some of us will demonstrate more of an aptitude in one area of competences. If Gardner is correct in his theory – and he has had significant challenges to his work – what he is claiming is that we all possess not one indicator of intelligence – our ability to solve problems by abstract, logical reasoning – but the capacity to solve multiple problems, as we have multiple intelligences.

Multiple intelligences and school-based teaching and learning

In the previous section we have seen how Gardner has identified seven forms of intelligence. The concept of multiple intelligences and how it might be applied to helping children achieve in school has, until recently, been more widespread in north America. In his book *Seven Ways of Teaching*, David Lazear explores how the usual day-to-day learning activities, intended to cover the set curriculum, can be planned in such a way that children's differing learning styles, or intelligences, can be used to enhance their achievement. Lazear outlines four elements that must be considered in planning a lesson activity that will teach with multiple intelligences (Lazear 1991:xx).

Four stages for teaching with multiple intelligences

Stage 1

Being aware that we possess multiple ways of knowing and learning and that there are various ways of *triggering* an intelligence within the brain/mind/body system.

Stage 2

We must learn how particular intelligences, or ways of knowing, work, that is the capacities and skills that are attached to each intelligence and how to access them. We must also learn how each intelligence expresses itself. For example, the 'language' of body/kinaesthetic intelligence is physical movement, not words, sentences, writing and speech.

Stage 3

We must learn how to teach content-based lessons that apply different ways of knowing to the specific content of a given lesson. Therefore, we must learn how to use the intelligences as the teaching as well as the learning process.

Stage 4

We must help children understand their learning styles and how their predominant intelligence will help them improve their achievement (ibid.).
Lazear works from the hypothesis that:

> in the normal person the intelligences operate in concert with each other, generally in very well orchestrated ways, although certain of the intelligences do tend to be stronger or more developed than others.
>
> (ibid.:xxi)

In respect of this notion, Lazear suggests that in planning a learning activity all the intelligences will be triggered through how the activity is planned, even though activities are designed to focus on and use one intelligence specifically. In particular, he suggests, as a rule of thumb, that at least three ways of knowing, over and above verbal/linguistic and logical/mathematical, are involved (ibid.). Ways in which learning activities can be presented, enabling the seven intelligences or ways of knowing to be triggered, are given below.

Verbal–linguistic

- reading;
- word banks or vocabulary linked to the learning expected from the activity;
- writing – including a range of genre, narrative, recount, report, instructions and poetry;
- debate and 'hot-seating';
- humour, jokes and storytelling.

Logical–mathematical

- use of abstract formulae and symbols;

- using graphic and diagrammatic ways of presenting information;
- number sequences and calculations;
- encoding and decoding;
- exploring relationships;
- problem-solving and exploring patterns and games.

Visual–spatial

- guided imagery – visualising images in response to ideas/stories being discussed and explored;
- actively engaging the imagination;
- representing knowledge and understanding through use of colour schemes;
- patterns, designs, painting, drawing;
- mind mapping;
- pretending;
- sculpture.

Body–kinaesthetic

- formal dance steps and creative, expressive dance;
- role playing;
- physical actions and gestures;
- drama;
- martial arts;
- physical exercise;
- mime;
- inventing games;
- conventional sports.

Musical–rhythmic

- rhythmic patterns;
- vocal sounds – singing;
- musical composition;
- use of percussion instruments;
- humming;
- music as an environmental background;
- musical performance.

Interpersonal

- giving feedback;
- receiving feedback;
- 'picking up' on others' feelings;
- co-operative learning strategies – group work;
- 'jig-sawing' activities;
- group projects.

Intrapersonal

- silent reflection – as a opposed to an expectation to 'do' something;
- thinking strategies;
- focusing and concentration strategies;
- higher-order reasoning – analysing and philosophising;
- independent work.

(Adapted from Lazear's *Seven Ways of Teaching* (ibid.:xxiii))

While each of the intelligences listed above has its own body of skills, knowledge and understanding, they can be used as a means to gain knowledge in areas beyond itself (ibid.). Following the 'triggers' in the list above, we might, for example, use music to learn spellings and mathematical times tables; use body movement to bring to life and explore different periods of history; and the skills of comparing and contrasting to analyse characters in a story (ibid.). And, if children are taught about multiple intelligences and their own multiple intelligences, 'how to access them, how to strengthen them, and how to actively use them in learning and in everyday life' (ibid.), then it is likely that they will more motivated to learn and achieve more.

Activity 9.3: Planning learning activities that include a range of learning styles

- While working with children over the next few days keep with you a checklist of the seven intelligences.
- Keep a record of the learning styles, or intelligences, that lesson activities trigger.
- Do some intelligences and learning styles dominate the way activities are planned?
- Are there any intelligences and learning styles that are never used?
- At your next planning meeting see if there is an opportunity to explore introducing a wider range of ways in which learning can be accessed.

TABLE 9.1 Lesson-planning ideas using a body–kinesthetic approach learning (adapted from Lazear's *Seven Ways of Teaching* (1991 : 62)

History	Mathematics/ numeracy	Language/ literacy	Science	Geography
Perform and/or create dramas from a period of history.	Use different parts of the body to measure things.	Act out the meaning of vocabulary specific to the topic being studied.	Role play the parts and dynamics of an electric circuit.	Explore – through touch, artefacts from places. Recreate the artefacts in dance.
Re-enact scenes or moments from history, for today.	Carry out computations using groups of children.	Write or devise a story to explain the learning being studied.	Create the solar system and the rotation of the planets with the class.	Try food from different places. Wear clothes from different cultures.
Hold a historical period costume and food day.	Make up a 'playground' game that uses maths concepts and operations.	Learn spelling, phonemes or other aspects of language through games and associated body movements.	Dance the different states of matter.	Explore different places through dance. What is it like to climb a mountain? Walk across hot sand in the intense sun?
Learn dances from the past.	Make geometric shapes with the body, or in groups, or by running/dancing around the hall or playground.	Explore aspects of a narrative, for example characters/contexts, through dance.	Ensure as much science learning as is possible is 'hand on'.	Explore distances between places – imagine the whole school is the world; whose classroom would be England? Whose class would be Australia?

Excellence and Enjoyment

A major thrust of the government's education policy since 1997 has been to raise the level, or standard, of children's achievement, particularly in literacy and numeracy. In seeking to do this, the government introduced the National Literacy Strategy (NLS) in 1998, the National Numeracy Strategy (NNS) in 1999, revised the National Curriculum in 2000 and introduced Curriculum Guidance for the Foundation Stage in 2003. While the levels of children's attainment did rise from 1998, the initial momentum was not maintained and national levels of attainment seemed to plateau. However, the government continues to maintain the target of '85% of all primary school children to reach L4 at KS2 as soon as possible' (DfES 2003 : 4). The rationale given for this target is that 'we know that performance at age 11 has such a huge impact on how children are likely to do in later life' (ibid.). There has been some evidence that the focus on raising standards, particularly in literacy and numeracy, has led to a narrowing of the curriculum. Schools have found that in designing their curriculum to ensure an hour a day to teach literacy and an hour to teach numeracy, time available for other curriculum subjects has been squeezed. This has been particularly true for foundation subjects like geography where, for example, Ofsted has commented that standards are low in many primary schools. Often this is due to inadequate time allocations (Ofsted 2002). For some schools, having a curriculum that is focused on literacy and numeracy seems at odds with the government's policy of inclusion and meeting the learning needs of all children. That is to say, concentrating on particular subjects and ways of learning – those centred around linguistic, mathematical and logical reasoning skills – would seem to preclude children who, for example, learn kinaesthetically, visually or interpersonally.

However, while the NLS and NNS have set objectives for each term, they are *frameworks* and *strategies* for enabling children to become literate and numerate. The NLS and NNS are not statutory; schools do not have to use them as teaching tools by law. The only statutory skills, knowledge and understanding that must be taught are those required by the National Curriculum. The NLS and NNS provide a very comprehensive guide and set of objectives that, if used and if delivered through some of the ways suggested in the training material, do enable schools to cover a large part of the National Curriculum for English and maths. However, if we take the NLS, for example, there are no objectives therein for speaking and listening; but if we look at English in the National Curriculum, one third of children's English-learning entitlement is centred on speaking and listening (DfES/QCA 1999:44–50). Therefore, if schools use the NLS only to teach English, they will be struggling to cover the whole of the National Curriculum programme of study for English. What, indeed, has happened in many schools is that as they have become more familiar with the strategies they have continued to plan learning activities around the framework of objectives, and have devised the activities in ways which do consider the range of children's learning styles and different educational needs.

In 2003 the government published *Excellence and Enjoyment* (DfES 2003). This document stated:

> Primary education in England is in a strong position with improving results and good comparisons internationally. We want to build on that success, and challenge primary schools to take the lead themselves in going further.
>
> (DfES 2003:4)

Excellence and Enjoyment recognises the hard work schools have put in to raise the standards in literacy and numeracy, and its publication is as a result of the DfES working with Ofsted to research what constitutes good practice in literacy and numeracy by analysing the inspection reports of schools that have had particular success in these curriculum areas and presenting the evidence to help all schools improve. One of the significant aspects of *Excellence and Enjoyment* is the notion that while schools must continue to focus on raising standards, they must not be 'afraid to combine that with making learning fun' (ibid.). The document also emphasises that schools 'have much more freedom than they often realise to design the timetable and decide what and how they teach' (ibid.). Therefore, nothing that has been discussed already, throughout this book, is at odds with the government's expectations of what should be happening in schools. Indeed, as the National Curriculum states, 'an entitlement to learning must be an entitlement for all pupils' (DfES/QCA 1999:3). The National Curriculum's over-arching statement on inclusion makes it clear that what this means is that schools must ensure that all pupils have the chance to succeed, whatever their individual needs and the potential barriers to their learning might be (ibid.).

Activity 9.4: How are literacy and numeracy taught in your school?

While working with children who are undertaking literacy and numeracy activities ask yourself the following questions:

- What are the learning styles and intelligences that are being focused on?
- Are all children able to access the learning intended?
- Could the activities be made more accessible to more children if other learning styles were used?
- Do I have the opportunity to discuss this with colleagues, or influence the planning of activities, thereby removing the barriers to learning being experienced by some children?

The Primary National Strategy

it is important that children have a rich and exciting experience at primary school, learning a wide range of things in a wide range of ways. Our new Primary Strategy will support teachers and schools across the whole curriculum.

(DfES 2003:27)

The Primary National Strategy (PNS) is a response to the success of the NLS and NNS in 'improving the quality of teaching and raising standards' (ibid.). The features of the NLS and NNS that have contributed to the raising of standards have been evaluated and, through the PNS, are to be applied across the whole curriculum. Below are the principles of good learning and teaching that underpin the PNS and should, therefore, underpin all teaching.

The principles of learning and teaching

Good learning and teaching should:

- ensure every child succeeds;
- build on what the learner already knows;

- make learning vivid and real; and

- make learning an enjoyable and challenging experience.

(ibid.:29)

Alongside the introduction of the PNS, the DfES has produced a range of materials to support its implementation. The materials are designed to help those working with children plan learning activities underpinned by the principles above. The materials provide advice and support on:

- creating effective learning environments;

- securing motivation and concentration; and

- providing equal opportunities.

These materials are very useful in that they can help in planning a rich curriculum that removes barriers to learning by enabling those that work with children to meet specific learning needs. However, perhaps even more significantly, they are the first example of government documentation that acknowledges that the way to meet diverse needs is to plan for a range of individual learning styles and to consider the range of intelligences children are brining to the learning environment.

Meeting diverse learning needs through visual, auditory and kinaesthetic learning styles

Section 3 of the PNS *Excellent and Enjoyment: Learning and Teaching in the Primary Years* (DfES 2004) discusses the concept of learning styles and states that, 'as the result of heredity, upbringing and current environmental demands', individuals have a tendency to perceive and process information in a variety of ways (ibid.:52). In particular, Section 3 explores how many schools are using the visual, auditory and kinaesthetic, or VAK, approach to learning. The VAK approach encourages schools to plan activities that are varied in their response to a range of learning factors (ibid.). It is suggested that schools use ideas about learning styles to consider how:

- lessons can be varied and interesting to engage children in using visual, auditory and kinaesthetic modes;

- different subject disciplines can promote and develop particular ways of learning, for example, art and design could support and develop visual perception, and PE could support and develop kinaesthetic learning;

- mixing different types of materials, elements and explanations can aid children's attention and help them learn more effectively.

(DfES 2004:53)

Visual learning takes place through the use of pictures, charts, diagrams, video and ICT images, and may also include the written word. A learning activity that incorporates visual learning would:

- ask children to collect information from carefully selected visual sources that support the intended learning;

- follow up their initial hypothesis with further research, conducted independently, or through carefully selected support material; and

- explore their new knowledge and understanding by representing it in a visual way.

(ibid.)

Auditory learning takes place through:

- listening to explanations;

- taking part in discussions;

- giving oral presentations.

(ibid.:54)

Kinaesthetic learning takes place when learners are physically engaged in a task:

- through role play; and

- practical tasks.

(ibid.)

Case study 9.3: A history lesson taught through VAK

The children are learning about Victorian schools. They are working in groups.

Visual learning: each group is given a picture of a Victorian classroom. Different groups are given a specific focus to research:

- How is the classroom organised, including how the children and teacher are seated?
- What do they seem to be learning and how do you know?

Having agreed the answer to their question the group must then use other sources available to research two other facts about Victorian schools and make a poster showing what they have learnt. Each group then presents the poster to the rest of the class, role playing a child in the Victorian class, or the class teacher. Depending on the age of the children, provide a timer for each group and ask them to ensure their presentation does not last more than the time allotted.

The learning activity takes place across a number of lessons. Those supporting the learning help the class and individual groups structure completing the task by providing specific instructions in manageable 'chunks' and by conducting 'mini-plenaries' throughout the teaching sessions to re-focus on what learning is taking place, allow groups to share interim ideas with each other, highlight good practice and ensure learning is progressing at an appropriate pace.

Auditory learning: the auditory learning happens through the children being given the opportunity to discuss the pictures and their ideas. When they have completed their posters they present them to the rest of the class, explaining what they have found out and what their poster shows.

Kinaesthetic learning: this learning style is used as the task is a practical activity, involving moving around to collect resources and make a poster. Rehearsing the presentation of the poster through role play and the final presentation also reinforce kinaesthetic learning.

The ALPS approach – Accelerated Learning in Primary Schools

Using the ALPS approach as a method for helping children learn is being adopted in an increasing number of schools. Smith and Call, the current leading exponents of the method, explain that as an approach to learning it focuses on providing the most supportive learning environment for children, including paying attention to physical and social factors that affect learning (Smith and Call 1999 : 7). Lessons that are planned through the ALPS approach contain the following features:

- providing children with the opportunity to connect to, and building upon, prior knowledge and understanding;
- the presentation of an overview of the learning challenges to come;
- describing the outcomes through setting learners positive outcomes and defined targets;
- providing input through presenting information in visual, auditory and kinaesthetic modes;
- activating understanding;
- demonstrating understanding through 'mini' plenary sessions throughout the learning activity, not just at the end of the session;
- ensuring the activities end with the opportunity to review and recall the learning that has taken place.

(ibid.:25)

That lessons structured in this way will provide for maximum learning opportunities for all children is based on what Smith and Call (ibid.:33) denote as nine 'brain-based' principles.

The nine 'brain-based' principles on which the ALPS approach is founded are:

1 The brain develops best in environments with high levels of sensory stimulation and sustained cognitive challenge.

2 The optimal conditions for learning will feature sustained levels of cognitive challenge alongside low threat.

3   Higher-order intellectual activity may be diminished in environments that are emotionally or physiologically hostile, or that are perceived to be so by the learner.

4   The brain thrives on immediacy of feedback and on choice.

5   There are recognised processing centres in the hemispheres of the brain.

6   Each brain has a high degree of plasticity, developing and integrating with experience in ways unique to itself.

7   Learning takes place at a number of levels. An ALPS teacher engages both conscious and unconscious processing through suggestive methods, varieties in questioning strategies and personal goal-setting.

8   Memory is a series of processes rather than locations. Processes to access meaningful long-term memory must be active rather than passive.

9   Humans are 'hard-wired' for a language response. They may also be hard-wired for a musical response.

(ibid.:34)

Further to the nine principles above, Smith and Call emphasise the importance of the 'deliberate creation and maintenance of a positive and supportive learning environment' (ibid.:36). Such an environment is essential to ensuring learning is taking place, since little learning of long-term benefit happens in classrooms where children are experiencing anxiety, uncertainty, ambiguous relationships or where there is an emphasis on punishing unwanted behaviours, rather than praising and encouraging wanted behaviours (ibid.:35). A positive learning environment is one that: 'produces opportunities for every child to demonstrate what we are calling the new three Rs. These lifelong learning attributes are the new three Rs of responsibility, resourcefulness and resilience' (ibid.:36).

For Smith and Call, these 'three Rs' epitomise not only the necessary attributes that should underpin a child's attitude to learning, but also to life in general (37). The three Rs help a child to be successful in their learning as they provide children with understanding of how to learn.

Smith and Call's 'three Rs': Responsibility, Resourcefulness and Resilience

Responsibility is the recognition that actions have consequences. Managing impulsivity, delaying immediate gratification and thinking in terms of success outcomes are characteristics of the responsible learner. Responsibility is the ability to see things from another's point of view and locate one's own actions within the larger scheme of things.

Resourcefulness is to be able to adapt to different learning challenges. It is about learning the tools of what it is to be a good learner and being able to deploy those tools to suit any given situation. That is, being able to use what you already know and can do to tackle the new learning task. Resourcefulness includes taking risks and managing the challenge of making mistakes, finding out what went wrong and trying again.

Resilience is about being able to persist in the face of frustration or set-backs or when complexity is seemingly overwhelming. The resilient learner is one who has developed a range of coping strategies and does not internalise or externalise the blame. The coping strategies of a resilient learner are supported by a positive self-image and strong self-esteem. These attributes allow the learner to be able to place failure in context and to be able to see possibilities for learning within the experience (ibid.).

Teaching using the ALPS approach

The basic format of a lesson that follows the ALPS approach is outlined above. ALPS-based lessons are those where it is evident to the children how their learning is connected to things they have already learnt, that the target learning for the given lesson activity is explained to them and that as the lesson progresses they are provided with feedback on how they are reaching the lesson's target or aim. There is also time at the end of the lesson to recall what has been learnt. Within this lesson format we have seen how those planning the activity need to give consideration to other things that are going on in terms of the learning. Taking on board new knowledge and understanding or trying new skills are only part of what is happening when learning is taking place. Those planning the activity need to be mindful of the ways in which the learning is presented to the children. In terms of stimulating learning, Smith and Call suggest that in planning a learning activity the planners need to: 'think VAK; think whacky and plan for brain breaks' (ibid.:66). Smith and Call also emphasise the importance of using 'memory-mapping' as a planning system.

Think VAK

As has already been discussed in this chapter, if information is presented to children in a variety of ways, and they are allowed to record their learning in ways other than writing, it is more likely that they will engage in their learning and be motivated to complete tasks. This is not to say that using a recording method other than writing is somehow 'easier' or does not constitute real learning, but that it provides a recording medium for a child which is more in tune with its own learning style, and therefore better enables the child to take on board the intended learning for any given activity. Therefore, in planning any lesson activity how the learning can be presented, and recorded – visually, aurally and kinaesthetically – needs to be thought through.

Think whacky

Smith and Call suggest that where key facts need to be learnt, 'think of slightly absurd ways of teaching them and installing them in memory' (ibid.). This gives the children's memory a 'key' or 'handle' to attach the new information to. An example they give is of a teacher who used a foam hand, the sort sold at concerts and sports events, to help embed subject-specific vocabulary in a science lesson. When she held it as a 'thumbs up' sign the class stood up and chanted 'Up with evaporation'. When it was held in the 'thumbs down' position they sat down and chanted 'Down with condensation' (ibid.).

Plan for brain breaks

Brain breaks are based on the notion that human beings are naturally active creatures. Children's attention will wander, and this may affect behaviour if children are expected to remain still and silent over a period of time. Indeed, planning brain breaks into lesson activities usually has the effect of preventing any unwanted behaviour occurring. Brain breaks help keep the children in the most receptive state for learning, since a brain break involves physical activity which, in turn, increases the oxygen supply to the brain and releases neurotrophins, which are natural neural growth promoters. Movement also promises some relief from stress (ibid.:153). Knowing when to have a brain break is a matter of professional judgement. It will depend on the physical attentiveness and energy levels of the pupils. This you will come to know through experience. The best approach is to have a number of brain-break activities in mind and use them as seems appropriate (ibid.:155).

What are brain breaks?

Cross crawl – In turn, children lift the left knee and touch it with the right hand, then lift the right knee and touch it with the left hand, and repeat the process a number of times.

Rub-a-dubs – Children circle their stomach with the right hand while the left hand pats their head. Then they change and reverse the circling.

Chop-chop – In pairs, children take it in turns to massage a partner's back and shoulders and conclude with the sides of the hands, chopping in a gentle firm movement.

(ibid.:152)

It has only been possible to give a brief overview of the ALPS method here. However, for those of you who are interested in finding out more about using ALPS strategies to plan learning activities, two contact address are given at the end of the chapter.

Conclusion: providing children with the opportunity to demonstrate what they can do

The overriding theme of this book has been about understanding where individual children are 'coming from' in terms of the skills, knowledge, understanding and attitudes they bring to school. It has been discussed how understanding the needs of individuals can enable those who are planning and devising learning activities to provide better teaching and learning support. The focus of this chapter has been on the learning styles that all children share, whatever individual cultural and gender attitudes they come to school with, or whatever their learning ability may be. If learning is planned to meet how the child learns, it is more likely that the child will have a positive experience of learning and achieve the standards which he or she is capable of.

Children need to be engaged in learning that develops and stretches them and excites their imagination. As the government document *Excellence and Enjoyment* states:

> Children enjoy learning – not just learning different things, but learning in many different ways: out-of-doors, through play, in small groups, through art, music and sport, from each other, from adults other than teachers, before school, after school, with their parents and grandparents, formally and informally, by listening, by watching, and by doing. They develop socially and emotionally. They take pride in their learning and want to do well.
>
> (DfES 2003 : 9)

Below is a final activity you might like to try. If you have attempted to better understand the potential barriers to learning for just a few of the children you are working with, and have sought to support them to feel more included in school life, then record your achievement on a 'feeling good about ourselves' display, as described below.

Activity 9.5: A 'feeling good about ourselves' display

Decide on the theme for your display – a plant with lots of leaves and petals; a tree with apples; a line of cars or trucks; a train with lots of carriages; etc.

Each member of the class – children and adults – has a leaf, or a petal, an apple, a car etc., and writes on their leaf something that has happened recently that makes them feel good about themselves. Help those children who struggle with writing; allow the children to write in whatever language they wish (you might want to write an English translation with it); the emphasis of the activity is on helping children recognise the good things that are happening for them.

Help the children think about what they want recorded by giving examples from your own life and writing your own leaf.

The 'feel-good' notes will say things like: 'My mum said she loved me'; 'Aziz played football with me at play'.

Assemble the leaves into a display.

Repeat the exercise frequently. Add to the display and let it 'grow' around the room.

The activity can also be done verbally, particularly if you want to focus children if they are excited or very lively after some particular activity.

(Developed from an idea in Wetton and Cansell 2001 : 13)

Bibliography

Alfrey, C. (2003) *Understanding Children's Learning*. London: David Fulton Publishers.

DfES (2003) *Excellence and Enjoyment*. London: DfES.

DfES (2004) *Primary National Strategy Excellence and Enjoyment: Learning and Teaching in the Primary Years: Section 3 – Diverse Learning Needs*. London: DfES.

DfES/QCA (1999) *The National Curriculum: Handbook for Primary Teachers in England KS1 and 2*. London: HMSO.

Fontana, D. (1995) *Psychology for Teachers* (3rd edn). Basingstoke: Macmillan.

Gardner, H. (1993) *Frames of Mind* (2nd edn). London: Fontana Press.

Joyce, B., Calhoun, E. and Hopkins, D. (2002) *Models of Learning – Tools for Teaching*. Buckingham: Open University Press.

Lankshear, C. and Knobel, M. (2004) *New Literacies*. Buckingham: Open University Press.

Lazear, D. (1991) *Seven Ways of Teaching: The Artistry of Teaching with Multiple Intelligences*. Palatine, IL: SkyLight Publishing.

Ofsted (2002) *Primary Subject Reports 2000/01: Geography* (HMI 360). London: Ofsted.

Ofsted (2003) *Yes He Can: Schools where Boys Write Well* (HMI 505). London: Ofsted.

Smith, A. and Call, N. (1999) *The ALPS Approach*. Stafford: Network Educational Press.

Tilstone, C. and Rose, R. (2004) *Strategies to Promote Inclusive Practice*. London: RoutledgeFalmer.

Wetton, N. and Cansell, P. (2001) *Feeling Good – Raising Self-esteem in the Primary School Classroom* (2nd edn). London: Forbes.

Wilson, A. (2005) *Creativity in Primary Education*. Exeter: Learning Matters.

Further resources/contacts

Accelerated Learning in Training and Education (ALiTE)
24 Abbotsford Road
Cotham
Bristol BS6 6HB
Tel: 0117 974 3669
www.alite.co.uk
Training in school and classroom approaches as described in this book.

Accelerated Learning Systems Ltd
50 Aylesbury Road
Aston Clinton
Aylesbury
Bucks
HP22 9AH

Index